THE AWAKENING MINORITIES

The Physically Handicapped

Duane F. Stroman

UNIVERSITY
PRESS OF
AMERICA

LANHAM • NEW YORK • LONDON

85-1531

Library of Congress Cataloging in Publication Data

Stroman, Duane F.
The awakening minorities.

Includes bibliographical references and index.
1. Physically handicapped. 2. Deviant behavior. 3.
Minorities. I. Title.
HV3011.S75   1982   305'.90816   82–40235
ISBN 0–8191–2694–2
ISBN 0–8191–2695–0 (pbk.)

All University Press of America books are produced on acid-free
paper which exceeds the minimum standards set by the National
Historical Publications and Records Commission.

Dedication

This book is dedicated to the physically impaired in the hope that it will enlighten all citizens with regard to the abilities, the aspirations, the rights and the problems of those who are either physically different or impaired.

Acknowledgements

Grateful acknowledgement is made to the following publishers and/or authors for the permission to quote copyrighted materials:

-Frances Cook Macgregor for quotes from <u>Transformation and Identity</u>: The Face and <u>Plastic Surgery</u>. New York: The New York Times Book Co., 1974.

-"Vital Speeches of the Day" for quotes from Kenneth Jernigan, "Blindness: of Visions and Vultures," <u>Vital Speeches</u> 43 (Oct. 15, 1976), pp 20-21.

-John Gliedman & William Roth, <u>The Unexpected Minority</u>. New York: Harcourt Brace Jovanovich, Inc., 1980.

-Leo Buscaglia for quotes from <u>The Disabled and Their Parents</u>: A Counseling Challenge. Thorofare, N. J.: Charles B. Slack, Inc., 1975.

Table of Contents

List of Tables and Figures

PREFACE

For nearly a century sociologists have been studying groups or groupings of people who have been identified as minority groups and deviant groups. The study of such groups has diverged along two lines as sociologists have become specialized into many different specialities within the general discipline of sociology. Thus, minority group theorists and researchers have centered on studying what they have designated as minority groups. At first their attention focused on nationality groups, racial groups, and ethnic (cultural) groups. More recently women have been categorized as a minority. And even more recently, other groups such as the aged, youth, physically impaired, mentally retarded and mentally ill have been designated as minority groups. Such groups are designated as the "awakening minorities" in this book because of the growing awareness of their minority status by both themselves and others. During the same time period deviance theorists have widened their focus from the study \of criminal deviance to other types of deviance some of which is marginal to the breaking of the law. Thus, deviance theorists have subsequently studied a variegated array of behaviors and bodily characteristics from deviation from religious codes of behavior to homosexuality, transsexuality, drug abuse, mental illness and participation in communal living arrangements.

The simultaneous expansion of both of these subfields in sociology, minority group and deviance studies, has led to an overlapping focus of the groups studied but yet a sizeable diversity in the conceptual approaches and use of terminology.

The purposes of this book relate to this overlapping but divergent focus of minority group and deviance theory. The first purpose is to compare minority group theory and deviance theory in terms of their focus, terminology, assumptions and explanatory theories. The second purpose is to apply minority group theory to a number of groupings of people who have been the focus of study primarily by deviance theorists rather than minority group theorists. It is believed that while both approaches are valid in offering insights into the variety and causes of diverse human behavior, the application of minority group theory to people whose behavior or traits differ sub-

stantially from others (usually a majority of the population and those who are more powerful) offers insights
that deviance theory does not.

Two major types of minority groups are conceptualized in the first chapter: physical attribute
minorities and cultural-behavioral minorities. The
physical attribute minorities are those whose physical
differences make them visibly identifiable. These
differences as well as other alleged individual and
group characteristics are held in low esteem by the
dominant members of society. In most instances physical attribute minorities are also involuntary minorities; that is their differences are ascribed or given
to them at birth or occur as a result of an accident
and are usually unalterable. This is true for racial
and sexual minorities and for age-related minorities
such as youth or aged people. It is also true for
the physically impaired minorities like the blind,
hearing impaired, orthopedically impaired and facially
disfigured. It is also true for dwarfs and midgets
who are born with their condition of short stature.

Cultural-behavioral minorities are distinguishable
from the dominant group primarily by their displaying
behavior which is held in low esteem, usually because
it deviates from certain social norms or customs. Historically, ethnic groups have been conceptualized as
a cultural-behavior minority. It is also possible to
conceptualize a number of other groups as cultural-
behavioral minorities: the mentally retarded, the
mentally ill, fat people and homosexuals. In addition,
such groups may also be analyzed as either voluntary
or involuntary minorities depending upon the origin of
their behavior. For example, in most instances mental
retardation is regarded as a genetic condition that is
fundamentally unalterable and therefore involuntary.
But homosexuality and many forms of mental illness are
usually interpreted as nongenetic in origin, as
alterable, and therefore as voluntary behavior. At
first glance, fat people would appear to be a physical
attribute minority because they are visible by their
size and shape. But closer analysis will reveal that
usually they are pictured as a behavioral minority
because they engage in excessive eating behavior. As
a rule, they are not held blameless for their condition as is true for the blind, deaf, ugly, short or
lame individual.

Before turning to an analysis of six physically different groups in chapters 2 through 7, we begin chapter 1 by analyzing and comparing the characteristics of minority groups and deviant individuals. In the six chapters which follow particular attention is given to how these six physically different minorities meet the four criteria of a minority group. These four criteria are: identifiability, pejorative stereotypes about and discrimination directed toward the minority, their lower socioeconomic status, and the level of their individual and group awareness of their lower status and the kinds of responses they make to their lower status and the discrimination directed against them.

In writing a book such as this many people should be thanked. But the list would be too long. But I do want to give thanks to Lois Fluke for typing the manuscript at a time when she had many other job responsibilities.

PART I   THEORETICAL PERSPECTIVES

CHAPTER I

SOCIOLOGICAL PERSPECTIVES OF DEVIANT AND MINORITY
STATUSES: A COMPARISON

One of the fascinating aspects of the human
species is the extraordinary physical and cultural diversity of its members. At the same time these two
kinds of diversity, sometimes singly and sometimes in
combination, are often the source of conflict and inequality in human relations. The differences rather
than the similarities of humans have been a source of
war, prejudice, curiosity, antagonism, murder, im-
prisonment, banishment, discrimination and great social
inequality.

For nearly a century sociologists and anthropologists have been studying the physical and behavioral
diversity of humans and how people react to such diversity. One of the most common reactions is that
people with distinctive behaviors and/or distinctive
physical characteristics are perceived as inferior or
threatening and therefore should be controlled. But as
sociologists studied such individuals and groups they
have diverged into two specialties within the field.
One field has been deviance theory which largely concentrates on why individuals depart from cultural
norms of behavior and societal reactions to such behavior. The other field has been minority group theory
which focuses primarily on the distinctive physical or
cultural differences of groups of people and the resulting social processes between such groups. For about
the last fifty years each of these two specialties has
expanded its focus to look at other individuals and
groups to the point where these two specialties are beginning to overlap substantially. While they overlap
to a certain degree in the kinds of behaviors and physical traits they focus on, differences remain in
terminology and the kinds of explanation they offer as
to the origins and solutions to human diversity and inequality. Before turning to a definition of minorities
and deviance, typologies of both types of groups, and
explanatory models of deviant and minority statuses, I
will look at the influence of basic assumptions in
studying human behavior.

1

CONSENSUS AND CONFLICT PERSPECTIVES

A critical element in sociology, as in other
sciences, is the organizing framework by means of
which concepts are delineated and data organized around
them to test hypotheses. This organizing framework is
called a theory. Of the three major theoretical approaches in sociology--the functionalist, the conflict,
and the interactionist, most deviance and minority
group theorists have utilized either a functionalist or
conflict perspective.

The functionalist or consensus perspective sees
society as made up of a number of interrelated parts
much like a biological organism. Each of the parts or
institutions of a society plays a function in maintaining the whole system or of returning the system to
relative balance when it is thrown into disequilibrium
as a result of social change. The consensus perspective of society was particularly used by earlier
deviance theorists. This consensus model of society
assumes that either a society is relatively homogeneous
in the types of people who make up society, or more
likely, that there is a high consensus on what the
dominant and approved norms of society are. The consensus model of society assumes there is a relatively
high degree of agreement on what are acceptable and unacceptable behaviors and that the various institutions
of society could and do (1) socialize their members
into accepting these behaviors as right and wrong, and
(2) sanction those persons who engage in behaviors
that deviate from the norms of society in order to control such behavior.

The consensus perspective in the area of minority
studies is found primarily in the assimilationist position that an ethnic group should become culturally
like the dominant group or that society should adopt a
pluralistic value structure that tolerates racial and
cultural differences.

The conflict perspective, traceable to Karl Marx,
finds that society is made up of a mosaic of groups
with different values, interests and statuses which
conflict with one another. These groups vie for the
scarce resources of society--power, wealth and prestige. Social change is not an occasional event but an
ongoing process marked by hostility, disagreement,

2

competition and sometimes violence as the less powerful try to maintain or enhance theirs. Social order is maintained by the powerful through the propagation of an ideology which serves its interests and by the threat and use of force to maintain its superior status. There is little consensus on many values except that which comes through social conformity and compliance with the social control system's agents managed by the rich and powerful.

The conflict perspective has become the dominant model among both minority and deviance theorists. Among conflict deviance theorists there is an assumption that deviance does not inhere in the nature of the activity or the person doing it, but, like beauty, exists in the eye of the beholder and his relative power in being able to define and enforce his views of deviance. Definitions of deviance often vary with the tolerance of society toward certain actions. While the functionalist perspective assumes there is nearly an absolute consensus on society's central values, the conflict perspective views deviance as relative to time, place, circumstance and power. The functionalist perspective concentrates on locating social agreements which define what behaviors are considered deviant and what forces are at work which lead some people into deviant behaviors. The average citizen has been extensively socialized into this model of deviance. In contrast, the conflict perspective is primarily concerned with how some behaviors become defined as deviant, the power characteristics of those who do the defining, and how they influence social processes which define and control deviant behavior.

Among minority group theorists who assume that no racial, cultural, or sexual grouping is innately inferior, there is widespread acceptance of the conflict theory to explain the differentials in power, prestige, and privilege evident among such dominant and minority groups. The dominant group utilizes its superior education, jobs, income, political power, and usually numbers, to gain and maintain a disproportionate share of society's scarce resources.

3

DEFINITIONS OF DEVIANT AND MINORITY STATUSES

Definitions of both deviant and minority group status may be made either broadly or narrowly depending on the purpose of the definer. They may also be arrived at either inductively or deductively. The inductive approach would involve looking at all the individuals or groups who are defined that way by society and then developing a definition that was inclusive enough to cover all of them. The deductive approach involves postulating a set of criteria and then using them arbitrarily or perhaps later refining them to make a closer fit between the definition and empirical reality. The inductive approach often results in a broader definition.

A narrower definition of deviance is that it is a departure or variation from the behavioral norms of society. This definition limits deviance to overt behavior. It is probably this definition which is used by most laymen and sociologists. A wider and more inclusive definition is that deviance is a departure or variation from the normative standards of society.[1] These normative standards cover not only behavior but physical criteria of normality. While most of the sociological literature on deviance is focused on deviant behavior such as crime, prostitution, homosexuality, substance-abuse and the like, some of it is focused on deviation from normative standards of physical and mental being such as found among dwarfs, the facially disfigured, fat people, the mentally retarded, or those with misshapened bodies. This wider definition of deviance as a departure from the normative standards of society will be used because of its empirical inclusiveness--reflecting both popular and considerable sociological usage.

The concept of minority group started from a rather narrow base and has been expanded over time to be more empirically inclusive of groups both popularly and sociologically called minorities. The concept of national minorities arose in Europe where it was used to identify the national origin of a group of people not residing in their original homeland and who constituted less than half of the population in their adopted country.[2] The term "minority" was coined by Donald Young in his 1932 book on intergroup relations,

4

<u>The American Minority Peoples</u>. He used the term as
popularly used in Europe and the United States to refer
to national minorities not living in their original
homeland.[3] In 1945 Louis Wirth developed a definition
of a minority group which has been widely used in the
literature ever since. Wirth states,

> We may define a minority as a group
> of people who, because of their
> physical cultural characteristics,
> are singled out from the others in
> the society in which they live for
> differential and unequal treatment
> and who therefore regard themselves
> as object of collective discrimination.[4]

Wirth clearly understood that minorities do not
have to be a statistical minority. Rather, their
relative powerlessness in dealing with the discrimination they faced based on their stigmatized physical
or cultural characteristics were the critical factors.
Because of this discrimination they develop an awareness of their inferior status. This definition is
sufficiently broad that it may include both racial
minorities, which are distinctive in their color and/or
physiognomy, and ethnic minorities whose cultural tra-
ditions such as language, dress, national origin, and
religion are distinctive from the dominant group.
This definition is sufficiently broad that it may include women, the handicapped, the aged and other physically identifiable groups as well as persons whose
behavior departs from the culture of the dominant
group.

In 1958 two anthropologists, Charles Wagley and
Marvin Harris developed a widely used but narrower
definition of a minority. They arrived at their
definition by looking at a number of commonalities
that racial, ethnic and racial-ethnic groups had in the
new world. Their definition includes five distinguishing characteristics:

> (1) minorities are subordinate
> segments of complex state societies;
> (2) minorities have special phy-
> sical or cultural traits which are
> held in low esteem by the dominant
> segments of the society; (3) minor-
> ities are self-conscious units bound
> together by the special traits which

their members share and by the
special disabilities which these
bring; (4) membership in a
minority is transmitted by a rule
of descent which is capable of
affiliating succeeding generations
even in the absence of readily apparent physical or cultural traits;
(5) minority peoples, by choice
or necessity, tend to marry within
the group.[5]

Two weaknesses are evident in this definition.
The concept of endogamy--marriage within a specified
racial or ethnic group in this case, restricts the definition to certain groups so that it cannot be applied
to women, the aged or other physically identifiable
people where no such marital restrictions exist.
Neither is membership in such groups based on a rule of
descent. A second weakness in this definition is that
it does not explicitly point out the discriminatory
practices of the dominant group although it is hinted
at by the phrase "special disabilities" that membership in a minority group brings.

While many other definitions of minority groups
have been made, the one developed by Anthony and
Rosalind Dworkin will be used because of the inclusive
universality of the criteria it adopts and therefore
its applicability to minorities which are not racial or
ethnic in nature. Their definition is that "a minority
group is characterized by four qualities: identifiability, differential power, differential and pejorative
treatment and group awareness."[6] Each of these four
criteria is a somewhat measurable variable that can
range from high to low along a measurement scale. Thus,
a minority group may have a relatively high, interme-
diate or low identifiability, power, group awareness
and the discriminatory treatment directed toward it may
range from severe to slight. This variability in minority group status along these four criteria mean that:
(1) different groups of people designated as minorities
could be ranked according to their total minority status,
(2) any particular minority group may have different
scores on each of the four criteria, and (3) the
relative stigma and oppression of a minority group may
change over time and be measured by a series of empirical indicators of their status.

The first of the four qualities of a minority

group the Dworkins cite is their <u>identifiability</u>.
Minorities may be identifiable in either a physical
sense or a cultural-behavioral sense or in both of these
simultaneously. If a minority group is physically different it is visually identifiable by such factors as
skin color, type and presence of head and body hair,
body stature, facial contours, lip and nose size, eye
openings--the major factors associated with race. But
there may be other physical differences such as sex,
age or physical handicaps which could be used to identify people. The cultural differences associated with
ethnicity include national origin, lineage, religious
affiliations, the use of another language or speaking
the language of the host society with an accent, and
many other differences ranging from dress patterns and
family life style to affiliation with ethnic organizations. The physically different minorities are
distinguishable by their physical attributes while for
the most part ethnic groups are distinguishable by
their <u>cultural behavior</u> which sets them apart. This
behavior is often not as quickly visually distinguishable as is true for physical differences. The concept
of behavioral minorities means that any group that acts
differently in a behavioral sense can be analyzed from
the perspective of minority group theory. In some
cases both racial and ethnic differences are present in
the same group. For example, Chinese Americans,
Japanese Americans and American Indians are all racial-
ethnic groups.

The second quality the Dworkins use in distinguishing a minority from its reciprocal, the dominant
group, is <u>differential power</u>. Minority groups possess
fewer resources to influence and control others than do
the dominant group. Many indices have developed to
measure the power of minority groups in comparison to
dominant groups such as numerical size, property
holdings, levels of income, years of education, number
and type of political offices held, and the number,
size and power of organizations that represent their
interests and the extent of membership in such organizations.

The third criteria of a minority group listed by
the Dworkins is <u>differential and pejorative treatment</u>.
This is not a quality intrinsic to the group but rather
defines their discriminatory treatment by the more
powerful dominant group. This treatment may range from
genocide to mild forms of stereotyping and discrimination. Differential and pejorative discrimination

7

against a minority group produces measurable outcomes in the forms of less average education, lower percapita income, less property ownership, less office holding, lower status jobs, and degrees of physical segregation from the dominant group in schooling, work, housing, organizations and leisure pursuits.

The fourth quality minority groups possess is group awareness. This group awareness develops as a result of the stereotypes the dominant group holds about the minority and the concurrent discriminatory practices aimed at keeping the minority in its inferior economic, political and social position. The stereotypes about the minority group act as an ideology which justifies their differential treatment and lower status. The sense of "we-ness" and "they-ness" that develops among both dominant and minority groups calls social attention to and makes significant the physical and cultural differences among people. This sense of group awareness may be thought of not only as an individual experience of minority group members who know they are thought about and treated differently but as a shared experience which they discuss with one another. Group awareness is most likely to be heightened when minorities organize to discuss and take common action to alter their treatment. Self-awareness may range from low to high. The kinds of responses a minority group will make individually and through various groups will reflect not only their degree of self-awareness as a minority, but the assessment of how the dominant group will respond to any challenges they make to the whole system of dominant-minority relations in that society.

TYPOLOGIES OF DEVIANCE AND MINORITY GROUPS

I have already suggested that in the literature on deviance two major types of deviance exist: (1) behavioral deviance in which some overt action is judged to deviate from more or less widely shared norms about how people should act, and (2) physical attribute deviance where the physical and mental attributes of a person deviate from what is considered normal or whole or pleasing. Dinitz, Dynes and Clark have developed a typology of deviance which posits five normative orders, deviation from any one of which results in one of five types of deviation. Their typology of deviance includes:[7]

8

1. Deviation from physical, physiological or intellectual ideals. The nature of this deviation is statistical or aberrant in being. This type of deviant is a freak of some type: midget, dwarf, ugly, fat, disfigured, mentally retarded. While the condition is morally evaluated as being undesirable, its origin may be blameless, that is, not due to human irresponsibility.

2. Deviation from religious or secular ideologies. The nature of this deviation is to deviate either from religious or secular ideologies and proscriptions. This type of deviant is the sinner, heretic and apostate. The sinner violates the proscriptions and prescriptions of a particular religious group or secular group. The heretic rejects the dogma of the group, the rationale for its basic prescriptions and proscriptions. The apostate goes one step further than the heretic. He not only rejects the dogma of the group but accepts an alternative and "alien" set of principles. Commonly shared religious beliefs often become the basic morality of a society that is fundamentally secular rather than theocratic in its structure. To deviate from the relatively highly shared norms in a society is to be immoral; to reject them for alien principles and betray them is to be a traitor.

3. Deviation from legal codes. The nature of this deviation is to break the laws of society. This type of deviant is the criminal. Generally there are three types of criminal acts proscribed by law: (1) Mala in se acts are those that are intrinsically bad and usually bring harm to a victim such as in robbery, murder, rape or treason; (2) mala prohibita acts are not necessarily immoral or harmful but are still illegal such as misdemeanors in traffic violations and breaking curfew restrictions; (3) status offenses typically enforce moral conceptions and values but involve crimes without victims or with willing victims such as in drug addiction, homosexuality and prostitution, abortion and gambling.

4. Deviation from cultural definitions of
    mental health. The nature of this deviation
    is to be aberrant in action to a degree that
    is socially unacceptable. This type of dev-
    iant is the mentally ill or crazy person.
    This deviant is sick in a behavioral sense
    from assumed mental functioning just as a
    person can be sick in a particular organ
    system from an infection. As part of the
    medical model, the sick patient is seen as
    confused rather than willfully deviant as a
    rule. He has a reduced capacity for "normal,"
    rational and affectively appropriate decision-
    making. As a schizophrenic or maniac de-
    pressive psychotic with pathological internal
    problems that affect his behavior, the men-
    tally ill person may or may not be treatable.
    But that the sick person should be treated
    insofar as possible rather than punished is
    part of the medical model of deviation from
    mental health. Problems exist in defining
    what is mentally ill behavior in view of
    cross-cultural, intracultural and longitu-
    dinal cultural variations in the symptons and
    assignment of causes of aberrant action. And
    whether mental illness is simply unsuccessful
    coping behavior rather than pathological con-
    duct stemming from internal states of
    confusion remains a central issue.

5. Deviation from cultural ends and/or means.
    The nature of this deviation is the rejection
    of the dominant cultural ends or means of
    getting there as typified by bums, tramps,
    Hippies, or suicides. This type of deviant
    is the alienated. In this type of deviation
    the focus is shifted from a sick individual
    to a sick society whose values the alienated
    rejects. This sense of alienation may have
    many and multiple sources--a sense of power-
    lessness about making critical decisions that
    affect their lives, a sense of meaningless
    about their work and life, the rapidity of
    technological and value changes, and a lack of
    involvement in activities that creatively en-
    gage their energies.

Dinitz, Dynes and Clark's first type of deviance
is comparable to what I have defined as physical

attribute deviance while the remaining four are more detailed delineations of what I have defined as behavioral deviance.

Several other points should be made about the typology of deviance developed by Dinitz, Dynes and Clark. First, the typology does not set up mutually exclusive categories of deviation. A person may be in two or more of their categories simultaneously. Or a particular type of deviant act, say homosexuality, may be classified as departing from several types of normative regulation. Thus the homosexual can be conceptualized as sinful for breaking religious proscriptions on sexual behavior, criminal for breaking laws prohibiting sodomy, mentally sick because he pursues actions defined as pathological, or alienated because he pursues sexual satisfactions in a way that is not culturally approved. The way in which he is defined as deviant says more about the definer's conception of the world than that of the defined.

A second point about the Dinitz, Dynes and Clark typology is that it is a useful tool in defining institutional value orders from which individuals may deviate in various degrees. In the same vein this typology also helps to illustrate the relative nature of deviation in historical or cultural perspectives. At one point in history, sin, apostasy and heresy were serious social offenses in western society. But with the development of multiple religious groups and the attenuation of the importance or even relevance of religion to many, sin and heresy have become group specific and irrelevant or relatively meaningless to others who are not involved in religious institutions.

A third point should be kept in mind about this typology of deviant behavior and its use in studying deviance. Not all deviance is equally stigmatized and controlled. Research studies of public opinion and normative sentiments show a strong consensus supporting legal codes that outlaw certain crimes against persons like murder, robbery, rape and assault. But the conflict model has more support where a variety of dissenting groups disagree over the legal control of drugs, abortion, and sexual activities like homosexuality and adultery.

Another typology of deviance that cross cuts behavioral deviance and physical attribute deviance is

11

the distinctions between involuntary and voluntary deviance made by Sagarin and Montanino. <u>Involuntary deviance</u> is that which occurs beyond the capacity of the individual to control. An involuntary deviant is one who is not held responsible for his condition under normal circumstances, although victims of involuntary conditions are sometimes blamed or stigmatized for the characteristic even though they did not willfully create them. Examples of involuntary deviants include the mentally retarded, the physically handicapped, dwarfs and midgets, the misshapened and ugly, and some types of mental illness traceable to genetic origins. The involuntary deviant can blame circumstances beyond his control for his physical conditions or perhaps his behavior. Because of bad luck or an accident, the involuntary deviant gets stuck with a status he would not desire and which is usually unalterable.[8] As Sagarin and Montanino point out,

> These persons can be described as the purest of society's victims, disvalued not for what they choose <u>to do</u>, but for what they have no choice <u>in being</u>; not for their violation of formal codes of conduct but for their inability to satisfy informal, unspoken expectations held by a mass of society's normals.[9]

The disability that such people experience leads to a social disvaluation of them rather than a personal disapproval of them. The social disvaluation of them comes from the lack of ability to do or to be what normal people do and are and the discomfort normals feel in their presence. Involuntary deviance cannot be reduced by increasing negative sanctions of social control. However, some of it may be prevented by certain medical measures. But normals often avoid them or segregate them in order to lessen their own discomfort.

<u>Voluntary deviance</u> is that which deviates from normal or approved behavior which is also assumed to be under the control of a person. Assumptions are made about the origins of such behavior to the effect that the deviant is held responsible for his actions. It is further assumed that the offending behavior can be dropped or altered. However, the stigma associated with the overt deviant behaviors is often transferred to the "being" part of the actor so that the stigma

may remain even if the person stops engaging in the deviant behavior. Thus a person who commits a crime may be seen as a criminal even if the criminal act was done years earlier and not repeated since then. Greater stigma is usually applied to the voluntary than the involuntary deviant because it is assumed that the voluntary actor can avoid or overcome his deviance and that clear public policies and sanctions will aid in controlling such behaviors.[10]

Sociologists have given primary attention to voluntary deviance and behavioral deviance which overlap extensively. Less attention has been given to involuntary deviance which also extensively coincides with physical attribute deviance.

Several typologies of minority groups have been developed which are analytically useful in distinguishing subtypes of them. Earlier in this chapter I made the dichotomous distinctions between physical attribute minorities (racial minorities, women, age-related minorities, physically impaired) and cultural-behavioral minorities. This last typology has been applied historically to ethnic groups but could be logically extended to other groups or individuals who display behaviors that distinguish them from the dominant group. The physical attribute minorities can also usually be classified as involuntary minorities since they either are born with their physical differences or acquire them as a result of inevitable aging processes or are the victims of accidents or diseases over which they have no control. However, the cultural-behavioral minorities are not so easily described as voluntary minorities. The cultural behavior of ethnic groups is predominantly learned at very young ages through complex socialization processes that lead to lifetime personal characteristics that are not easily altered. Thus, the process of ethnic assimilation or becoming like the dominant group, even when desired, may take several generations. However, the conceptualization of other groups such as the mentally ill or homosexuals or transsexuals as voluntary minorities may be more feasible if their behavioral differences can be shown to be acquired and perhaps acquired at a later age.

Graham Kinloch identifies four types of minority groups in his definition of a minority. He defines a minority as "any group that views itself and/or is de-

fined by a dominant power elite as unique on the basis
of perceived physical, cultural, economic and/or
behavioral characteristics and is treated accordingly
in a negative manner." (Emphasis in original.)[11]
Kinloch thus distinguishes four major types of minorities: "(1) Physical: race, sex, age; (2) Cultural:
religion, ethnicity; (3) Economic: social class; (4)
Behavioral: deviation."[12] In addition he points out
that any particular group of people may have two or
more of these characteristics at the same time. This
raises questions of whether minority statuses are ad-
ditive and if an individual has multiple minority
statuses which one will be predominant? Kinloch suggests that in our society the racial classification
has been predominant. His last three classifications
of minorities--cultural, economic and behavioral, are
all cultural-behavioral as I have defined the term.

     This analysis of typologies of minority and
deviant statuses shows both differences and similarities: (1) both minority group and deviant theorists
make general distinctions between physically different
and cultural-behavioral deviant groups or minority
groups; (2) both recognize the distinctions between
voluntary and involuntary deviants or minorities,
although there are groups such as ethnic minorities
or homosexuals or fat people or the mentally ill who
sometimes have both voluntary and involuntary com-
ponents in their statuses--depending on the individual
case; (3) historically, deviance theorists have
focused their major research on deviance that can be
classified as behavioral and voluntary while minority
group theorists have focused their major attention on
groups that are physically different and whose difference is voluntary in origin; and (4) deviant
theorists have focused their major attention on
personal/social processes that lead to individual deviance while minority group theorists give more
attention to processes that lead to individuals being
considered members of groups which are collectively
oppressed. Some of these distinctions will become
clearer as we examine the explanatory models of deviance and minority group formation and their response
to dominance.

EXPLANATORY MODELS OF DEVIANCE AND MINORITY STATUS

     Models are used in the social sciences to explain
how certain social developments occur and the processes
involved. In this section of the chapter I will first

look at one theory--the conflict model, to describe
the formation and interaction of dominant and minority
groups. Following that I will look at a number of
models used to describe the origins of deviant behavior. Models of deviance are under two general
types: individualistic and social explanations of
deviance. The most useful and widely used model of
the origins of minority groups is the conflict model.
In the conflict model racism, sexism, handicappism,
and other comparable isms are viewed as the outcomes
of competition between different groups for scarce
resources. For racism or its variants to develop
three fundamental conditions must usually be met:
(1) There must be two or more groups, identifiable by
visible physical or cultural differences; (2) There
must be competition between or among such groups for
limited but valued resources such as jobs, land, education, political and economic power; (3) These
groups must be unequal in power, enabling one to claim
more resources for itself while denying the other
group(s) equal access to them.[13] Over time as these
inequalities become structured into the institutions
of society, an ideology is developed by the dominant
group which justifies its superior status due to the
alleged inferiority and difference of the minority
group. And concomitant with the rise of structured
inequalities in a society will come value conflicts
over whether such inequalities are legitimate. As
minority groups become aware of their oppression,
they often take a wide range of individual and group
actions to rectify or escape from what they perceive
as social injustice.

    The range of actions and policies taken by the
dominant group and the counter-responses by the minority group are too complex to analyze fully here.
However, I will briefly list the kinds of dominance
that have been exercised by the powerful groups in
society and briefly describe the kinds of responses
minority groups make to their oppression. The following list of policies toward and treatment of
minorities are ranked in order of their decreasing
severity: (1) extermination or genocide, (2)
slavery, (3) population transfer or forced migration,
(4) segregation coupled with subjugation, and (5)
various degrees of discriminative subjugation. In
addition to these five structured patterns of inequality are three patterns of equality in intergroup
relations which may eventually prevail:

(1) _assimilation_ of the minority into the dominant group by means of ethnic acculturation or racial amalgamation, (2) _cultural or racial pluralism_ with egalitarian integration into the social structures of that society, and (3) _cultural and/or racial hybridization_--the melting pot theory of an emergence of a new race or culture. These various kinds of treatment and outcomes take on many variations within each classification and the treatment of a minority at any one time may involve more than one of these sets or practices.

The range of responses that a given minority will make to its oppression are quite varied and complex and will be influenced by a variety of other factors such as the general norms of that society, the type of government that exists, the level of education of both the dominant and minority group, the communications network of the society, the type of economy that exists, and the past history of dominant-minority relations in that society. The behavioral responses that either individual minority group members or organized groups of them make to their oppression or discrimination fall into three very general patterns (1) _acceptance_ of the system of inequality, (2) _avoidance of the_ system insofar as is possible, and (3) _resistance_ to the system with a goal of either overthrowing it or ameliorating it.

In the pattern of _acceptance_ the minority generally complies with the expectations of dominants in the system. They know how they are to act and their behavior is molded by both socialization processes and the use of sanctions by the dominants if they act in ways contrary to the norms governing minority behavior. Acceptance of the status quo in intergroup relations may vary, however, from whole-hearted acceptance in which the minority believes it is inferior, to situation-specific acceptance, to acceptance of the system with bitter resignation. In the latter case, the minority is aware of its unjust oppression but believes itself powerless to change that oppression or that the cost of trying to change it might be excessive.

The pattern of _avoidance_ ranges from individual minority group members running away from societies which subjugate them to minimizing contacts with dominant persons. Or groups of a minority may voluntarily self-segregate themselves into their own communities to minimize contacts with oppressive dominant persons. Or

16

a minority group may engage in mass migration to another society where they believe their chances for equality are better.

The response pattern of <u>resistance</u> to inequalities ranges from simple non-compliance with the system, to violent aggression or revolution to undermine or over-throw the system, to peaceful reform efforts to make the pattern of intergroup relations more egalitarian. The tactics of both individual and organized group resist-ance to subjugation may range from organized guerilla warfare, to boycotts, demonstrations, political lobbying, and cooperation with dominants to change <u>de facto</u> and <u>de jure</u> forms of segregation and discrimina-tion.

The conflict model of the formation of unequal minority and dominant groups thus focuses on complex social processes wherein groups unequal in power and often in size end up treating categories of people differently because their physical or cultural at-tributes are labeled as inferior. But such inequalities often produce normative strains in a society. Values emphasizing the humanity of all people, equality before the law, and the desirability of equal opportunity for each person to maximize his potential conflict with oppressive patterns of treatment. Social processes are often subsequently set in motion, primarily by the minority group, but sometimes with the help of dominants sympathetic to the plight of the minority, to rectify inequalities.

While models of the origin and continued pattern of intergroup relations focus heavily on <u>group</u> forma-tion and interaction, models of deviance focus primarily on <u>individual</u> departures from normative standards and subsequent societal responses to such departures. As mentioned earlier, the functionalist perspective emphasizes individual deviation because it assumes extensive consensus around social norms. In contrast, the conflict perspective emphasizes the ideo-logical and processual conflicts between elite groups which have the power to define and sanction deviance and those labeled and treated as deviants. These two schools of thought respectively yield <u>individual</u> and <u>social</u> <u>explanations</u> of deviance.

<u>Individual</u> <u>explanations</u> of deviance are those which center the cause of deviance in the internal

17

workings of the deviant person. Individual explanations center on the personality "disturbances" that led
to unacceptable behavior. According to Gwynn Nettler
bad behavior almost always has to be explained by pre-
ceding events such as a limited learning experience or
a distorted personality structure. In contrast, "good"
or conforming behavior usually does not need to be
explained except as an expression of free choice.[14]
Thus, if we ask a person why they became a dentist,
we'll probably be satisfied if they say, "I wanted to
because it interested me." But if we ask a bank robber
to explain why he robbed a bank, a purposeful explanation, like "That's where the money is at," may not be
satisfactory. Thus, in everyday life and to a large
extent in social science, purposeful or willed explanations are adequate for good behaviors but not bad
behaviors. Three variants of individualistic explanations of deviance which will be discussed next are
the psychiatric model, the psychoanalytic model and the
personality trait theory of deviance.

The Psychiatric Model of Deviance. This model of
explanation is central to most of the 24,000 American
psychiatrists, many psychologists and many citizens and
popular media writers. In this model, deviant behavior
is the result of some disturbance within the person
whose inherent personality needs have not been adequately met during the critical years of childhood development. Deviant but not non-deviant persons are believed
to have emotional disturbances that arise from childhood deprivations such as unresolved emotional
conflicts, lack of parental or especially maternal affection, feelings of inadequacy, or uncontrolled
aggression. Deviant behavior is an outcome of such
personality traits or emotional problems. Deviant behavior such as crime, alcoholism or homosexuality may
provide coping techniques with which to deal with these
personality disturbances.[15] As a social control
mechanism, psychiatry primarily uses individual and
group psychotherapy to help disturbed individuals to
discover the roots of their disturbances and work out
new identities and coping skills by means of which they
can control their conflicts, aggression and emotional
insecurities.

Four major criticisms have been made of the
psychiatric model of the explanation of deviance.
First, the model does not clearly distinguish between
the sickness and the deviation itself. The sickness is

often attributed after the deviation and because of it.
Thus, circular reasoning is used to infer that sickness
exists because of some aberrant behavior has occurred.
Second, psychiatric diagnoses are said to be unreliable
because they are subjective, rather than objective.
Because psychiatrists often disagree with one another
both in theory and in particular diagnoses, because
they are largely unable to predict deviant behavior
before it occurs, and because they are unable to distinguish between "mentally healthy" and "mentally
unhealthy" criminals, their diagnoses are called unreliable. A third criticism is that psychiatric
theory overemphasizes childhood family behavior as a
determinant of adult behavior and thereby underemphasizes the continued development of people throughout
the life cycle and the importance of many other roles
and role conflicts during both childhood and adulthood.
Lastly, psychiatric theory and research is criticized
on scientific and methodological grounds because it
concentrates on individual case studies using verbal
recall of patients rather than using scientific samp-
ling, control groups and other standards of evidence
seen as critical in the development of science.[16]

The Psychoanalytic Model of Deviance. The
psychoanalytic model of deviance is difficult to sum-
marize because of its complexity, use of a terminology
that is sometimes obscuring, and because of the many
varied interpretations given to it by the followers of
Sigmund Freud, its inventor. It has had a major impact
on psychiatric theory and a significant but declining
impact on psychology. Most deviant behavior is traced
to the first of the three parts which make up the personality: id, ego, and superego. The id is the
unconscious mind which is a large reservoir of animal
drives including life affirming drives, particularly
the libido or sex drives, and destructive drives and
instincts. Conduct which is antisocial originates
here and is not always controlled by the ego, one's
conscious mind, or the superego, one's conscience de-
rived from socialization, particularly that in the
early development of the child. Anti-social behavior
develops out of unresolved conflicts between the id's
instinctive drives for sensual satisfactions and the
requirements of society not always fully internalized
into the superego. Thus criminal or anti-social behavior is basically not learned but an expression of
the uncontrolled biological self that expresses itself
in four somewhat sequential but overlapping stages of

19

development: anal love of self, oral love of self, love of the opposite-sexed parent and love of an opposite-sexed person outside the family. As the child grows, the ego needs to successfully adjust the impulsive pleasure demands of the id with the moralistic and restrictive requirements of society. The activities of deviants thus represent regressions to infantile desires or unresolved conflicts in the development process. Interpretations of the deviant behavior of particular deviants or particular types of deviants is highly individualized according to the psychoanalyst giving the interpretation. For example, homosexuality in males may be explained by an unresolved Oedipus complex where the male child's rivalry with the father for his mother's affection brings fear of castration and guilt feelings for his incestuous desires. By participating in homosexuality, the deviant avoids the incestuous desire of all women including his mother. And the social ostracism he receives because of his homosexual escapades assuages his guilt.[17]

The criticisms of psychoanalytic theory are many. It overemphasizes biological drives, termed the id, and correspondingly underemphasizes the heavy role of learning in human behavior. It assumes deviant behavior is a given rather than determined by social and political processes and therefore variable over time or cross-culturally. It overemphasizes the role of sex as an element in human conflict. Like psychiatric theory, except more so, its practitioners vary widely in their interpretations of the same case. Its subjective methodology, limited nonrandom samples, convoluted explanations and unmeasurable concepts all subject it to the charge that it is unscientific. While psychoanalytic case studies make interesting and provocative reading, they rarely yield hypotheses which are then subjected to rigorous scientific testing.[18]

The Personality Trait Theory of Deviance. Many laymen believe that deviants have certain traits that incline them to their non-conforming behavior. Many psychologists and sometimes other social scientists or psychiatrists have developed dozens of rating scales, personality trait tests and projective tests to determine if criminals or other types of deviants ranging from alcoholics to homosexuals can be distinguished from conformists. The results have been disappointing. While some studies have revealed low levels of correlation between some traits and behavior in some

20

situations, they have not revealed a "criminal mind" or a "deviant personality syndrome" that links individual personality traits to certain types of behavior. And while the concept of a "psychopathic personality," an anti-social habitual deviant, is frequently used in the literature, it is really nothing more than a statement that some people are chronic offenders of some norm. In the words of Clinard and Meier, "No evidence has been produced that so-called personality traits are associated with deviations from disapproved norms. Comparisons with control groups have revealed that no series of traits can distinguish deviants from non-deviants in general."[19]

These three models of individual deviation and similar variants are sometimes grouped together under the term medical model of deviance. The medical model of deviance assumes that some mental aberration in the individual leads to non-conforming behavior just as inflammation of bodily tissue leads to fever. Thus moral problems are medicalized and subject to medical treatment rather than punitive action. The medical model is pervasive in today's society and on the face of it is imputed the objectivity of science. Yet it lacks it because it simply cloaks the term deviance under the concept of sickness. It is prone to tauto-logical reasoning because it labels nonconforming behavior as evidence of some prior personality traits or disturbance as the causes without being able to measure these independently of the behavior itself. It has little to say about the social nature of deviance: the politics of defining deviance and controlling it and the relationship between social norms and the types of sanctions applied to behavior that may be learned rather than unfolding of basic drives or internal conflicts.[20]

In the last eighty years, a number of social models of deviance have been generated in the social science literature. Like the individual models of deviance, there is overlap among them and certainly the borrowing of ideas over time. Yet a number of distinctive emphases exist within different models to justify looking at how they attempt to explain deviance. Several earlier theories like social disorganization and social pathology theories will not be examined because of their dated and limited conceptualization about both the nature of and origins of deviance.

21

The Anomie Theory of Deviance. This theory
draws on the seminal work of Emile Durkheim, Merton's
elaboration of anomie theory, earlier conceptions of
social disorganization and recent formulations of the
theory of Cloward and then Simon and Gagnon. According
to Robert Merton's formulation, anomie occurs when there
is a discrepancy between individual goals or the means
to achieve those goals and the cultural goals of being
successful or using the acceptable institutional means
to achieve the success society inculcates in its
members. Part of the value structure in American
society is to be successful in a socioeconomic sense.
Citizens develop high and sometimes unrealistic aspirations. Anomie in the social structure occurs when
success-goals for the population at large are extolled,
but there are limited means to achieve that which is
emphasized. This disjuncture between the emphasis on
success and a deficiency in the educational and occupational channels to achieve success, lead, in many
individual cases, to feelings of alienation or anomie.
Thus anomie is a cultural/structural phenomena, anomia
the individual counterpart of this.

Because there are disjunctures between social
goals and the means to achieve it, there are four
deviant ways a person can deal with the situation if he
is unable to conform by accepting both the goals of
society and the accepted ways of getting there. One of
these is innovation where societal goals are accepted
but illegitimate means used to reach them. Most crimes
against property are an illustration of the innovative
approach. This type of criminal wants economic success but uses illegal methods to achieve it. Ritualism
often involves less deviance because it involves using
acceptable legal channels to seek goals that are not
highly valued, such as simply holding on to a job by
going through the motions of work without aspirations
for advancement. Thus cultural goals are substantially
abandoned. Retreatism abandons both cultural goals and
the accepted means of achieving success. These people
abandon the success goals of society for private satisfactions like alcoholism, drug addiction or mental
illness. Rebellion is not only the rejection of cultural means and ends but involves attempts to replace
both with new goals and new structures to replace
existing unsatisfactory structures and goals. Merton
labels the rebellion typical of political radicals and
revolutionaries as nonconforming behavior while ritualism, retreatism and innovation are depicted as

22

aberrant behavior. This theory locates the origin of deviance not in individual attributes but in the social structure which does not provide sufficient opportunities to reach the success goals strongly emphasized by society. This disorganized state of society takes its heaviest toll on the powerless poor where rates of deviance are highest.[21]

Cloward extended Merton's theory to include not only social differentials in access to legitimate opportunity structures but also to illegitimate means. Thus the poor, particularly those living in urban slum areas, have more opportunity to learn criminal and other deviant roles because of the greater presence of deviant subcultures and deviant role models.[22]

Several criticisms are made of this theory. One is that the deviants identified in this theory are those who are officially treated as deviants; but this may not apply to those who are not detected. It also contains both an absolutist and class bias. It is absolutist in the sense that it assumes there is a universal consensus on what is success and what are both the legitimate and illegitimate means of achieving it. But in fact deviance is a relative concept that varies by a wide number of class and social factors. This formulation of deviancy has a class bias in that those who control the defining of deviancy are in the middle and upper classes and often work as the social control agents of society by defining what practices are sick, illegal or immoral. Thus it locates more deviancy in the underclass of society. Lastly it does not adequately explain the process of becoming deviant and the role of deviant subcultures, role models and the like. In the final analysis, it is a general but rather simplistic theory of the role of anomie in society in inducing strain in individuals, but does not adequately describe a variety of other factors like labeling that may be influential in the development of deviancy.[23]

The Conflict Theory of Deviance. The conflict theory of deviance stands in contrast to the consensus model of deviance which generally assumed a high societal consensus on the meaning of deviancy. The conflict theory of deviance says that the identification of the meaning of deviancy varies by the relative power of a group in a pluralistic society marked by a variety of interest and/or ideological groups. The

stronger groups become the more or less official de-
signers of deviancy with varying degrees of political or
occupational power to define, control, treat or punish
deviancy. The consensus model of society, while extensively supported by the lay public, is seen by social
scientists as not reflecting the diverse power struggles
for control of morality that in fact occur in a hetero-
geneous society. In the conflict model the most
powerful groups create rules, often laws, to serve their
interests by controlling behavior which threatens their
statuses. In a sense this power elite assumes their
definition of criminal or aberrant behavior is the consensus of society and act upon it. Law and the rules
which govern mental health care institutions, drug
control agencies, and the criminal justice system, and
the welfare system are established by the power elite.[24]

Conflict theorists regard crime as a rational act.
Persons who steal and rob have been forced into these
acts by social conditions brought about by the in-
equitable distribution of wealth, while corporate crime
is directed at protecting and augmenting the capital of
its owners. Organized crime is a rational way of supplying illegal needs in a capitalist society.[25]

Evidence of the inequality of the enforcement of
the law is seen as confirming evidence of this theory.
Not only are the more affluent and powerful less likely
to be arrested, convicted or sentenced for their breaking of the law than the poor; if they are convicted
they are more likely to be put on probation or given
lesser sentences than the poor for comparable crimes.[26]

Who is deviant or criminal often depends on which
of a variety of groups are most successful in convincing the public of their view and gaining the power
to change public views or the law. While the elite
capitalists usually have dominance in maintaining law
and order to protect their property interests, at other
times, challenge groups, such as groups of homosexuals,
prostitutes, drug addicts, former convicts or the physically handicapped, organize to protest the conditions
of their lives, oppressive laws and discriminatory
regulations. Their expressive protests, sit-ins and
challenges to the system sometimes do lead to changes.
These changes do show that elitist control agents sometimes must yield concessions to maintain control or
occasionally avoid their overthrow by strong revo-
lutionary groups.[27] Conflict theory is thus helpful in

explaining (1) how powerful groups are central in defining and controlling deviance and (2) how the meaning
of deviance is variable by one's location in the class
and power structure of society. But the theory has
several important limitations. It does not describe
the process by which particular individuals become deviant. It tends to concentrate on conflicts between
social classes to the exclusion of racial conflicts,
conflicts among groups with different views of what the
moral order of society should be like, or age and sex
group conflicts. It tends to assume conflict in all
areas of social life while in fact there is extensive
consensus supporting the law which deals with serious
crimes. While the conflict theory helps to explain who
is central in defining deviance, it does not explain
why some become deviant while others do not. Lastly,
this theory has tinges of ideology in it. In practice
its theorists often select case material which support
the theory rather than testing hypotheses as to the
validity of the conflict theory.[28]

The Labeling Theory of Deviance. Despite the fact
that labeling theory does not contend to be a complete
theory of deviancy, it has received much attention in
recent years because it is a new approach that offers
insight into the process of becoming confirmed as a
deviant and the importance of interpersonal and societal
stigmatizing labels in this confirmation process. It
starts with the basic assumptions of the conflict
school--that deviance is relative in society and primarily relative to the status and power of the definer
opposite the person who is defined as deviant. It then
goes on to examine what effects the application of a
deviant label has on the person who is labeled.

Central in the symbolic interactionist perspective
on deviance is the distinction between primary and
secondary deviance. Primary deviance is the original
behavior that led to the individual being labeled as
deviant in the first place. Labeling theory has no
explanation of why the primary deviance first occurred;
rather it focuses on the nature and consequences of
interpersonal and societal labeling processes. Secondary deviance are those behaviors adopted by the labeled
to cope with the labeling and related actions directed
toward him. Often the emphasized effect of labeling is
to push the labeled person deeper into deviancy. Secondary deviance is seen as an outcome of stigmatiz-
ation.[29]

According to Becker, the interactionist perspective emphasizes the relativity of deviance at the
outset according to the situation participants find
themselves in, who is violating rules, and who is
making the judgment about the degree of harm done and/or
severity of the rule breaking. Thus, for rule breaking
to be converted into deviance, the person applying the
label makes a judgment under the circumstances of occurrence (where and when it happened, who was involved,
whether it happened before, if the person is liked)
whether the behavior is serious enough to warrant some
deviant label that the act is sick, criminal, perverted,
obscene or whatever.[30]   Becker writes,

> Deviance is not a simple quality,
> present in some kinds of behavior
> and absent in others. Rather, it
> is the product of a process which
> involves responses of other people
> to the behavior.... Whether a
> given act is deviant or not depends
> in part on the nature of the act
> (that is, whether or not it violates
> some rule) and in part on what other
> people do about it.[31]

This process thus shifts attention from the rule
breaker to the audience who creates deviance by defining when it has occurred and how it should be
reacted to.

Secondary deviance focuses not on the characteristics of the primary deviance but the labeled person's
reaction to a variety of stigmatizing stereotypes and
contacts with formal and informal agents of control.
Labeled norm violators may respond in a variety of ways.
They may accept the label because they accept the
legitimacy of the norms they have broken and the authority of the labeler to label them. This is probably
truest of those who in fact have violated a serious
legal norm and not merely or unjustly been accused of
doing so. This societal reaction may lead them to end
their deviance--the intended effect of some labeling is
deterrence. But the disgrace of public labeling,
rather than deterrence, may encourage further deviance
by several interrelated processes. First, the label
may be applied not just to an act but the person who
does it. The person is stereotyped as a deviant and
this label is applied to his whole person. He is no

longer an artist who occasionally engages in homosexual acts but a homosexual. The global key to the person is his deviancy and not his other varied interests and non-deviant activities. Secondly, the labeled person may come to adopt societal attitudes toward him and see his deviancy as central to his own self identity. This becomes a psychological self-fulfilling prophecy. What started out as a minor element in his life style and self identity engulfs him in its entirety. Third, as a result of these developing stigmas and altered self identity, he may be pushed toward participation in a deviant subculture which further confirms both the stigmatized label and his self identity. Concomitant with these feedback processes are his growing social isolation from normals who continue their negative evaluation of him and his growing participation in a subculture which is more likely to give him positive reinforcements about his labeled abnormalities. The deviant subculture provides him with a new ideology and value set from which he can condemn his condemners.[32]

An illustration of this process can help illustrate the interactive nature of it. Imagine a homosexual who has engaged in homosexual acts for many years without being detected by straights. Then he is caught by police engaging in a homosexual encounter in a public restroom. His name appears in the newspapers so that parents, employer, landlord, and friends discover his sexual identity. He is labeled by his former hetero-sexual friends as a "faggot," "queer," and "gay queen." As his true and imputed central identity becomes known, his straight friends drift away from him partly out of the fear that association with him may lead to public questioning of their own sexual identities. Now known as a homosexual, he increasingly is pulled into the homosexual subculture where he finds friends, an ideol-ogy that rejects the sickness society attributes to him, and a life style and sexual identity in which he feels comfortable. Thus, the labeling by society and signi-ficant others pushed him deeper into the deviant role. Yet he was "deviant" before found out but not labeled as such. Thus labeling affected his subsequent be-havior.

The concept of primary deviance and secondary deviance was originated by Edwin Lemert. In his words, "When a person begins to employ his deviant behavior or role based upon it as a means of defense, attack or adjustment to the overt and covert problems created by

27

the consequent societal reaction to him, his deviation is secondary."33 This process involves a number of steps over time. Howard Becker introduced the idea of a "deviant career sequence" which involved a number of contingencies or factors each of which was necessary for the deviant career to go on to the next stage. One of the most important of these factors was to be public- ly accused of being deviant.34

While labeling theory has become one of the most important and discussed theories of deviance, it has a number of shortcomings. First, it does not explain how the primary deviance got started and what role it plays in the continuation of deviant behavior once it is labeled as such. This is a fairly serious deficiency. Second, it often assumes that labeling will help con- firm deviancy with little discussion or research on how much of the time or under what circumstances it may deter it. Third, it does not identify who does the labeling--whether it is the society as a whole, a par- ticular group, or particular social control agents invested with the authority to label. Does it matter who does the labeling, how, and with different degrees of severity? Fourth, it tends to contain the class bias found in consensus theories of deviancy that the elite of a society do most of the labeling and then of the lower classes. Fifth, it may overemphasize the importance of labeling. Some career deviants freely choose to continue their career without discovery or labeling processes being applied to them. Sixth, the theory needs much more rigorous empirical testing to determine the degree of support for it and under what conditions or with what types of personalities or de- viancy it is best supported.35

Social Control Theory of Deviancy. Like other theories of deviancy, there are variants on this theory. But all of them start from a different assumption than the other theories. Instead of asking why people do not conform, it starts by asking why do people conform or conversely why do not more people deviate from norms. "The basic assumption of control theories is that crime, delinquency, and other forms of deviance are not so much caused by forces motivating people to violate norms as they are simply not prevented."36 Thus some deviant acts are not adequately contained by social control mechanisms and processes. However, for most people socialization is effective;they feel that either they do not want to deviate because they believe in the

28

norms or they fear the social, political, legal and economic consequences if they are detected violating the norms. People are internally and externally rewarded for being good citizens. And perhaps, more importantly, they are not stigmatized or penalized when they conform to social expectations.

Travis Hirschi argues there are essentially four bonds between an individual and society that are developed in the socialization process and help to maintain conformity. These four bonds are (1) <u>attachment</u> to the norms of the group, fostered by learning them, (2) a <u>commitment</u> to them which leads to avoiding behaviors which could jeopardize valued goals, (3) <u>involvement</u> in activities which are normatively approved, thus leaving little time for deviant behavior, and (4) <u>belief</u> or allegiance to the value system of his group.[37] Social control may break down where internalization of the norms of society is incomplete, or where the value system is unclear as in disorganized slum areas, or where an individual is socialized into a deviant subculture. Thus, either internal or external controls may break down and not contain deviant behavior.

There are several limitations to control theory, one of which is its having been tested almost exclusively on juvenile or adult crime. It too assumes that deviancy is defined whereas it is a problematic area in all deviancy theories. By focusing on conformity it gives inadequate attention to the processes leading to nonconformity. It is a general and rather simplistic theory that does not spell out in detail how the social control system operates.[38]

<u>Social Learning Theory of Deviancy</u>. This theory comes in a number of variations reflecting the formulation of it by a particular writer and whether he is a criminologist, social psychologist or operant condition learning theorist. While it does not attempt to define how certain acts become defined as deviant in the first place, it is relatively comprehensive in its formulation of the process by which a person becomes a deviant. Some call this the socialization theory of deviance. Edwin Sutherland's sociological construction of his theory of <u>differential association</u> to explain crime will be slightly modified here to make it applicable to all deviant behavior. The following nine statements in italics are his except I have substituted the word

29

"deviance" wherever he used the word criminal or delinquent.

"1. <u>Deviant behavior is learned.</u>" Deviance is not inherited, or a result of a sickness, or invented (except as to technique).

"2. <u>Deviant behavior is learned in interaction with other persons in a process of communication.</u>" This communication may be verbal, written or nonverbal.

"3. <u>The principal part of the learning of deviant behavior occurs within intimate personal groups.</u>" Television, the mass media and other sources of information play a minor role in the genesis of deviancy.

"4. <u>When deviant behavior is learned, the learning includes (a) techniques of committing the deviancy, which are sometimes very complicated, sometimes very simple; (b) the specific direction of motives, drives, rationalizations and attitudes.</u>" This principle does not exclude the existence of norms which condemn deviant acts, but focuses on personal explanations which help to justify those acts.

"5. <u>The specific direction of motives and drives is learned from definitions of the legal codes as favorable or unfavorable.</u>" Sutherland recognizes in this proposition a certain amount of culture conflict. Individuals are often surrounded by some definitions which are favorable to the violation of norms such as nobody will get hurt, a big organization won't miss the money, etc.

"6. <u>A person becomes deviant because of an excess of definitions favorable to violation of law over definitions unfavorable to violation of law.</u>" This key proposition in the theory recognizes contradictory learning experiences, but the predominance of definitions favorable to violating the law or other norms predominate. Associations may be either with deviant definitions or deviant persons. Conformists, conversely, have an excess of definitions favorable to obeying the norms.

30

"7. Differential associations may vary in fre-
     quency, duration, priority and intensity."
     Frequency and duration are self explanatory
     while priority refers to earlier learning in
     comparison to later learning while intensity
     has to do with the prestige of the source of
     non-conforming behavior. The terms fre-
     quency and duration give this proposition a
     quantitative orientation, while the priority
     and intensity terms, although quantifiable,
     appear to give it a qualitative orientation.

"8. The process of learning deviancy by assoc-
     iation with deviant and nondeviant patterns
     involves all of the mechanisms that are in-
     volved in any other learning." Contrary to
     some popular opinion that the learning of
     deviant behavior has to be explained by some
     unique learning process is this view that it
     is learned just as is any other behavior.

"9. While deviant behavior is an expression of
     general needs and values, it is not explained
     by those general needs and values since non-
     criminal behavior is an expression of the same
     needs and values." Thus the need for money
     can be satisfied by honest work or theft while
     satisfaction of the sex drive can be satis-
     fied by either heterosexual or homosexual
     experiences.[39]

This general theory of deviancy has been subjected to extensive testing, usually with criminals and
juvenile delinquents. This research has usually confirmed the differential association principle. It
helps to explain how persons learn deviancy over time
in a psychological sense and how this is frequently related to the ecological distribution of deviancy by the
existence of a subculture of deviancy or the definitions
favorable to its commission. While it does not explain
some deviancy, like physical disability or the origins
of mental retardation, it helps to explain that which
is voluntary and behavioral.

One variation on this theory is that developed by
Burgess and Akers on the learning principles of operant
conditioning. Unlike Sutherland's theory which assumes
that behavior is thought about and often verbalized in
terms of motives and goals, operant learning theory

31

makes no assumptions about mental processes. Rather,
it argues that deviant behavior, like conforming behavior, is a function of both positive and negative
reinforcement and positive and negative punishment. It
argues that differential association--reinforcement, is
the basis of deviant behavior.[40]

COMPARISON OF DEVIANCE AND MINORITY GROUP THEORY

Deviance and minority group theory can be compared
and contrasted along a number of dimensions. Table 1.1
shows five dimensions along which the two general
theories can be compared. It should be noted that different theorists emphasize selected elements while
giving other aspects less attention.

Groups Studied. Deviance theory gave its early
and primary attention to criminals and juvenile delinquents and then somewhat later to victimless
criminals like homosexuals, transsexuals, prostitutes,
pornographers, and substance abusers. Later, deviance
theory was applied to mental illness and mental retardation. Lately, minor attention has been given to
those who deviate physically from the rest of the
population such as with dwarfs, midgets, fat people and
the physically impaired. In contrast, minority group
theory had its origin in studying ethnic and racial
groups, then somewhat later women as a minority group.
In the last two decades some beginning attempts have
been made to apply minority group theory to other
groups like homosexuals, the physically handicapped,
youth and old people, the mentally ill, the mentally
retarded and fat people.[41] Increasingly these two
fields of analysis are overlapping in their interests.

Identifying Attributes of Subjects Studied.
Deviance theory focuses primarily on that deviance
which departs from norms of behavior and only secon-
darily around physical or intellectual deviations from
norms of "being." In contrast, minority group theory
has given about equal attention to physical attribute
minorities, especially racial and sexual minorities,
and cultural-behavioral minorities, especially ethnic
groups. But in the last two decades both of these two
categories have been extended to new groups like the
aged, physically handicapped, homosexuals and fat
people.

32

Minority group theory has generally used the principle of <u>visual physical identifiability</u> as a critical characteristic of a minority while deviance theorists have critically focused on <u>non-normative behavior</u>. Deviance theory early in its development used a consensus model of society when its focus was primarily on criminals. But with a more inclusive study of other deviant groups, deviance theory has substantially shifted to using social models of the explanation of deviance many of which frequently assume a conflict perspective on social processes. In contrast, minority group theory has always centered on a conflict model of society to explain intergroup relations.

<u>Responses to Deviant Individuals or Minority Groups by Dominant Groups</u>. The conceptualization of how dominant and/or powerful groups respond to either deviant or minority groups is substantially different in the two types of theory. In deviance theory attention is given to how the more powerful and norm-defining groups in society try to prevent, control and treat (sometimes "therapeutically") non-normative behavior. Much of the focus is upon how institutional control agents such as teachers, police, court and prison officials, social service agency personnel, physicians, legislators, and even the media define non-normative behavior and use a variety of sanctions and therapies to minimize or prevent its occurrence or treat or contain it when discovered. Attention is also given on how the labels that both citizens and these institutional control agents apply to deviant behavior may reduce it but more likely confirm primary deviancy. The critical point here and one especially emphasized by conflict theorists, is that the power to define and control deviancy tends to be differentially located in the upper strata of society or their social agents.

In minority group theory the social processes are much the same but the terminology is somewhat different. The dominant group is defined as those who have the power to define and reward those racial, ethnic, sexual, and other characteristics which are judged as superior and inferior. The dominant group is often numerically larger, but not always. Dominant groups develop a number of stereotypes about the differentness and inferiority of minority groups. These stereotypes act as rationalizations for a variety of forms of discrimination against minority group members which in turn

Table 1.1 Comparison of Devnance and Minority Group Theory

Basic of Comparison	Deviance Theory	Minority Group Theory
Type of Group or Individual Usually Described	1. Behavioral departure from normative standards: criminals, substance abusers mentally ill, mentally retarded, homosexuals, transsexuals 2. Physical departure from normative standards of being: dwarfs, midgets, physically handicapped	1. Physical attribute minorities: race, sex, age, dwarfs, physically handicapped 2. Cultural-behavioral minorities: ethnic groups, mentally ill, fat
Identifying Attributes of Subjects Studied	1. Behavior which varies from legal/moral norms set by the socially powerful 2. Physical characteristics like size, appearance or impairments which depart from aesthetic or functional norms	1. Physical attributes: color, sex, age, physical handicaps, size 2. Cultural-behavioral: dress, lineage, religion, language, group memberships,

Responses to Deviant Individuals or Secondary Groups by Dominant and/or Powerful	1. Labeling behavior or appearance as unacceptable, immoral, illegal, ugly, sick, etc. 2. Control, prevention and correction of deviant behaviors or appearances through institutions of social control: education, justice, medicine, law	1. Labeling the physical and/or cultural attributes of a group as inferior 2. Oppressive behavior ranging from annihilation of the minority to discriminatory behavior directed against it
Socioeconomic and Political Power	1. Usually lower in socio-economic and political power	1. Usually lower in socio-economic and political power
Range of Adaptive Responses of Deviants or Minority Groups	1. True conformity to behavioral or physical norms 2. Outward conformity but retain degrees of deviant life-style 3. Try to change social system to make deviance more acceptable or treated less harshly	1. Acceptance of inequality with efforts to become like dominants 2. Avoidance of or separation from discriminatory system 3. Resistance to system either to overthrow it or make it more equalitarian

35

helps to perpetuate their inferior status.

However, one critical difference remains in this regard. It has to do with moral judgment. From the perspective of minority group theory, the differential treatment of minority group members, discrimination if you will, is seen as being unfair or unjust, although not necessarily seen as unfair by all dominant group members. Discriminatory practices are based on largely unfounded stereotypes and/or differences due to nurture stemming from centuries of racist and sexist practices. By the moral standards of equal opportunity, the dominant group restricts equal opportunity because of its own prejudices and the financial, ego and power gains it acquired by not promoting it. Therefore the dominant group is often judged to be wrong. It is strategically advantageous to be considered a minority group for they have been mistreated. This mistreatment can be rectified by the elimination of discrimination and the unfounded prejudices which support it. The problem of moral judgment is more problematic in deviance theory. For the absolutist theorists, the deviant group, not "moral society," is wrong. However, the conflict theorist is closer to the minority group theorist. This is because the very definition of deviance is extensively a function of power in society. Those who define deviancy come primarily from the elitist segments of society and acquire ego, financial and power gains by being the definers and enforcers of the morally acceptable. This relativist position recognizes that some behavior is not inherently moral or immoral but simply the result of differential definitions by the more powerful.[37]

Insofar as a deviant group can define itself or be defined by others as a minority group, advantages accrue to it. If it can argue it is unjustly discriminated against, then the moral onus is on the dominant group. The dominant group is seen as violating the socially and/or legally defined rights of the minority group. These socially defined rights center around equal opportunity to the goods of that society: education, jobs, promotion in work based on merit, housing, political power, recreation and leisure pursuits. If irrelevant characteristics are attributed to the minority group by the dominant group, it is seen to be acting unfairly. Shifting the definition of a group from a deviant to a minority group converts pejorative labeling as "justified" different treatment into "unfair" discrimination. It shifts the burden of moral responsibility from the deviant group to the dominant group. It enables a formerly clandestine deviant group (like many homosexuals) to come out in the open to accuse the dominant group of unfair practices toward it. It bolsters the self-identity of deviant group members by redefining them as persecuted individuals rather than morally reprehensible or sick ones. It paves the way for the deviant group to redefine its mission from furtive self-satisfaction to a group attempting to correct the discriminatory injustices of a society. Thus, a group formerly considered deviant by many people, may want to redefine itself as a minority group for strategic reasons. This self-redefinition, however, does not necessarily make it a minority. But it gives a public relations advantage.

Lower Socioeconomic Status. The lower social, political and economic status that accrues for most deviant and minority group members follows from the way they are labeled, discriminated against and their own self identities. However, insofar as normative deviant group members can disguise their behavior or other characteristics to appear as normal, they can escape the consequences of discrimination. But this does not hold true for either physical attribute deviants or minorities who are easily identifiable.

Range of Adaptive Responses of Deviant Individuals and Minority Groups. Earlier I identified group awareness as the fourth of four minority group characteristics. This awareness of being a minority group is the predecessor of taking action to do something about it. The three major responses that have been formulated are (1) to try to become like the dominant group (assimilation and/or amalgamation), and thus avoid the penalities of being a minority; (2) avoidance and separation from the abusive dominant group, often encouraged by emphasizing ethnic or racial identity; and (3) changing society so that all groups (dominant and minority) may both retain their distinctive identity and yet have equality of opportunity (pluralism), or develop a "new" society (hybridization). Any one group or individual may take any of these responses nearly simultaneously or over time. Deviant groups or individuals actually make similar responses but the phrasing of them is frequently different in deviance theory. (1) One option is for the deviant to conform, for the alcoholic to give up booze and for the homosexual to go straight. This is often the goal that social control agents want to achieve but are never totally successful in doing so. True conformity is rather comparable to the concept of assimilation in minority group theory. In essence, the deviant comes to behave like normal or nondeviant people. Of course the racial minority cannot quickly be blended into the dominant group by amalgamation any easier than the amputee or blind person can overcome his physical limitation. Thus, insofar as a minority or deviant status is entirely dependent on an involuntary physical condition, this route is closed as an adaptive response. Even for physically different minority persons or deviants, however, many of the pejorative characteristics attributed to them are not part of their physical being but socially invented stereotypes that apply to controllable or voluntary behavior. These differences or stereotypes about differences can be altered if they exist or the limited opportunities that flow from stigmatizing attributes can be reduced.

The tactic of accomodative avoidance and separation used by the minority group is somewhat comparable to the outward conformity of many deviants who in varying degrees also participate in a deviant subculture where a disguise of their behavior is unnecessary. Thus the criminal, drug addict or homosexual may try to give the appearance of being norm-abiding when with conformists. However, they may reduce many of their contacts, especially leisure contacts with the conformists. They spend more time in the deviant subculture not only for the gains inherent in those contacts but to avoid deviance labeling and possibly consequent actions aimed at controlling or treating their behavior. Most deviant groups follow this pattern of apparent outward conformity. This is because they recognize the power of the controlling group to levy sanctions on them even if they do not accept definitions of themselves as sick, criminal, immoral, or whatever. With their behavior morally and legally sanctioned, they often try to remain underground and out of incriminating contact with those who can penalize them in some way.

A third tactic the deviant individual or deviant group may use is to try to change society's opinion of what is deviant. They want less exacting definitions of conformity just as those who push pluralism want less demeaning definitions of what is superior in racial, ethnic or gender characteristics or attributes.

The deviant group may want to see certain actions de-
criminalized, like homosexuality or marijuana use, or
more tolerance for nonconformity in "being" characteristics such as fatness, ugliness or physical impairment.
Whether this is a realistic possibility depends on
whether the dominant or powerful group can have its
values and beliefs changed. It is not likely that
criminal acts which brutalize people or confiscate
their goods are likely to be redefined. But redefining the relative deviancy of sexual acts, mental
illness or substance abuse may occur over time. The
tactics used by deviant groups are much like those
used by minority groups: consciousness raising, boycotts, "civil" rights demonstrations and political
lobbying pressures. The use of such tactics by so-
called "deviants" is generally less prevalent than
among minorities and also less studied by deviance
theorists. This is so at the present time because most
deviancy continues to have a greater stigmatism attached to it. Therefore the pattern of outward
conformity remains the predominant response pattern of
some deviants. However, social changes may increasingly
politicize deviant groups, especially non-criminal
deviants.

Summary and a look ahead

This chapter has been concerned with first
looking at deviance theory and then comparing it with
minority group theory primarily because both types of
theorists have studied many of the same groups but with
somewhat different perspectives and terminologies. Deviance theorists have focused primary attention on
nonconforming behavior, especially law-breaking behavior, which in the Sagarin-Montanino typology is
voluntary deviance. Minority group theorists have
focused almost exclusively on racial and ethnic minorities and more lately women whose identifiable
differences are less behavioral than physical in nature.
In the Sagarin-Montanino typology their deviance is
primarily involuntary deviance although the attributed
social and personality differences that distinguish
racial, ethnic and gender minorities in fact are
heavily social in origin. While both types of theorists
have looked at other groups like the physically impaired, blind, deaf, mentally retarded, mentally ill,
homosexuals and aged, the deviance theorists have paid
more attention to these groups than have minority group
theorists. In succeeding chapters I hope to correct

39

that balance by investigating physically different groups from the minority group perspective. This is not to say that the analytical tools or terminology that minority group theory provides is better than that of deviance theory, only different. But in contrast to most deviance theory, minority group theory gives greater emphasis to: (1) a conflict model of society and the relative powerlessness of persons who behave or look differently, (2) questions about the fairness of negative stereotypes and discrimination against such persons, (3) the self-awareness and self-identity of physically different people, and (4) the patterns of response of such persons, particularly civil-right types of group-organized responses which assume unjust discrimination rather than moral nonconformity.

In succeeding chapters I will apply the framework of minority group theory to six physically different minorities: the physically handicapped, the blind, the hearing impaired, dwarfs and midgets, the facially disfigured and fat people. All but one of these groups, fat people, are physical attribute minorities. Fat people, however, while having a physical attribute which sets them apart, are described primarily as a behavioral minority. This is so because their eating behavior is usually seen as a voluntary and alterable behavior unlike the physical attribute minorities whose condition is neither voluntary or usually alterable.

In analyzing these six minorities, particular attention will be given to their identifiably different appearances and sometimes their behavior, stereotypes about them and attitudes toward them, the discrimination they experience, their relative power, the extent to which they have developed a group awareness about their differentness and/or being a minority, and the kinds of responses they make to their stigmatized status.

PART II

PHYSICALLY IMPAIRED MINORITIES

In this section of the book I will concentrate on those who depart from the normal population in their being--their physical being other than racial differences. This section will not cover every type of difference in physical being. But it will attempt to cover some of the major categories of difference: the physically impaired, the hearing impaired and deaf, the visually impaired and blind, the facially disfigured, dwarfs and midgets, and fat people.

Several comments need to be made about categories. Many authors include nearly all the groups listed above, with the exception of midgets and dwarfs, under physical impairment. In looking at the physically impaired in Chapter 2 I will be concentrating on those who have motor control problems or mobility problems due to the loss of limbs or their use stemming from damage to the central nervous system. The problems of these people are somewhat distinct from those experiencing blindness or deafness. The problems of the facially disfigured have little to do with physical impairment per se; rather their problems stem almost solely from the handicapping conditions imposed by society because of their marked departure from aesthetic norms of attractiveness. Fat people are primarily handicapped by the attitudes and practices of society rather than their proportions. A second comment is that physical impairment comes in many degrees--it ranges from mild to profound hearing loss, from mild arthritis which limits some mobility to quadraplegia, a paralysis of all limbs. Associated with the degree of impairment is the degree to which it involves handicapping limitations imposed by society.

A third comment is that some persons have multiple handicaps. For example, one survey of children aged 9 to 11 living in one district in England showed that 2.7% were intellectually retarded, 5.3% displayed some type of psychiatric (emotional or mental) disorder, and 5.5% had some physical impairment. Of those who were mentally retarded, 18% showed one or more of the other disabilities: 2% were psychiatrically impaired, 4% were physically impaired, 12% were both psychiatrically and physically impaired. Of those who were emotionally disturbed, 10% had other problems; 1% were retarded, 7% were physically impaired, and 2% were both physically

41

and mentally impaired. Of those with a physical impairment, 17% showed one or more other disabilities; 2% were retarded, 7% were mentally disturbed and 8% were both retarded and disturbed.

Figures on the rate and numbers of people with physical and mental impairment are not always precise. Often they are made on estimates based on various types of surveys carried out by different offices of the U.S. government. These offices use various definitions that define conditions that range from minor impairment such as partial deafness in one ear to total paralysis. Table II.1 indicates that in the time period 1970-73 around 58,882,000 million Americans or nearly 30% of the population had some physical impairment. However, these figures are somewhat misleading because some people have multiple impairments (which would reduce this figure since some people are counted more than once in them), while others have only one minor impairment. A more realistic figure is that somewhere around 15% of the population has a physical impairment (about 30 million people in 1970) which affects their mobility or normal social functioning. In addition about 3% of the population is estimated to be mentally retarded and 10% mentally ill. Many of the chronic impairments that people experience do not have their beginning at birth. Many of them come late in life as the physiological aging process takes its toll upon older people. Some are caused by home, traffic, and work-related accidents which may occur at any point in the life span. Thus, the physically impaired are an involuntary minority that anybody can become a member of as a result of an accident or disease.

Defining who is handicapped is problematic. In 1973 Congress passed Public Law 93-112, better known as the Rehabilitation Act of 1973. It was not until 1977 that the regulations implementing this law were drawn up. One of the regulations had to do with defining who is handicapped. The Department of Health, Education and Welfare defined a handicap as any mental or physical impairment that limits at least one "major life activity" such as walking, seeing, hearing, speaking, breathing, learning, working and performing manual tasks. HEW included all the conditions listed in Table II.1 as handicaps as well as alcoholism, drug addiction, cancer, diabetes, epilepsy, dyslexia, minimal brain dysfunction and developmental aphasia. This broad and inclusive definition enlarges the number of people

Table II.1

ESTIMATES OF PHYSICAL DISABILITIES, CHRONIC DISORDERS, MENTAL RETARDATION AND MENTAL ILLNESS IN THE UNITED STATES, 1970-1973

	Number	Percent of Total Population
PHYSICAL DISABILITIES AND CHRONIC DISORDERS		
Severely visually impaired or blind	1,306,000	.6
Hearing impaired or deaf	14,491,000	7.1
Chronic obstructive pulmonary disease	14,000,000	6.9
Rheumatoid arthritis	5,000,000	2.5
Partial or complete paralysis	1,392,000	.7
Other orthopedic impairments	8,018,000	3.9
Chronic heart conditions	10,291,000	5.1
Speech defects	1,934,000	.9
Parkinsonism	1,000,000	.5
Cerebral palsy	750,000	.4
Multiple sclerosis	500,000	.2
Muscular dystrophy	200,000	.1
Subtotal	58,882,000	28.9
MENTAL ILLNESS	21,500,000	10.0
MENTAL RETARDATION	6,000,000	3.0
Total	86,382,000	41.9

Adapted from Robert M. Goldenson (ed.). Disability and Rehabilitation Handbook. New York: McGraw-Hill, 1978.

who are considered handicapped, often beyond what some people consider a "legitimate" handicap. In any case, how handicaps are defined will not only affect the numbers of people who are considered impaired but eligibility for benefits under federal, state, and local laws.

  ✳   The study of persons whose difference stems from their physical being is rewarding in developing an understanding of the relationship of the impairment to conceptions of self-worth and social worth. It is also rewarding in understanding how society is increasingly recognizing the role it has in causing and preventing some impairments and in dealing with those who are impaired. ✳

Chapter 2

The Handicapped Minority: The Physically Impaired

In this chapter attention will be given to those who
are physically impaired other than the mentally retarded or visually and hearing impaired.   In 1980 around
35 million persons, about one in seven, had some type
of impairment which restricted some major life activity
such as walking, breathing, or muscle control.   The
types of impairments considered here include muscular
dystrophy, poliomyelitis, multiple sclerosis, epilepsy,
black lung disease, chronic heart conditions, cerebral
palsy, heart disease, stroke, paralysis (paraplegia and
quadriplegia), amputees, arthritis and a variety of
other crippling diseases or conditions.   The range of
such functional impairments is great.   It ranges from
some minor limitations in mobility or coping skills
such as mild arthritis or limited stuttering to severe
cases of cerebral palsy and quadriplegia.   Thus, unlike
some minority statuses where one is either included as
a minority group member or not included, the physically
impaired have varying degrees of impairment.   In analyzing the physically impaired, therefore, it is important
to recognize that minority group theory in general may
be relatively more or less applicable to particular
individuals depending upon the extent of their single or
multiple impairments.   Gliedman & Roth estimate that
somewhere around half of all disabled individuals have
a "serious" impairment.[1]

Impairments, Disabilities and Handicaps

In both the professional literature and popular
references, the terms impairment, disability and handicap are frequently used interchangeably.   They are used
to define an anatomical, physiological or mental deficiency.   However, in some of the more recent
sociological and psychological literature, a distinction
is being made between disability or impairment, the
biological or physical impairment, and handicap, the
social stigma which is often attached to those with a
physical impairment.   Thus, a disability or impairment
is something that a person carries with them, whereas
a handicap is the psychological component of an impairment that is a product of the prejudice and
discrimination that comes from others.   In this and
subsequent chapters we will use the terms disability or
impairment to point to a non-psychological medical con-

dition. In contrast, a handicap is the emotionally or
intellectually debilitating effect that an impairment
may have on an individual. If the impairment does not
bring obstacles to being self-directing and autonomous,
either from society or the self, then the person is not
handicapped but only disabled. However, most disabilities bring derogatory attitudes and restrictive
practices from others. Beatrice Wright argues that a
physical attribute becomes a handicap only when it becomes a significant barrier to the accomplishment of
one's goals. Some physical attributes or deviations
may become handicaps because they effect self conceptions or social relationships even though they are
not physically limiting in themselves.

   Figure 4.1 illustrates the three kinds of limitations that impaired people may experience. The first
of these are intrinsic limitations. Intrinsic limitations are biological or physical givens that impaired
people experience in a variety of ways. If they have
emphysema, or black lung disease or chronic heart conditions they may be unable to engage in much movement
without creating pain or gasping. If they have epilepsy they may not be able to get a driver's license
and have the personal mobility that comes with being
able to drive one's own car. If they are paraplegics
or quadraplegics they may be confined to a wheelchair.
If they have cerebral palsy they will have varying degrees of muscle control so that they may have to be
confined to a wheelchair, have little use of their arms
or legs and perhaps an inability to talk.

   Extrinsic social limitations or social handicappism
are the second kind and are those imposed by society.
They reflect stereotypes about impaired people and
often result in a variety of forms of discrimination.
This discrimination may range from normal people keeping
their distance from abnormal people to institutional
discrimination in areas of employment, housing or the
provision of medical and social services. The term
handicappism is similar to the term racism in this
regard. It refers to cultural stereotypes and discrimination which go beyond the social treatment
warranted by people's intrinsic disabilities. Whether
a certain treatment is warranted is a complex judgment
that will be discussed more fully later. Typically
what happens is that a person with a physical disability
is seen as a physically disabled person -- that is, the
disability rather than the person becomes the focus.

Rather than seeing them as having a limitation, they are seen as being a limited person. The impairment is globalized to their whole being rather than perceived as a facet of their physical being. In a society where it is idealized to have a sound mind in a sound body, they are seen to be deficient in significant ways. This stigma underlays their differential treatment as being less than whole persons. This stigma may not only be attached to impaired persons but sometimes to the persons who associate with them or their parents. Their "defect" is carried over to the parents.

Extrinsic social limitations often become self-fulfilling prophecies or vicious circles. If disabled persons are defined as having few employment possibilities or learning skills they will not be given such opportunities. They then become as they are labeled and treated, underemployed and undereducated, which confirm the originally false definition of their unemployability or uneducability.

Robert Burgdorf summarizes how those who have studied the plight of the physically impaired describe them:

They have been described as "second class citizens", "the forgotten minority", "society's stepchildren", "the most discriminated minority in our nation", "social fugitives", "the silent minority", "human discards", and "most misfortuned citizens". They have been pitied and abused, occasionally deified but more frequently viewed as demonical, they have been hidden, ignored, and generally shunned by society, but recently they have engendered the concern of presidential committees and government agencies. They have been the recipients of charity and special public services but have also been denied many rights and opportunities available to the general public. In literature and real life, they have been heroes and villians. Some have made great contributions to our civilization and culture, while others have lived wasted lives in deplorable and dehumanizing conditions. They are a minority that has been present in all countries at all stages of history, and yet they have remained largely invisible.[2]

47

Figure 2.1

Three Types of Limitations
Related to Physical Disabilities

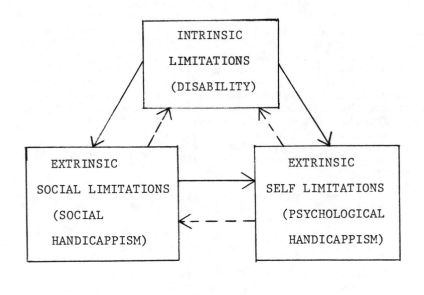

The third type of limitation is <u>extrinsic self-limitation</u>. Basically it occurs when society defines <u>disability</u> as a handicap and the responding disabled person also interprets his condition as a handicap. If the disabled person takes on a definition of himself as handicapped, this works as a psychological self-fulfilling prophecy. He defines himself in terms of his own limitations and not his other assets. This may exacerbate his original impairment by compounding it with lack of development of other or compensating skills and personality traits. Thus the impairment becomes an emotional and intellectual handicap which sustains his dependence on others rather than leading to the development of autonomy skills. To the extent that impaired individuals adopt the handicappism mind set of the larger society they reinforce the social mechanisms which helped to create it in the first place. As indicated in Figure 2.1, if impaired individuals feel they are handicapped, this has a feedback influence on both the impairment itself and the social limitations imposed by others.

The Story of One Quadriplegic

Bruce Hilliam was born in 1961. When he was fifteen years old he dove into a pool of water, following another person. When he floated to the surface his whole body was asleep. Medical examination revealed his fifth, sixth and seventh vertebraes were cracked and that he would remain paralyzed from the armpits down for the rest of his life. This realization came slowly to him as he was subjected to medical tests and surgery in hospitals for a period of time. Depression set in but he was fortunate to have a close knit family that gave him a lot of support. He underwent tiring physical therapy to learn how to write since his fingers in each hand are locked together as a result of the accident. He stayed two years in the hospital before he returned to school. While initially greeted with ovation, his social life soon ground to a standstill. He observed, "the handicapped person, I

49

learned, didn't count for anything. I
had been labeled one of life's losers."
But strong family support enabled him to
finish high school, college and get a
Ph.D. in mathematics. But industry didn't
want him. He found interviewers took a
greater interest in his electric wheelchair
than they did in him. He heard a litany of
excuses about insurance rates, architectural
barriers and inability. So he took a job
in college teaching where students soon
adapted to a teacher in a wheelchair. He
hires two part-time live-in attendants who
shave him, put him to bed, get him up, and
dress him. He does get irritated when he's
put alone in a banquet room in a restaurant
so other customers won't see him, or when
other people address the person he is with
as if he were not there or incapable of
responding or when religious fanatics in-
sist he can be healed if he had enough
faith. He gets around in a van with a
special lift for wheelchairs and hand controls. He says about his life, "I think
my life is as complete as anyone else's.
Life to me is very worth living. I can't
see any reason for resenting that I'm alive.
People have come up to me and said that if
they were me they'd commit suicide. I
just smile. I'm in love with life."

Abstracted from Sonny Kleinfield, The
Hidden Minority: America's Handicapped.
Boston: Little Brown & Co., 1979;
quotes from pp. 10, 21.

Identifiability

One of the characteristics of a minority group is their identifiability. There is a considerable range of easy visibility of the handicapped. Those who are in wheelchairs, or amputees, or move with orthopedically different motions are quite visible. But some with handicaps like cardiac patients or epileptics are not easily visible unless they have an attack in front of others or engage in self reports about their disabling condition. But it is probably safe to say that a majority of the physically handicapped are visibly different. For the smaller proportion who are not visually discernible as different, many come to be known about because of medical exams, employment interviews which probe into a person's medical history or various testing or self-report forms used in our society. A person's deviance from normality is often known in his home community whether or not it is visually apparent.

⚹   One of the problems faced by most visibly physically impaired people is that they are seen as less attractive which in turn inhibits interaction with them in some way. One researcher tested Erving Goffman's hypothesis that persons with a "spoiled identity," in this case a disability, would be less accepted in social interaction than a non-disabled person. ⚹The researcher tested his hypothesis at an airport. In about half the situations a confederate of the researcher was seated in an airport terminal in a wheelchair with a rubber tube inserted in his left nostril. He approached 34 persons and asked them "Which way is it to the San Diego Freeway? A nonimpaired person asked 29 persons at the same airport the same question. The subjects responding to the impaired person maintained a greater distance than they did to the nonimpaired person. The interpretation given to this study was that respondents wanted to maintain a greater distance from a "contaminating" individual.[3] Similar studies have found that high school students felt less comfortable emotionally when interacting with a person who was impaired than a nonimpaired person.[4] Robert Kleck in an article entitled, "Reactions to the Handicapped -- Sweaty Palms and Saccharine Words" found that in brief encounters nonimpaired persons reacted differently to impaired persons. While the unimpaired persons verbally reported thay liked the handicapped person they had talked to in an experimental situation and enjoyed the interaction, their bodies told a different story. They maintained more eye contact with them than usual (to show their interest), but engaged in more nervous motor behavior and maintained a greater physical distance from them than usual. Because they felt uncomfortable about being uncomfortable around such impaired individuals, they smiled more, said more friendly things that they really did not agree with. They tried to make the impaired individuals feel good but ended up not treating them as full human beings.5 Kleck has found that persons stay further away from people who are described as epilpetics. He also found that among adolescents, persons who were physically attractive were ascribed a higher socioeconomic status. Other studies have yielded similar results. People seen as attractive are more likely to be seen as having a number of positive psychological traits. People who are dissimilar from ourself are seen as less attractive.6 Consequently, part of the cultural visibility of a handicapped person is that he or she is seen as less attractive.

Many disabilities are highly visible. However the response to the disability is a form of "surplus discrimination" -- a discrimination unwarranted by the extent of the disability. The individual who is handicapped is often taught that he is less than a whole person and therefore inferior. To a large extent this very inferiority is a learned inferiority.

Attitudes Toward the Handicapped

Attitudes toward the handicapped lay the basis for discrimination toward them in both personal and institutional encounters with the mentally and physically able. This discrimination in turn reinforces the stereotypes which help to justify it. A number of studies about attitudes toward the handicapped reveal they are complex, deeply embedded in norms of interaction, and fundamentally wrong.

One of the attitudes toward disability is that it is an encompassing condition. People tend to think in terms of a handicapped person rather than a person who is handicapped. It is imagined or perceived that it is the central life experience of that person and influences all his other mental and social abilities. As Gliedman and Roth write, it is terribly difficult for the handicapped to pass over into the world of normals.

"In nearly all instances the cripple, the
blind man, even the adult who admits to a reading
disability, must contend with the belief that,
until proven otherwise, the handicap renders him
less capable than an ablebodied person of similar
age, sex and social background. Overcoming this
presumption of inferiority is not impossible, but
it may require a very special kind of sociological
tour de force. Defined by society as a conspicuous failure, one way is open to all: the
possessor of a negative handicap can always prove
that he is the exception to the general rule _if_
he can achieve conspicuous success in some area
of life."[7]

But the exception mechanism is hard to change. We
do remember Roosevelt as a great President and not as a
cripple. We remember Alexander the Great and Julius
Caesar as great leaders, and not as epileptics. But
cripples are seen first as cripples and only later with
continued contact is there humanity recognized.

"Nor do we remember that Lord Bryon had
a club foot and Alexander Pope had curvature of the
spine. Elizabeth Barrett Browning was a para-
plegic. Milton was blind when he wrote _Paradise
Lost_, Beethoven was deaf when he wrote the
Ninth Symphony, Nietzsche was a syphilitic, and
Dostoevsky was an epileptic. Edison was deaf,
and Freud spent the last sixteen years of his
life wearing a prothesis on his jaw. To speak
of these men and women as handicapped seems a
contradiction in terms. It seems so, we believe,
because success defines a chronologically adult
individual as carrying out certain adult functions so well that his inability to carry out
other adult social functions is judged irrelevant.[8]

While some disabled persons can overcome the handicaps placed on them by society, for others the barriers
are too high to surmount. Part of this is due to the
fact that people without disabilities tend to focus on
the disabilities of others. They want to know how they
get around in wheelchairs, how they cope with blindness,
how they prepare for epileptic seizures. They forget
they like movies and music, must contend with bills and
bosses, and have a wide range of experiences unrelated
to their impairment. A comparable situation in race
relations would be for whites to only want to talk to

blacks about race relations and civil rights rather
than baseball, presidential candidates, crabgrass and
foreign affairs. Jerome Dunham and Charlis Dunham
write, "Some who assume that living with disablement
must be an almost unbearable cross reason that the disabled should be cared for and have a chance to be as
happy as possible, but should not attempt to compete or
participate in the mainstream of life."[9]

A second attitude toward the handicapped is that
they are like children. It is often assumed they have
fewer responsibilities and different concerns than
adults. Rather than calling them Mr., Mrs., or Miss,
we call them by their first names, "Charlie" or "Joey"
or "Linda." A soliticuous tone of voice is sometimes
used to display a power differential between those who
are independent and those assumed to be dependent on
others. When the media portray handicapped people they
usually show children. They usually show people who
need help rather than success stories of people who
have overcome their handicap. Many disabled people are
upset by the portrayal they receive in the mass media
during March of Dimes and United Cerebral Palsy solici-
tation campaigns. They show pitiful cripples who need
money rather than adults who become capable workers and
citizens who sometimes need extra financial assistance
for expensive wheelchairs, vans and home assistance.[10]

A third attitude is that the handicapped need
spokespersons to represent them. Assumed to be of a
childlike nature, and of limited ability, not responsible for their own condition, they need adults who know
how to get things done and who are more cognizant of
what is going on in the world. Until they prove otherwise they are assumed to be basically incompetent in all
things. Their impairment has been expounded to their
total personality and range of skills. This attitude
fosters dependence and learned helplessness among many
disabled as well as bringing resentment from many.

A fourth attitude shared by many laymen and especially professionals in the field of rehabilitation is
that the impaired are in a sickness role. This conception underlays societal policy toward the disabled.
But to equate sickness with a handicap has some dele-
terious consequences for impaired individuals.
According to Talcot Parson's formulation, the sick
role contains four elements: (1) the sick person is
not held responsible for his illness -- it is not due

54

to malingering but to biological causes over which he has no control. (2) While sick (usually seen as temporary for most conditions), the patient is exempted from normal role obligations (working, carrying on family responsibilities and the like). (3) The sick role is seen as a legitimate condition, if (4) the patient cooperates with medical personnel in attempting to work for his recovery. But several flaws are apparent in the sickness role if it is applied to a handicapped person. In most instances there is no recovery from a handicap -- it is permanent unlike most temporary illnesses. Because of this, the handicapped person is permanently exempted from normal role obligations. This means he more or less is seen as occupying permanently the second of the four role elements of the sick person. Thus, if the disabled person is seen as sick his condition is tolerated as a form of deviation -- deviation from health. But since he is not expected to return to health, his status carries a stigma with it because he is not expected to carry on normal role obligations of being a parent, worker, citizen or responsible adult in the community. Gliedman and Roth contend that the application of the sick role to the handicapped produces three "oppressive traditional stereotypes about the social ability of handicapped people."

* The sick role's grant of a temporary exemption from normal role obligations changes into a permanent exclusion from normal opportunities -- a reprisal on the part of able-bodied society to believe that the handicapped person is capable of leading a normal social life.

The sick role's decision not to hold the patient responsible for his state becomes a generalized inability to take seriously the handicapped person's attempts to assert his social abilities: instead of recognizing that when the handicapped person refuses to behave like a good patient it is because he is not just a patient, we treat legitimate acts of self-assertion as lapses of conduct for which the patient must not be held morally responsible and which require psychiatric assistance. That is, they are considered <u>symptoms of maladjustment</u>.

The sick role's insistence that the patient actively cooperate with the source of help to

achieve his own recovery turns into a permanent
denial of a person's rights and dignity as a human
being: we see nothing wrong with placing him
under the perpetual tutelage of those experts who
provide him with help, and we believe that the
patient should constantly, subordinate his own
interests and desires -- which include leading a
normal social life -- to the therapeutic goals
and programs decreed by the professional who is
providing the help.[11]

This transformation of the handicapped into a sick
role reinforces the presumed pervasive incompetence of
the disabled. Unable to overcome his sickness he is
permanently assigned to a status of powerlessness over
his own life.

Why Are The Disabled Feared?

Several interesting explanations have been for-
warded as to why normal people tend to withdraw from
the disabled. Each of the following theories has some
merit to it even though taken singly each is not adequate in itself.

Disability is a Symbolically Feared Condition.
The disabled are in fact limited in some way. They
symbolize that which restricts the freedom to lead a
normal life -- movement, speech, seeing, hearing,
thinking, sickness. They symbolize the uncertainty and
mutability of life -- that any of us could have their
condition. They represent to us a loss of some power,
a partial death by their deficiency in being whole.
The evil which has caused their disability is beyond
our comprehension to understand. By distancing ourselves from this condition, possibly contagious in our
fantasies, we protect ourselves physically, socially,
psychologically and morally.

The Disabled are not understood. Ignorance of
what is involved in the hundreds of different origins
and types of disability is beyond the learning experience of many. Children are often warned about the
terrible consequences of accidents in order to prevent
them from happening. Much of our socialization about
disabilities comes from such warnings and not from contact with the disabled. Thus, many people have
stereotypes of what it is like to be disabled. The
disability becomes the person blotting out the many

56

normalities of their life. The impaired are pitied and feared because their experience and condition is not the experience or state of being of the able bodied.

Disability interferes with norms of interaction. Related to a general ignorance of the disabled's limitations and abilities is the uneasiness of interacting with somebody who is different. Norms of interaction often assume all people are equal and to be treated humanely and kindly. How does one interact with somebody who is unequal in their capacity to move, to see, to talk? To be patronizing, to offer help when it is not needed, is to break the norm. But not to offer help when it is desired or needed could be seen as callous and equally norm breaking. Therefore by avoidance of the disabled, the normal person also avoids making interpersonal blunders that could either hurt the other person's feelings of making himself look ignorant (which he may be) of the person's capabilities or look generally socially inept. One avoids awkwardness by not seeking out the strange or strangers.

The calculations of inconvenience. Most human encounters are normatively guided by reciprocity, a symmetry of what is given and expected. But relations between people with different amounts of power, status or physical mobility are marked by asymmetry. More is often situationally demanded of the more powerful. Will the disabled draw the able into the helper role while the helped has nothing to offer in exchange? The disabled often go out of their way to maintain their independence by not asking for help when it would make life more convenient. A few disabled, however, take advantage of their helpers, sometimes counting on the gains they can make from altruistic persons. At the same time, the able bodied may count the cost of his time that the disabled wants as beyond what he can give. Again, distancing avoids the uncertainty of asymmetrial power exchanges and the awkwardness it could raise on both sides of the exchange.[12]

Discrimination Against the Handicapped

Perhaps the central feature of a minority group is the way it is treated differently by the dominant group. While many able-bodied adults treat the impaired as full human beings bothered by some disability, many others treat them in handicapping ways, ways that limit their access to the good things in life: education, recrea-

57

tion, work, family life and sexual experiences. In the introduction to their excellent book, The Unexpected Minority: Handicapped Children in America, Gliedman and Roth give a general overview of the disabled as a minority group:

> A new idea -- simple, yet wide-ranging in its ramifications -- informs our vision of disability. It is that handicapped children and adults are an oppressed minority group. Their oppression takes many forms: outright prejudice against handicapped people of all ages, job discrimination against disabled adults, and well-meaning but destructive misconceptions that exaggerate the true limitations of many handicaps. Frequently oppression is compounded by professionals who define the child's academic and psychological needs exclusively in terms of deviations from the norms of an able-bodied childhood and heavy-handed experts who alienate and demoralize the child's parents in the name of a spurious idea of professionalism. Increasingly, handicapped adults are themselves adopting a civil rights analysis of their problems. They are demanding better social services, but they are demanding more: an end to prejudice and discrimination against people with different bodies.[13]

Discrimination comes in a variety of forms. In this section of the chapter we will look at two categories of discrimination -- the interpersonal and the institutional. The first refers to contacts between the able and disabled in informal contacts while institutional forms of it come in organizational settings: educational and rehabilitation agencies, employment centers, in health care centers and in political arenas where the agents of discrimination are acting in some official role as a teacher, physician, rehabilitation counselor, personnel director, politician, or some other role. Of course people acting in official roles are often influenced by their personal attitudes. But personal attitudes and actions are often shaped in part by what is the formal or informal policy of their employing agency or firm.

As we have already seen, interpersonal treatment of the disabled are influenced by such attitudes as their helplessness, the exaggerated centrality of their impairment, their assumed childlike nature, and their inability to assume many adult responsibilities and tasks because of their "sickness". They are assumed to be different in many ways from other adults.

ᴚ   The behavioral outcomes or correlates of such attitudes range from isolation of them into separate institutions, to social distancing to over-solicitous assistance which creates dependence. Leo Buscaglia, who works with the handicapped, relates the following incident which is a not infrequent occurrence to the handicapped.

> We'll never forget, one family related, when we took our son, Tom, to a local restaurant for his birthday. He was ten. We were all dressed up in our Sunday best and were all set to have a real celebration. To say the least, Tom's palsy doesn't help to make dinner the neatest happening, but we've learned to live with it and it doesn't seem to matter anymore. What does matter is that he can eat by himself and that's a big thing. Aside from getting food all over his mouth and chin, and a little drooling, he does a pretty good job. Anyway, he was doing particularly well on this occasion and we were having a great time. Then, at one point, just during the main course, the people rose in the booth next to ours and stomped out. As the woman passed our table she looked directly at us and spat, "DISGUSTING!" We heard her continue mumbling as she left. "How do you expect decent people to eat with that sight going on?" When the cake finally came, the candles didn't seem so bright. Tom didn't care too much about blowing them out. That was his tenth birthday.[14]

> One of the frequent experiences that disabled people report is that they are treated as sexless human beings who do not have the same interests and drives as other human beings. Buscaglia reports,

> Most disabled persons will tell of their almost daily encounters with some form of overt or covert rejection. A college student confined to her wheelchair relates that each time she joins a group of girls actively engaged in girl talk, the conversation changes. They stop talking about boys, dates and sex, their favorite topics. They start talking about professors, school requirements

59

and books. I know they feel they're protecting me from a potentially painful situation, but in a sense, they are creating a more painful one. They're assuming I'm not interested in boys, dates and sex. They're, in their intended "kindness", rejecting me as a woman and relegating me to some sort of special world they've decided is more comfortable for me.[15]

Perhaps one of the harmful stereotypes to many adult paraplegics and quadriplegics is that they are asexual -- without normal sexual desires or capabilities. Sometimes they lack such capabilities but often they do not as the film, Coming Home, portrayed. One quadriplegic explains that he is capable of sex contrary to the beliefs that some people hold. He explains,

> I can't look at the centerfold of Playboy and have an erection. But if I handle my penis, I can. So I can satisfy a partner during intercourse. I can't appreciate it in terms of physical release, but my partner certainly has a climax. Sex is very much pleasing to me, and I feel the same drive toward an attractive woman as any other man. You know, I can't even unbutton my own shirt. So there has to be a lot of cooperation. The roles and methods expected of each partner have to be different. The woman has to be more active with me. But I enjoy sex.[16]

"It's not architectural barriers that pose the greatest obstacle to the handicapped. The real barrier cannot be seen or bumped into. And it can't be legislated away" writes Marcianne Miller. "The real barrier is an invisible emotional wall. Until this barrier is recognized and understood, the so-called 'wheelchair-power' movement will roll no further than to the edge of the curb." Miller argues that the able have an irrational fear of becoming disabled themselves by some twist of fate. They maintain a polite social distance from the disabled and do not engage them in meaningful conversations. Miller continues,

> I've heard the conversation in a room full of people stop dead when a wheelchair-bound person comes through the door. I've seen a mother grab her child and rush to the other side of the street to avoid passing a disabled veteran. I've had dinner invitations refused because people were

afraid to sit at the same table with my handicapped roommate. "I'll give you a check, " I've
been told when trying to drum up support for a
benefit, "but just don't ask me to meet any of
them."[17]

The polite tolerance but fear of the handicapped
has been around for centuries. In fact, a heavy bias
against the disabled is found in many children's books
and fairy tales. Some of the best loved children's
stories convey a scorn of freaks according to Shari
Thurer, a psychologist. Captain Hook wore a prosthesis;
Cinderella's stepsisters were fat, ugly and mean. Han-
sel and Gretel suffered under an arthritic witch while
Jack climbed the beanstalk only to be confronted by a
wicked giant. Chronic illness, physical deformities,
and other defects have become associated with inner defects, mental incompetence and villainous motives.
Deformity usually symbolizes immorality. In contrast,
good people in children's stories usually have intact
bodies, move with grace and have outward beauty and
sunny dispositions. Miller believes that such illus-
trations of handicappism are traceable to a subtle
prejudice in our Judeo-Christian ethic that fosters the
idea that success and riches go to the morally right and
productive while wrongdoers are rewarded with suffering,
physical defects and sickness.[18] Often parents feel
guilty for the handicaps of their children as if they
were retributions for their own transgressions.

> Maria French was diagnosed as having
> cerebral palsy at an early age. Because
> of great difficulty in walking, she spends
> much of her time in a wheelchair. At an
> early age her parents assured her she
> could become whatever she wanted to and
> got special help for her: speech therapy,
> physical therapy, and orthopedic aids.
> She found a paradox in how people treated
> her. On one hand they encouraged her to
> become herself, but on the other hand not
> to be a dreamer or expect miracles. While
> they wanted her to have freedom, they did

61

not want her to have the freedom to
fail. They tried to counsel her
against things they thought would be
too demanding for her: crawling,
walking like a drunk, eating with
her elbows on the table. They did
not want her to act like an impaired
individual who was different from
others: who drooled, who walked
funny, who talked funny. She per-
sisted in spite of her impairment
and the handicapping attitudes of
those around. She learned to type
and drive a car when this looked
like a foolish dream to others. Her
idea of getting a college education
seemed foolish to some, but after
nearly twelve years of being tutored
in closeted schools she saw that a
world of opportunities existed in
spite of the disbelief barriers raised
by others. In spite of obstacles she
went on to get a college degree and
then a master's degree.

Adapted from: Leo Buscaglia, The
Disabled and Their Parents:
A Counseling Challenge. Thorofare,
N. J.: Charles B. Slack Inc. 1975

The parents of handicapped children often suffer
from the same stigma attached to their deviant child by
society. They become a minority also. According to
Buscaglia,

    Their feelings of being in a minority result
mainly from their almost daily encounters with
socially derogatory attitudes. They are expressed
in patronizing inferences of friends and relatives,
in the avoidance response of strangers and often
covertly implied in the attitudes and treatment
given them by the professionals who purport to be

dedicated to the remediation of the physical and mental disabilities of their child. The professionals' impatience, condescension and skepticism toward them and their child, stated or imagined, and their insistence upon the relegating of their child into special categories and segregated schools and classes, seem to continually imply their inferior status.[19]

Different parents react in different ways to having a physically handicapped child. Their responses depend not only on the kind and severity of the handicap, but the physical and emotional demands made on them by it. And of course it is also influenced by their own attitudes toward handicaps, their work obligations and their coping skills. One common response to the first announcement of having a handicapped child is denial. They cannot believe that their child is handicapped. This is often accompanied by guilt feelings of whether they have done something wrong to bring this condition about. If denial continues it often results in "shopping behavior." This shopping behavior is characterized by visiting many experts -- doctors, specialized clinics and counselors in hope of finding a diagnosis that their child is not deficient in some way. The denial may take on other forms: denying the disability to the child, or to family and friends and avoidance of others so they cannot see it. They may try to protect the child by keeping him within the protected environment of the home.

Frustration is another response to the surprising presence of a physically disabled child. It has several roots. One source of frustration often comes from the medical system in which a series of specialists carry on their diagnoses behind doors closed to parents who don't know what is going on. The findings are finally disclosed to parents but often cloaked in medical jargon beyond their understanding. A barrier to communication is often raised by experts in the language they use, the condescension they convey, and the lack of concrete advice on the child's prognosis and what services will be needed. Some professionals give alarming advice: "let the child die," "there is no hope," or "put him in an institution." Such advice and prognoses are often wrong. Another source of frustration is where to go for help and what to do. Parents are not told what clinics or schools are available for

63

their child. They are frustrated because they do not know where to turn for help. They are frustrated too by dealing with the uncertainties of a new situation they have never experienced before.

A third reaction by parents is one of grief, sorrow, disappointment. An expected normal child is lost. Sadness and self pity may be compounded by feelings of guilt or of shame for the child's stigma is their stigma.

A fourth reaction that we will describe more fully later on is to fight the medical system and society at large for its handicapping practices which deny the family and the disabled child their rights. They push for more information from doctors, they seek the removal of architectural barriers, they seek better counseling and educational services, they organize with other parents to share common problems and seek solutions to them.[20]

In addition to the interpersonal discrimination that disabled children and adults experience are institutional barriers in the medical system, the educational system including rehabilitation centers, the employment system, and politics. Discrimination is a denial of rights. The United Cerebral Palsy Association has issued a "Bill of Rights for the Handicapped" that list ten rights for the disabled: (1) The right to prevention of disability, (2) The right to health services and medical care, (3) The right to education, (4) The right to training, (5) The right to work, (6) The right to an income, (7) The right to live where and how they choose, (8) The right to barrier-free public facilities, (9) The right to function independently, (10) The right to petition.[21]

The right to prevention of disability involves preventing, insofar as possible, both congenital and environment sources of disablement. Some gains have been made in this area in the last two decades, but much more remains to be done in this area for two reasons. One is that our health care system is more oriented to cure than prevention, partly because fees for curing are higher than for prevention. The other is that the regulations necessary to reduce environmental pollution, vehicular and industrial accidents are sometimes costly and resisted primarily on that basis. But an estimated one third to one half of all disabilities are prevent-

able. Some cost estimates on the savings that would
accrue by eliminating preventable disabilities indicate
that it would not only be financially advisable to do
so but would save millions of people from the unnecessary suffering, disfigurement and decreased opportunities that accompany disablement.[22]

A number of causes of congenital defects have been
identified: genetic abnormalities, prenatal damage to
the fetus stemming from disease, malnutrition, accident,
or the absorption of poisonous substances, and injury of
the child at birth. Other early childhood injuries
ranging from ingestion of lead-based paint to head injuries are causes of disability. Many of the resulting
conditions, like mental retardation, cerebral palsy,
blindness, deafness and deformity are either preventable or the degree of impairment lessened with
prevention and/or early treatment measures. Some of
these measures include genetic counseling of parents,
abortion, proper nutrition, immunization against disabling diseases during pregnancy, pre-natal medical
care of the mother and good health education. Yet only
about 3% of our health care budget goes for prevention
and 1% for health education. But if we look at the low
cost of preventing many disabilities in comparison to
the special health and educational care costs of these
disabilities and the high rates of dependency of the
handicapped on public welfare and the missed tax reve-
nues from potential workers, then the decision to
underfund prevention and health education measures appears unwarranted.

No one knows the toll that environmental pollution
has in leading to disability. But it may be substantial.
In addition, there are about 60,000 deaths from vehicular accidents per year and a far greater number which
result in either severe or minor impairments. While
much is known about how to make vehicles, highways and
crossings safer, new preventive measures are only
slowly being adopted because of their high cost. In
1971 there were over 3 million recorded job-related
injuries and illnesses in a work force of 57 million.
Around 10 to 15% of these resulted in disablement for
six months or more -- sometimes forever. In 1969 Congress passed the Williams-Steiger Occupational Safety
and Health Act which mandated that employers provide a
work place free from recognized hazards that would or
could cause death and serious harm to employees. The
Occupational Safety and Health Administration (OSHA) in

the Department of Labor has the responsibility of setting health and safety standards and insuring compliance
under this act. But gains under this law have been slow
because the understaffed department does not have the
manpower to detect non-compliance and many employers
are slow to voluntarily comply because of the perceived
cost of compliance with regulations.[23]

Handicapped individuals need not only the medical
care that other people get but special care for their
disabling condition. They frequently run into a number
of problems in this area -- lack of availability of services, especially if they live in rural America, lack of
information and counseling on the types of services both
available and needed, difficulty of accessing such services because of architectural barriers at some
locations, a lack of coordination of such services, and
the low quality of some of these services that are offered. Insufficient research has been done on a variety
of aspects of not only handicapping conditions but services to the disabled. More research needs to be
carried out on the origins of handicapping conditions,
the psychology of disablement, the provision, communication about and coordination of health and training
programs for the handicapped, and the development of
special prosthetic devices and learning aids for the
physically and mentally impaired.[24]

At the level of the delivery of educational and
medical services the handicapped person, and his parents
if he is a child, are caught in a professional model
where they are often treated as children who are unaware
of the clinical nature of their problem and the special
medical or educational services that only the "experts"
know about. Impaired individuals and their parents are
vulnerable to professional doctors, psychologists and
educators whose services they need but which are often
offered in an oppressive way. Clients are often caught
in a double bind by the experts. If they openly disagree with the procedures and conclusions of the experts,
they are often interpreted as maladjusted -- another
piece of evidence of the deviance model of handicappism
that prevails among service providers. Thus service
providers often coerce clients into accepting their educational or medical views even though in many instances
they are wrong. In this way medical and educational
institutions often treat disabled individuals as a
minority group according to Gliedman and Roth. Unless
they organize strong resistance to the treatment they

are getting, they are treated as inferior non-experts
by the dominant group -- the professional providers.[25]

   Until the 1970's the physically handicapped were
educated for the most part in special education classes,
by tutors if their parents could afford it, in separate
and segregated institutions, or not at all. For the
most part their education did not take part in the mainstream of public school education. But two court cases
and several federal laws have substantially, but not
fully, gained for the disabled their constitutional
right of equal treatment under the law -- in this case
equal educational opportunity.

   In 1971 the Pennsylvania Association for Retarded
Children (PARC) brought a class action suit against the
Commonwealth of Pennsylvania in federal court on behalf
of fourteen retarded children who had been denied free
public education. The federal district court ruled in
favor of the parents. It required that the state provide every retarded child with a free public education.
In 1972, in Mills V. Board of Education of District of
Columbia, a similar ruling was made except that it applied to all handicapping conditions. There the court
ruled that children who were emotionally, physically or
mentally impaired had the right to a free education in
public schools under the equal protection clauses of the
Constitution. A rash of similar suits then rapidly followed in many states. Several pieces of federal
legislation have progressively defined the public
school's obligation to educate handicapped children.
The Elementary and Secondary Education Act of 1965 included the handicapped in it but did not lead to major
changes. The Rehabilitation Act of 1973 (P.L. 93-112)
defined impairments in an inclusive way. The major
watershed came in the Education Amendments of 1974
(P. L. 91-230) which called for the education of the
handicapped in the "least restrictive environment."
The idea here was that handicapped children, insofar as
possible, were to be "mainstreamed" into the regular
public school system so that their education and contact with other children would be as normal as possible.
To be eligible for federal funding, each state was to
formulate a plan on how it was going to include the disabled in its educational programs.[26]

   The most inclusive and detailed federal legislation
on the education of the handicapped was passed in 1975
and went into effect in September of 1978. This 1975

legislation was the Education for all Handicapped Children Act usually referred to as Public Law 94-142. This piece of legislation has led to a major revolution in the education of handicapped children from the ages of 3 to 18 effective in September, 1978 and ages 3 to 21 effective September, 1980. This law requires a number of things of public school systems: (1) to provide a free public education to all including the handicapped, (2) to develop an individualized education program (IEP) for each child based upon individual diagnosis, (3) to keep as much of each handicapped child's education alongside able-bodied peers as is possible, and (4) to provide a procedure wherein parents of handicapped children are kept informed about educational decisions being made about their children and may appeal them when they are dissatisfied.[27]

Public Law 94-142 has created many issues in public education ranging from the unpreparedness of many teachers to have impaired students "dumped" in their classrooms, to the additional costs it is imposing on schools to make them architecturally accessible and to add special equipment and teachers. This legislation has paved the way for making major gains in the education of handicapped children. But some forms of discrimination are still occurring against handicapped children in spite of remarkable advances being made under this legislation. Many teachers and administrators continue to treat the disabled as deviations from normalcy that are bad rather than different. Such attitudes are often carried over into the attitudes of their students--both able and disabled. While parents are to be informed of changes in their child's IEP (individualized education program) and able to appeal it or changes to it, the content of it is often announced to them by the educational experts who claim to know what is best for their children. While parents can get outside counsel or expert opinion to protect their rights or buttress their views, they must pay for these services out of their own pockets. The use of a variety of testing mechanisms that are used on normal children may be discriminatory when used with the disabled: (1) these standardized tests may not be attuned to the differences in environment and learning experiences the impaired have had in comparison to normals, (2) the very disability that some students have such as in speed of writing or sensory ability or motor ability as true for cerebral palsy cases may detract from good test performance which reward speed and good motor coordination, (3) these tests, especially IQ tests, may be used for diagnostic purposes in assigning students to various educational groupings but are not valid for pinpointing the causes of the disability and special educational needs that the child has. In commenting upon the use of intelligence tests especially adopted for the handicapped, Gliedman and Roth point out that,

> Instead of seeking to identify the special characteristics of the child's cognitive strategies, they assess the child according to norms that make no allowance for these differences. Tests designed for able-bodied children assess the handicapped by norms that may have no relevance whatsoever to the child's intellectual development.[28]

Consequently, some handicapped children are mislabeled below their achievement potential by the use of standardized tests. Defined as intellectually inferior, educational processes of labeling and academic grouping are carried out which confirm the false definition in the first place. Because teachers sometimes see limited options for the handicapped following schooling, they treat them as disabled patients rather than the capable learners they may be. They expect less of them. Often this leads to a teaching by ability grouping in which many of the disabled end up in a low ability group. In this way, mainstreaming may be undermined by resegregating the disabled into the same ability grouping. It undermines one of the basic intents of mainstreaming -- to overcome the prejudice and discrimination toward the disabled by having both the abled and disabled overcome stereotypes by means of cooperative and extensive contact and by opening up educational opportunities for the handicapped that will better prepare them for life and work after school.[29]

Nicholas Hobbs summarizes well the problem of "exceptional" children:

> Children who are categorized and labeled as different may be permanently stigmatized, rejected by adults and other children, and excluded from opportunities essential for their full and healthy development.[30]

Hobbs then goes on to point out that,

We have a multiplicity of categorical
legislative programs for all kinds of children.
Yet the child who is multiply handicapped, who
does not fit into a neat category, may have the
most difficulty in getting special assistance.[31]

Employment is one of the major satisfactions in our
society. Being employed is the major route for financial independence. But by a number of indices, the
handicapped do not fare well in our work system: a
smaller proportion of them enter the work force; of
those seeking work, more of them are unemployed or
working part time only; on the average they make less
money; they are underrepresented in the better paying
occupations and they are frequently given fewer promotions. There are four major reasons why this
situation prevails although the relative influence of
each has never been accurately measured. Certainly one
of the reasons is that some disabilities are so extreme
and complete that they provide insurmountable obstacles
to competitive gainful employment. However most disabilities are not that severe and are situation
specific -- that is they may keep a handicapped person
from doing some types of work but not others. A second
reason is that the impaired suffer the same kind of
lower educational status that other minorities do. On
the average they have fewer years of education and
fewer resources than do the able, which puts them at a
competitive disadvantage. Often they have experienced
less job training and have less work experience to draw
on to gain employment. A third reason is that employers
discriminate against the handicapped for a variety of
reasons that we will look at shortly. A fourth reason
has to do with job accessibility because of a lack of
transportation or architectural barriers to getting
into or moving around within the place of work. This
may include doorways too narrow or steps which prohibit
the use of wheelchairs or a lack of bathroom facilities
for the impaired. All of these may help contribute to
both the impaired and employees learning to exaggerate
their limitations because they are so often socially
presumed to be dependent on others and unfit for work.[32]

One national study found only 23% of the nondisabled
men and women between the ages of 20 to 64 not in the
work force compared to 52% of the disabled. In this
same study, 95% of all nondisabled males and 54% of all
nondisabled females were working in the 20 to 64 age
category compared to 60% of the disabled males and 29%

70

of the disabled females.[33]

A 1966 survey carried out by the Social Security Administration found that among noninstitutionalized adults 18 to 64, 17.2% had some disability compared to 52.8% who did not. Of the nearly 18 million adults who are disabled, 34% had severe disabilities, 28% had disabilities only in some occupations while the remaining 38% had what were labeled as "secondary work limitations," only.[34] Thus a majority of the impaired could work but do not. The major argument made by Frank Bowe in Rehabilitating America is that we are rehabilitating too few disabled people. Rather than saving money by not spending it on rehabilitation programs, we are spending much more on the welfare support of many disabled people, especially the older disabled. He argues that we cannot afford not to rehabilitate people capable of working and whose lives would be greatly enhanced by such efforts.[35]

The critical factor that we want to look at are the facts of discrimination and the reasons for it. Under the Rehabilitation Act of 1973, any employer who is receiving federal financial assistance is prohibited from discriminating against the handicapped. Furthermore, they are to make "reasonable accommodations" in the workplace so that the handicapped can be employed. Each employer with federal contracts in excess of $2,500 as well as the federal government itself are to develop "affirmative action" plans to actively hire, place and promote the handicapped. However, a recent survey by the U. S. Department of Labor of 300 randomly chosen companies found that 91% were not in compliance with the Vocational Rehabilitation Act of 1973. Only 24% had affirmative action plans for the handicapped, only 18% made reasonable workplace accommodations for the handicapped, while 57% illegally asked prospective employees to identify the extent and severity of any handicaps they had. The Office of Federal Contract Compliance Program, assigned the responsibility of enforcing this law, was found to be doing little.

Three areas in which contractors tend not to be in compliance are (1) hiring qualified handicapped persons, (2) using proper reasons for terminating them, and (3) promoting them or even considering them for promotion.[36]

Certainly many industries and firms do hire the

71

disabled. But many are reluctant to do so for stereotyped reasons which turn out to be factually inaccurate
for the most part. Numerous surveys of a variety of
types of employers have revealed the following employer
beliefs which are in fact false:[37]

1. The handicap produce less quantitatively
and qualitatively with more absenteeism. Several
studies reveal that the handicapped actually produce more than their able-bodied counterparts and
are less absent from work. An Office of Vocational
Rehabilitation study of employers found that 24%
said the disabled produced more, 66% the same, and
10% less than their nondisabled employees. A
duPont study of its 1,452 physically disabled
workers showed that 91% of them performed as well
or better than the nondisabled and that 79% of them
had an average or above average work attendance.
The Office of Vocational Rehabilitation study found
55% of the disabled has less absenteeism, 40% had
the same absenteeism and 5% more absenteeism than
the nondisabled.

2. The handicapped have a higher turnover
rate. Because of training costs for new workers,
employers do not like to lose good employees.
Most evidence indicates that the handicapped are
less mobile occupationally than other workers,
partly because they often have fewer employment
opportunities than do other workers.

3. The disabled will have more accidents that
will increase the company's insurance rates and
their liability for compensable injuries. This
frequently cited reason for not wanting to hire the
handicapped is fundamentally economic. It is also
not verified. Most evidence points to the fact
that the handicapped are more cautious and safety
minded and have fewer accidents. The duPont study
of its 1,452 disabled workers found that 96% of
them rated average or better on safety both at work
and off the job. A study of over one hundred large
corporations by the U. S. Office of Vocational
Rehabilitation found the accident rate for the disabled lower in 57% of the companies, the same in
41%, and higher in only 2% of the companies.
Furthermore, accident insurance is not based on who
is hired, but on past accident rates for that company and the industry of which it is a part.

Therefore hiring the disabled with a generally
superior accident rate does not cost the company
more money. If anything, it may save it money. A
survey by the National Association of Manufacturers
of nearly 300 firms revealed that 90% of them did
not have their insurance rates altered by hiring
disabled employees.

4. Other employees will not accept the
disabled as fellow workers. In the first place
this argument is generally irrelevant in light of
the law preventing employment discrimination.
Secondly, it is generally untrue. Other employees
often become good friends with a fellow disabled
worker. Since they often have a strong dedication
to disproving the stigmas about them, the disabled
are frequently conscientious workers who boost
employee morale by showing what can be done in
spite of a handicap.

5. Expensive adjustments to the workplace will
have to be made to accommodate the disabled. This
stereotype cannot be responded to generally but
only on a specific case by case basis. By law employers are to make "reasonable accommodations" --
whatever that means beyond special parking spaces,
ramps, wider doors, lowered workbenches, and special
lavatory facilities. Undoubtedly it would be un-
reasonable to redesign one assembly line at a cost
of millions to accommodate one disabled worker.
But in many instances for the minimally disabled no
workplace alterations need to be made at all. For
many others the alterations are not prohibitively
expensive. Generally, fellow workers do not resent
special considerations being given to the handicapped such as earmarked executive parking
privileges near a firm's employee entrance. Some
firms often exaggerate the cost of making buildings
accessible. For example, the Kaiser Aluminum and
Chemical Corporation had architects visit its headquarters to estimate the cost of making it barrier
free. They came up with a cost of $160,000. Main-
stream, Incorporated, an organization set up to get
corporations to hire the handicapped, visited the
same building and came up with a cost estimate of
only $8,000. They pointed out that every bathroom
and doorway and hall didn't need alteration unless
every employee was disabled.[38]

73

In spite of the lack of evidence to support many of the reasons employers give for not employing the handicapped, many disabled remain unemployed. For example, special campaigns have been held to "hire the handicapped." These campaigns are usually ineffective even for veterans who are to be given special consideration. Over three million disabled veterans live in the United States with over 490,000 veterans of Vietnam. Most of the Vietnam Veterans had joint and bone impairments, muscle impairments or neuropsychiatric impairments with only 5% of them being either blind or amputees. Overall, disabled veterans had twice as high unemployment as able-bodied veterans of the same age. Many employers have argued that their jobs would have to be redesigned to accommodate the handicapped. Many employers continue a rather double standard toward the handicapped. Many say they would be willing to hire the handicapped, but their actual hiring practices tell a different story. They remain aversive and reluctant to hire them, especially if they are more severely disabled or if the employer is not engaged in manufacturing. Max Cleland, director of the Veteran's Administration, had both legs and an arm blown off in Vietnam. He says "It's bad enough to shut these handicapped men and women out of the economic system of the country they served. It is intolerable to waste their tremendous remaining potential on the basis of disabilities they incurred in that service.[39]

Because nearly one in seven noninstitutionalized adults between the ages of 20 and 64 has some chronic condition lasting six months or more and affecting his employability, the federal and state governments have cooperated to develop an extensive vocational rehabilitation program. In 1975 over 1,800,000 clients were served in this program at a cost of $1.7 billion. While these rehabilitation centers do help to rehabilitate millions, they too have been found to engage in several forms of discrimination. Because they are funded on the basis of the number of clients they actually place in jobs, they engage in "creaming." This involves selecting the least disabled clients for rehabilitation services because they will most easily be placed in jobs and thus insure the continuation of the rehabilitation agency at a high level of funding. Because of this the more severely disabled have less opportunity for rehabilitation. These agencies use various diagnostic tests to steer clients into rehabilitation programs and jobs which they consider

appropriate or realistic for them rather than on what
the client desires or what may be the client's real
potential. The most severely disabled are usually
steered into sheltered workshop employment -- permanent
employment in menial jobs for menial pay. While this is
often appropriate, it may not prepare some of them for
their real potential of holding a mainstream job outside the sheltered workshop.[40]

Tha handicapped are placed in triple jeopardy from
entering the mainstream of life by becoming independent
through their own work. They sometimes face limitations
from their impairment itself. Even worse are those
frequently imposed by society -- getting education or
training for work and finally getting a job itself.
The third jeopardy is that they may give up because of
the handicapping practices of society which tells them
they are second rate citizens.

Perhaps one of the most controversial areas involving the physically disabled is the creation of
re-creation of a barrier-free environment. Society has
not created physical obstacles to intentionally limit
the enjoyment or mobility of the disabled. Rather it
was by oversight. In many ways the handicapped were
considered non-persons who didn't move but were expected to stay in one place forever. But the number of
handicapped persons has been increasing and will continue to increase as our population grows older and as
contemporary medicine increasing salvages many persons
who would have died or died at earlier stages in earlier
times from a variety of crippling disorders. As their
numbers are increasing and they are organizing to present their claims to equal opportunity their cries for
a barrier free environment are being heard. Politically
they have already been heard in the matter for some
important legislation has been passed to help the handicapped. In 1968 Congress passed PL90-480, the
Architectural Barriers Act, which required that new
public buildings using federal funds in their construction be made accessible to and internally useable
by the disabled. The 1973 Rehabilitation Act established an Architectural Barriers and Transportation
Board of eleven members, eight of whom were to be handicapped, to enforce the 1968 act. And by 1974 all fifty
states had passed legislation to require all newly constructed public buildings be made accessible to the
disabled. But this leaves many older buildings inaccessible and even some of the new buildings are not

75

carefully designed to be totally useable by the handicapped.

✻   Cost is the major factor in making old public
buildings accessible. HEW put the estimate at $2.4
billion. For example, the cost to make the nation's
6500 hospitals barrier-free has been estimated at
$880 million, $3 million to alter the nation's 119
medical schools, $40 million to alter San Francisco's
schools. Exactly how many of the nation's impaired
have trouble gaining access to or using public buildings
is unknown. It may be in the neighborhood of 10 to 15
million or even more if we include the elderly. The
additional cost of making new buildings barrier free is
put at about 1% of the total cost of the building; it
may go as high as 2.4% to make older ones barrier free.
Altering public transportation systems is higher. It
would be prohibitively expensive to scrap all rolling
stock and start afresh. The State of Florida found
that to buy new 35-foot buses with low floors, wider
aisles and automatic lift ramps for wheelchairs increased the price of each bus from $130,000 to
$470,000.[41] However, the Urban Mass Transportation Act
Amendements of 1974 stated that it was the nation's
policy to make special efforts and special funding
available to make mass transportation facilities and
services available to the elderly and handicapped citizens. How far, if at all, should cost be a factor in
denying people the right to mobility and all that goes
with it -- work, education, recreation and personal
freedom?

     Some of the major barriers the handicapped face are:
steps; revolving doors; doors too heavy or cumbersome
to open from wheelchairs, walkers and crutches; doors
with unturnable handles for some with limited arm
motion or strength; doorways too narrow for wheelchairs;
cafeteria lines with aisles too narrow or food too high
to see and reach from wheelchairs; elevator doors too
narrow to enter in wheelchairs or insufficient inside
space to turn around in to reach the buttons; light
switches, elevator buttons, drinking fountains, food
store shelves and countertops (stoves, workbenches)
that are too high to reach; phone booths too narrow to
enter or with the buttons out of reach; narrow bathroom
and tub facilities lacking support bars; hangers out of
reach for those in wheelchairs; an inability to get onto
public transportation (buses, cabs, trains, subways and
airplanes); desks that are too low to wheel a wheelchair

underneath; curbs that prevent a wheelchair from crossing; and, of course, steps. Without making costly
changes, however, approximately 5 - 7% of the population will have trouble in shopping, going to school
or work, banking, voting, visiting ball parks, churches,
theaters, restaurants, museums and a whole range of
other places that most people take for granted. They
will be consigned to a much narrower social life and
kept in a second class citizenship status. They become
hidden--recluses in their own homes. Since all people
have the potential of becoming disabled, would they
want such a confined existence for themselves? Two
major values are at stake here. One is the intrinsic
value that would result to the handicapped by enlarging
their freedom of choice to do what others do. The other
value is the financial return to society by allowing
handicapped citizens to be economically productive tax-
payers rather than the recipients of disability and
welfare payments. Most benefit/cost studies of the re-
turns on vocational rehabilitation programs show a ratio
of about 10 to 1. This means that for each dollar
invested in rehabilitation there is a ten dollar return
on the investment. While such a ratio cannot be cal-
culated for making the environment barrier free, such
efforts do increase the chances for employment for some
of the handicapped. In addition, it adds to the quality
of their life in innumerable ways.

The Lower Status of the Handicapped

Perhaps little needs to be said about the lower
socioeconomic status of the physically impaired.
Because of barriers to full personhood due to their
disability and then impediments to education and training and finally jobs, the disabled end up as a minority
group with lower incomes, fewer assets and less
political power than we might expect from a group that
makes up around a tenth or more of the population.
Presumed by many to be poor workers because of a disability that may be unrelated to work productivity, they
are relegated to a childlike status or inferiority unless they can prove against tough odds that they are
productive citizens in a society that values the work
ethic. In the epilogue to the Unexpected Minority,
Gliedman and Roth point to paralyzing handicaps that
society has imposed on those who are only impaired:

Thus, what many social critics have perceived
as a future threat for society at large has long

been a bitter reality for many handicapped children
and adults: the disabled already live within a
therapeutic state. In this society of the "sick"
there is no place for any of the hallmarks of a
present or future adult identity; no place for
politics, no place for work and sexuality, no place
for choice between competing moralities. All
political, legal, and ethical issues are transformed
into questions of disease and health, deviance and
normal adjustment, proper and improper management of
the disability. Language itself changes, "Respect-
ing the child's individual needs" means focusing
upon the child's deviance to the exclusion of everything else. "Special education" means providing
the child with schooling that usually is neither
special nor education in the ordinary sense of the
words. "Maturity" means learning to accept one's
social oppression as well as the true limits of
the body. "Portraying with sensitivity and understanding the problems of handicapped people" becomes
an Orwellian euphemism for perpetuating the handicapped role's vision of disability in the media.
Is it any wonder that the minority-group characteristics of the disabled so often come as a surprise,
that the handicapped child and the handicapped
adult are an unexpected minority? ... of all
America's oppressed groups, only the handicapped
have been so fully disenfranchised in the name of
health.[42]

The above quote which describes the medicalization
of the impaired's deviance is quite akin to scientific
racism which attempts to use "objective evidence" like
IQ tests to show the inferiority of blacks. While both
are carried out under the banner of medicine or science,
both contain a sophisticated oppression by using evidence to show the differentness of groups rather than
their similarity with all humanity. A complex vocab-
ulary and world view contain this obfuscating
oppression. As a result, 36% of the handicapped were
in the poverty category in 1970 compared to 20% of the
rest of the population.

The Disabled's Reactions to Impairments and Handicappism

Whether a person is disabled from the point of birth
on or is disabled at some point later in life as a result of an injury or disease, both are exposed to a
whole lifetime of socialization into the attitudes and

practices called "handicappism." We might expect that
the person handicapped from birth is more exposed to
the oppressive medicalization of his impairment than
the person whose impairment comes at age 18 or 37 or
54. But little research bears on this question of
whether the person who is impaired later in life has
more resistance to handicapping practices than the person born impaired. Research evidence does show,
however, that those who have an acquired handicap see
themselves in the same way that those who were born
with one do. But most of them are aware that the nondisabled feel uncomfortable around them, don't know
what to talk about except their impairment, and often
shun them because they are seen as lesser individuals.

In this section we want to look at the disabled's
reactions, individual and group reactions, to their
impairments. But we are strongly suggesting this does
not occur in a vacuum. It occurs in a setting where attitudes and a whole range of educational, medical,
rehabilitational, employment and architectural practices
and services strongly influence how the individual will
react to his disability and the handicapping attitudes
of society. With the same variety of responses that a
black person reacts to his skin color in our society,
the disabled will react to his impairment. He may deny
it, feel guilty about it, try to change it, succumb to
the idea he is inferior or rise above the imposed barriers to success. Perhaps the major difference is that
the impaired come in more varieties and face more degrees of severe restrictions than do social and ethnic
minorities.

Since the handicapped is often treated as a sick
person whose illness is not reversible, he tends to be
treated as an immature person who can expect a lifetime
of dependence on others. Often he is protected and
sheltered from experiences that contribute to ego
identity, personality growth, intellectual growth and
social awareness. Because of barriers to mobility and
to normal classroom experiences the impaired have
lesser opportunity to play a variety of roles that contribute to growth--leader roles, follower roles,
athletic roles, sexual roles, homemaking roles, work
roles. Frequently they are given fewer experiences in
which they can succeed or fail and from which their
self-identity can be constructed. Because of both their
disability and the handicapped barriers imposed on them,
they tend to become passive types of people. As

Andre Lussier writes,

> So far as physically disabled people are
> concerned, surface observation shows that, ac-
> cording to their reactions, they can be divided
> into two categories, the active and the passive
> ones, the doers and the dreamers. Apparently, in
> the analytic literature, more attention has been
> paid so far to the passive than the active type.
> Veterans' hospitals are still caring for many
> patients described as "passive dependent person-
> alities." Typically these patients use their
> congenital handicaps, consciously or unconsciously,
> as justification for passivity and dependence.
> They stop striving for attainable achievements and
> make inaction morally acceptable by considerations
> of self pity. The handicap becomes the pivot for
> a multitude of unfruitful fantasies and excuses
> for resignation.43

However, as we noted earlier, some impaired individuals do not see their disability as society does-
as a significant handicap. They get an education and
go on to make significant contributions by typing with
their feet, creating artistic productions by holding
paint brushes or pencils in their mouths, or using
sign language and computers to communicate with others.
They overcome the architectural and employment barriers
to become independent.

The attitudes of society and the correlated behavior of the impaired toward themselves with regard to
sexual development illustrates the repressive nature of
handicappism. Speaking of the impaired, Charlis Dunham
says,

> Prejudicial thinking and active suppression
> have combined to deprive them of a successful
> sexual existence, one that meets their need not
> only for physical stimulation and satisfaction, but
> for a feeling of self-worth and acceptance, expres-
> sion of tenderness, and a sharing of both the joys
> and sorrows of life with a loved one. One of the
> greatest obstacles to achievement of these en-
> riching relationships is the idea that the disabled
> are not sexual beings, that they are of a neuter
> gender. Myths of nonsexuality surround spastic,
> blind, deaf, paraplegic, and retarded individuals,
> just as they are imposed upon children and the

elderly. Too often these myths have the effect of denying the disabled the very foundations on which social sexual life is built--early experiences with the opposite sex, masturbation without guilt, basic information on the "facts of life" and the privacy that is necessary if romantic attachment is to develop.[44]

The needs of the handicapped are the same as others--relating to others, recreation, work, sexual relationships and parenting. While some do become passive in these regards, others do become fully developed human beings. But they often need to develop special mechanics to engage in either work, learning or sexual contacts.

Following the medical model of the handicapped, most of the 250 some national voluntary agencies dedicated to research and services for the handicapped were created and are manned principally by the able-bodied to help the handicapped. Even patterns of employment discrimination against the disabled have been found in these organizations which we might expect to operate in a more enlightened fashion. Nevertheless, partly as an offshoot of the civil rights era of the 1960's some of the handicapped have begun organizing and demonstrating on their own behalf. Thus, one of the earmarks of a minority group is the developing awareness of their minority status and the growth of self-help groups to protest that status. Some of the national, state and local organizations which have been developed were founded by the parents of disabled children who in significant ways share with their children the stigma of disability and minority status.

The major goals these self help groups have attempted to reach are the elimination of architectural barriers in public buildings and private housing, improved accessibility to public transportation, improved educational, medical and rehabilitation research on and services for the disabled, improved job placement and implementation of affirmative action legislation, establishment of recreational opportunities and facilities for the handicapped. In addition they have established information, referral and counseling self-help groups to better understand how to influence the legislative process, deal with insurance and social security problems and engage in peer counseling activities and consumer rights activities for the disabled.

81

According to James Haskins,

> In the late 1960's a quiet revolution began
> to spread across the nation, spearheaded by dis-
> abled activists and their supporters. Disabled
> Americans started to come out of their pockets of
> isolation to band together to fight for the cause
> they hold in common--the elimination of the pre-
> judice and discrimination that have prevented them
> from leading lives of dignity and independence.[45]
> In the 1970's this militancy spread as more diabled
> got involved in new groups they formed for them-
> selves rather than being formed for them by parents,
> advocates and teachers. These new groups included
> the Paralyzed Veterans of America, National
> Paraplegia Foundation, Disabled in Action, Inc.,
> and a national coalition called American Coalition
> of Citizens with Disability. This later group was
> formed in 1974 by 150 disabled persons. It has
> since concentrated on securing implementation and
> enforcement of legislation.

The first really militant organization was Disabled
in Action formed in 1970. Some of the statements by
this group or its members make their points sharply:

-- "You gave us your dimes. Now allow us our
dignity."

-- "We have been denied our rights. We want them
and we're not going to shut up until we get them."

--"All we want is our day in the sun."

-- "Everybody seems shocked by what we want. Why
is it so shocking about wanting to get around and
have a social life? What's so shocking about
wanting to hold a job and earn one's keep? What's
so shocking about wanting to see more of the world
than what shows up through a hospital window?"

-- "The able-bodied hold all the cards. We feel
it is high time we got dealt a hand."

-- "They embarrass us until we want to slip through
the cracks in the floor."

-- "We don't want dewy-eyed pity. We want our
rights."

-- "In the 1960's, a political and legal revolution began because there was a significant minority population that had to sit at the back of the bus. Today there is a significant minority that cannot even get on the bus."[46]

Governmental bodies have often been slow to act on the needs of the handicapped. According to Debby Kaplan, director of the Disability Rights Center in Washington, D.C., the number of handicapped federal employees declined by 3,350 in the two years ending December 31, 1975. She contends that the government is not taking the handicapped seriously. She believes that the government is slow in dealing with over 1500 job discrimination complaints filed by the handicapped before the Equal Opportunities Commission each year. There are also complaints that the federal government tends to keep the handicapped in stereotyped jobs such as the deaf in printing offices and the blind out of sight answering telephones.[47] While all public buildings are to be accessible to the handicapped, many of the buildings in the nation's capitol still remain inaccessible.

After the Rehabilitation Act of 1973 was passed, many disabled persons had their hopes raised that employer discrimination would lessen, that architectural barriers would be dismantled and that individualized educational programs would begin. To enforce this law, however, the Department of Health, Education and Welfare first needed to draw up a series of regulations that would specify what it meant and how it would be enforced. It did nothing for three and-a-half years. In the early winter and spring months of 1977 the American Coalition of Citizens with Disabilities organized thousands of disabled persons to stage repeated demonstrations and sit-ins at ten regional DHEW headquarters and in Washington to protest this unnecessary delay. Twenty two days later, on April 28, 1977, DHEW Secretary Califano signed the new regulations to become effective June 1, 1977.

Increasingly the disabled are taking their cases to court to protest the inaccessibility to voting places and other public buildings. They are also lobbying federal, state and local bodies to pass laws eliminating physical and social barriers to the handicapped. One illustration of the growing involvement of the disabled on behalf of themselves is that they made up over 80% of

83

the nearly 900 participants in the 1977 White House
Conference on Handicaps. They are putting pressure as
consumers on businesses as well. In 1980 Amtrack announced that it has wheelchairs available in 400 of its
524 stations, that progress was being made in making its
stations barrier-free, and that it was reducing certain
fares 25% for the elderly and handicapped.

Summary

    The physically disabled possess the attributes of a
minority group. Many of them are visible because their
disability leaves them without limbs, paralyzed, on
crutches, in wheelchairs or braces or otherwise noticeable in their motions or mobility limitations. They
have experienced many forms of discrimination including
those directed at historic minorities--unequal access
to education, training, jobs and other rights contained
in the constitution. In addition, many have had their
mobility curbed by thoughtlessly constructed architectural barriers which simply overlooked them because
they are a small numerical group who have been kept out
of sight as second-class citizens. Thirdly, they have
less power and lower socioeconomic status because of
the barriers erected against their full participation
in society. Fourthly, in the last two decades they
have developed a growing awareness of their minority
status and increasingly organized into self-help groups
to lobby for legislation and engage in other political
activities to press for their rights as citizens, as
workers and as people.

Chapter 3:   The Unseeing Minority: The Blind

The blind and visually impaired are one category of the physically handicapped. Since their sensory impairment is distinctive from those who have motor impairments, an investigation of them as a minority group in a separate chapter is undertaken to emphasize both the uniqueness of their impairment and to explore in greater depth the relationships between the able and disabled--in this case the sighted and the blind.

Defining Blindness

Defining blindness is quite problematic because it depends on who is doing the defining, what standards are used, and the reason for doing the defining. Essentially three different methods of defining blindness and visual impairments have been developed. Each produces different numbers and rates of blindness for the American population. These three techniques are ophthalmic, self-reports and administrative.

The ophthalmic definition of visual acuity goes back to Dr. Herman Snellen in 1868. He developed one test of visual acuity that is still widely used by opthamologists and optometrists today--the Snellen chart. On this chart are nine lines of letters or numbers of decreasing size. Visual acuity was measured as a fraction in which the numerator is always a constant 20 feet at which an object can be seen by a person with normal vision. Normal vision is described as 20/20, the ability to see at 20 feet an object that can be seen at 20 feet by a normal eye. The largest letter on the chart has a fraction of 20/200. This means that at 20 feet a person can see an object that a person with normal vision could see at 200 feet. The remaining seven fractions on the Snellen chart are 20/100, 20/70, 20/50, 20/40, 20/30, 20/15 and 20/10.[1]

In addition, Snellen also looked at whether a person had tunnel vision only. A person with tunnel vision can only see a particular spot in a visual field, say 20 angular degrees wide.

One of the difficulties with the use of a Snellen chart is that it does not make distinctions between total blindness, 20/200 vision, 20/100 vision or other finer distinctions. Thus, in dealing with vision problems, contemporary "eye doctors" want to look not only at finer degrees of impairment, but also at whether the pathology of impairment is remediable to some degree by glasses, surgery, or drugs and to what extent the impairment is functionally important for a particular person due to the nature of his work, recreation and other demands placed upon him.

Self report definitions of visual impairment are how people classify their own lack of visual acuity when several categories are given to them. For example, the National Health Survey of the U.S. Public Health Service has two levels of impairment which they define for people who are then asked to place themselves in one of them if they are applicable.

"Severe Visual Impairments" are defined as visual impairments in a person six years of age or older which renders him unable to read ordinary newspaper print with glasses or blind in both eyes for children under six who have never learned to read. "Other Visual Impairments" are visual "difficulties" for those over age six which are not severe enough to prevent him from reading ordinary newsprint with glasses or "trouble seeing" for children under six who have never learned to read. As one can see, fairly objective demarcations are absent in this definition of visual impairment which leads to a certain amount of subjectivity and relativity in determining the amount and severity of visual impairment in a population.[2] In the light of the stigma attached to severe visual impairment, we might expect people to underreport it in self-disclosure reports unless there were clear benefits for doing so like welfare payments.

Administrative definitions of visual impairment use categories of impairment that a person can either be assigned to or not. Typically, administrative definitions are used to determine if a person is or is not eligible for social security disability benefits, certain special types of "blind" educational services, rehabilitation programs and other benefits or services.

The section on Opthalmology of the American Medical Association developed five categories of visual impairment, which have been utilized for administrative decision-making:

1. Total Blindness: the inability
   to perceive any light at all.
   (Very few of the people designated
   as "blind" are totally blind.)

2. Light Perception: the ability
   to perceive the presence or
   absence of light.

3. Economic Blindness: the absence
   of ability to do any kind of work,
   industrial or otherwise, for
   which sight is essential. This
   is considered as less than
   20/200 visual acuity in the
   better eye with the best possible
   correction or an equally disabling loss of the visual field.

4. Vocational Blindness: impairment
   of vision which makes it impossible for a person to do the
   work at which he had previously
   earned a living. Of course,
   this does not preclude doing
   thousands of other jobs.

5. Educational Blindness: loss of
   sight making it difficult,
   dangerous or impossible to learn
   by the methods commonly used in
   schools. Two levels here are

   a) schools for the blind for
      which the admission re-
      quirement is 20/200 or less
      visual acuity in the better
      eye with best correction,

   b) sight saving classes for
      which the admission re-
      quirement is a visual
      acuity between 20/70 and
      20/200 in the better eye
      with the best correction.[3]

The third definition of blindness, listed above as
"economic blindness" has been slightly modified and
then used by most federal and state agencies serving

the visually impaired. It is usually called "legal blindness" defined as a person whose "central acuity does not exceed 20/200 in the better eye with correcting lenses or whose visual acuity is greater than 20/200 but is accompanied by a limitation in the field of vision such that the indirect diameter of the visual field subtends an angle of no greater than 20 degrees."

The adoption of this rather arbitrary definition of "legal blindness" has had important repercussions on who is classified as blind, who is and is not eligible for services. It includes as well those who are totally blind or who have only light perception. Thus the legally blind include many with some sight. But it is a somewhat more restrictive definition than the self-report definition of several visual impairments.[4]

Numbers and Demographic Characteristics of the Visually Impaired

As one reads the literature on blindness he comes across widely varying estimates on the numbers of people who are visually impaired. This is so for a number of reasons. One is that different studies use different definitions of blindness which greatly influence the numbers that will be reported. The second is that many studies use surveys based on either random or non-random samples that have varying degrees of reliability of being representative of the total United States population. Other studies use medical reporting procedures that may underestimate the number of blind persons.

Table 3.1 shows that the use of the more restrictive definition of legal blindness results in a lower estimate of the number of blind than does the self-reporting system used in conjunction with the more inclusive definition of severe visual impairment. According to these estimates there were 515,190 legally blind in the United States in 1978 but 1,478,626 with severe visual impairment. The reporting procedures and definitions used to determine the number of legally blind probably results in a substantial undercount. The estimates of blindness that most experts in the field would accept would probably be around 1,400,000. If this is the case it means that less than 0.6% of the population has severe visual impairment.

Table 3.1

Age Specific Prevalence Rates of Blind by Two Definitions of Blindness, 1978*

	Legally Blind			Severe Visual Impairment			
Age	Prevalence Rate Per 1,000	U.S. Total	% of Total	Age	Prevalence Rate Per 1,000	U.S. Total	% of Total
<20	0.541	38,870	7.5	≤24	0.528	48,523	3.3
20-39	1.127	74,577	14.5	25-34	1.23	41,545	2.8
40-64	2.375	133,012	25.8	35-44	1.68	40,858	2.8
65-69	5.462	47,166	9.2	45-54	4.88	113,104	7.6
≥70	14.37	221,565	43.0	55-64	7.28	150,463	10.2
				≥75	82.7	749,953	50.7
Total	2.1	515,190	100.0	Total	5.6	1,478,626	100.0

*This table is based on the 1978 U.S. population as reported in the U.S. Department or Commerce, Statistical Abstract of the U.S. 1978, Washington, DC 1979, of 218,059,000. The prevalence rates used for the legally blind are found in the Fact Book of the National Society for the Prevention of Blindness for 1965, and for the severely visually impaired in the National Health Survey of 1965 both of which are cited in Blindness and Services to the Blind in the United States, Cambridge, Mass: Organization for Social and Technical Innovation, 1971. The definitions of legally blind and severe visual impairment are given earlier in this chapter.

89

One other characteristic of the nature of blindness quite noticeable in this table is that relatively few youth are blind. Over half of the legally blind are 65 and over while over two thirds of the visually impaired are 65 and over. Thus few are born blind. Most blindness comes late in life with the deteriorative process of aging.

Several other demographic characteristics of blindness have also been noted. A higher proportion, around 60% of all blindness, is found in women. Part, but only part, of this difference is due to the greater longevity of women. Blindness is also more prevalent among blacks than whites.

Robert Scott has suggested there are four categories of blind people: about 67% are aged blind; about 15% are non-aged unemployable adults made up of those with little education, few skills, the multiply handicapped and women who do not seek work; about 15% are made up of employable adults, some of whom are working, while the remaining 3% is made up of youth.[5]

Causes of Blindness

Blindness can be caused by physiological conditions in the eyes themselves or in tissues surrounding them, by a number of diseases, or by accidents. One of the chief causes of blindness is cataract, a condition in which the normally clear lens of the eye becomes milky or clouded. With increasing opacity in the lens less light is able to enter the rear chamber of the eye and vision diminishes. Cataracts are usually easily removable. A variety of other diseases may contribute to or cause blindness-glaucoma, gonorrhea, retinitis pigmentosa, muscular degeneration, diabetes, syphilis, trachoma, smallpox and rubella (German measles). Only about 2% of all blindness is congenital or develops in early childhood. The 98% remainder is called "adventitious" or acquired blindness.[6]

Identifiability of the Blind

Most blind people are visibly identifiable by the sighted. But we must keep in mind that most of the legally blind are not totally blind. Of the roughly 400,000 legally blind in 1970, about 17% were totally blind, about 15% had some perception of light, 54% had sufficient sight to be able to be aware of motion and large objects and the remaining 14% had some reading vision with the use of large print or other aids. The latter group is not as easily identifiable as most blind people.

The blind are typically identifiable by their lack of ease in moving in strange locations and by the presence of canes, seeing eye dogs or reliance upon others for getting around. Some blind people wear sunglasses to cover unsightly eyes or have prosthetic (glass or plastic) eyes to replace those removed. In interpersonal contact the impossibility of engaging in eye contact is often a giveaway that the person is not sighted. However, many of those on the borderline of blindness try to hide their condition.

Stereotypes of and Discrimination Against the Blind

According to a 1976 Gallup poll, blindness was ranked next to cancer as the most feared aliment. "That contrasts sharply with our personal experience" says a blind man, Kenneth Jernigan. He continues,

> "We know that with training and opportunity, we can reduce blindness to the level of a mere inconvenience; but we also know that custodialism, discrimination, denial of opportunity, and putdowns can make our blindness a veritable hell-as terrible as it has even been thought to be."[7]

Most people do not conceptualize blindness as a "mere inconvenience" however. Michael Monbeck in The Meaning of Blindness: Attitudes Toward Blindness and Blind People reviews many literary and biblical works to determine the historical origins of our attitudes toward blindness and finds that most of them have a long history and still operate in society today. In summarizing these fifteen "attitudes" it should be noted that some of them also involve more than attitudes--they frequently imply, lead to, or involve differential treatment-discrimination if you will. It should also be added that many of these stereotypes and attitudes are overlapping in their meanings.[8]

1. The blind deserve pity and sympathy. This common feeling of showing pity to the blind was a mark of religious devoutness. In the early church and

throughout the history the blind have often been seen as wards of the church deserving special relief in hospices and cloisters along with other unfortunates. This pity is often lavished on the blind out of all proportion to their actual limitations because sighted people have little understanding of what it is like to be blind. Some people respond they would rather be dead than blind.

2. <u>The blind are miserable</u>. Sighted people often imagine the blind live in utter hopelessness and despair. Throughout history blindness was seen as an overwhelming tragedy, approaching death in the grief that it created from the loss. This calamity is envisioned as causing deep unhappiness, misery and forlorn depression. It has usually been considered inappropriate to tell humorous incidents about the blind and that any display of humor on their part showed fortitude or an occasional lapse from their melancholy.

3. <u>Blind people live in a world of darkness</u>. Darkness has historically been associated with evil, immorality, night and crime while seeing the light or living in the light symbolizes happiness, religiosity, morality, freedom. To be in the dark is to be outside of the mainstream of daytime living, to be alone as at night. It is interesting that many of the publications about or for the blind are given such titles as <u>Beacon</u>, <u>Light</u>, <u>Outlook</u>, <u>Illuminator</u> and <u>Lookout</u>.

4. <u>Blind people are helpless</u>. One of the common stereotypes is that the blind can do very little for themselves. In spite of the fact that they can often continue to do the things they did before blindness adventitiously caught them, they are described biblically as groping, stumbling and unable to find their own way. They are simplistically viewed by some as paralyzed, incapacitated and nonproductive. While few blind beggars are left in the United States, begging was a way to maintain their existence throughout history before the recent invention of public welfare.

5. <u>Blind people are useless</u>. This theme has occurred throughout history, depicting them as non-productive citizens that stems from their helplessness. Infantacide was often practiced on the congenitally blind in many societies; while those who had a productive life before becoming blind in later life were often simply tolerated. The attribution of uselessness

to the blind is the predecessor that they would be unable to use opportunities even if they had the chance. Such attitudes by others often leads to the blind having the same feelings about themselves.

6. The Blind are fools. The belief probably comes from the fact that the blind can be fooled, tricked and exploited in some situations because of their very lack of sight. That they can be taken advantage of is not startling; but it does not follow that they are fools simply because they can be duped due to their sightlessness.

7. The Blind are beggars. The theme occurs throughout biblical history and beyond to describe one of the economic roles they played. Often they were stationed near cathedral doors to sell trinkets or amulets or to be objects of charity. The concept of a "poor blind beggar" has decreasing meaning in societies which have public support systems for the unemployed handicapped.

8. The Blind are useful. Alongside the theme that the blind are useless goes another theme, often less pronounced, that the blind are able to function in productive lives in spite of their handicaps. This theme in literature has portrayed the blind as like other ordinary people in all regards except in their blindness. In the ancient world the blind were employed as prostitutes, rowers, laborers, scholars specializing in memorization of texts and law codes, vocal musicians, knitters, composers and even one as a king.

9. The Blind are compensated by other talents. The gift of compensating talents was often conceived of as a divine attribute in earlier times; later it was more likely to be conceived as the development of compensatory abilities. The blind have been variously conceived of as having different ways of thinking, added powers of concentration, better memories, more imagination and heightened musical sensitivities. Part of this view is that without sight the blind develop their other senses more to give them clues about their environment. Whether they are better developed or simply used more is unknown. But many blind do utilize their hearing to detect traffic and other movements and utilize tacticle stimuli to determine the nature of objects more extensively than the sighted.

93

10. The Blind are being punished for some past
sin. As part of the religious and moral code that evil
deeds have evil consequences is the idea that blindness
comes from wrongdoing. It is viewed as a punishment,
sometimes even upon the children of transgressing
parents. This view was prominent in classical literature and Biblical times. Blinding people was a
practice for some crimes in ancient times which further
lends credence to the view that blindness is caused by
or related to bad behavior. While this view is dimin-
ishing over time, some blind persons or their parents
often wonder what they did to deserve this fate or
punishment.

11. The Blind are feared, avoided and rejected.
This attitude and behavioral reaction varies considerably from culture to culture. In some societies
blind infants were put to death, in other societies the
blind were shunned as if they were possessed of some
evil or carriers of an infectious disease. Many
societies have segregated them into special or outcast
occupations and segregated them into separate living
quarters. In some societies they are educated in
separate groups or facilities. Today the blind are
feared by some out of ignorance of their capabilities
or their inability to relate to people who are different. Many blind still feel that they are not treated
as normal human beings. For example, one blind student
at the college where I teach, in response to a question
of what his biggest problem was reported, "Probably
socialization. To get to know people is the hardest
thing for me because people are afraid to approach me.
When I came here, a person was scheduled to room with
me, but that person's father told his son to change
rooms. Then my roommate moved after only three days of
rooming together."

12. The Blind are immoral and evil. One more recent view of the blind according to Monbeck is contained
in medieval literature and later literature where Satan,
the grand inquisitor, Pew in Treasure Island and many
other characters who are "malignant" or evil are also
blind. The blindness symbolically stands for the dark
cast of their character. One of the traditional
literary ways to imbue evil in a character is to handicap him with some deformity or sensory impairment.

13. The Blind are idealized. This literary view
has developed in the last two hundred years. In it the
blind are endowed with extraordinary talents, insights

94

and altruistic motives. This idea is related to their compensatory skills as well as the belief that the blind are good because they have less opportunity to be otherwise.

14. **The Blind are endowed with mystery and magical qualities**. Just as they may be touched by God with evil powers they also may be touched with magical powers of healing, prophecy, luck or psychic influence. They are fascinating to the sighted because they are seen as possessing a set of compensatory skills and an inner life that the sighted lack. In many societies, the blind are attributed mysterious power of divination and supernatural vision.

15. **The Blind are maladjusted**. This view is the most recent because the concept of maladjustment has a short history in social science. The fundamental idea here is that their lack of vision has led them to develop personality characteristics that are emotionally and intellectually warped. It is often assumed that the ordeal of becoming blind and attempting to adjust to the depression that typically follows it leaves the person troubled and disturbed. They are pictured as being envious of the sighted and unable to adapt to their sightlessness. They are seen as suffering from intellectual, physical and even moral lassitude because of the restrictions of blindness. They become bored, idle, aloof, self-pitying, paranoid, prone to petty angers, unfriendly and hypersensitive. Monbeck sees this as a secondary attitude that could develop among the blind because of the oppression they often experience. This is not to say it is true but to track its origin to outside sources if it does occur.

The presence of a wide variety of attitudes that have occurred throughout history suggests that blind people are not thought of as all alike. This may be true collectively for all people, but any one individual may select or be exposed to only some of these attitudes. Any one person however tends to think of blind people as all alike. The fact of their blindness and their reaction to it are seen as more significant than their individual abilities and idiosyncracies.

Many of the blind are treated as partial persons who are so desperate they will grab at any hopes that could bring them happiness. As President of the National Federation of the Blind, Kenneth Jernigan, reports he receives many letters from sighted people which impugn the normalcy of blind people. For example he got a letter from an Indian person who wanted to immigrate from India where the number of visas were already spoken for years in advance. However, if an alien marries a U.S. citizen he can become a U.S. citizen. This Indian offered to marry a blind person in order to gain entrance to our country. He received another letter from a middle aged prisoner who was willing to marry a "blind lady of virtually any age, who has never been divorced and who is reasonably secure financially. Objects: matrimony and the mutual happiness of two losers." The prisoner went on to write, If I cannot please you, blind lady, no man can. The need for your being reasonably secure financially is in line with my intention of having a full time job keeping you happy."[9]

Alexander Alexanian carried out an interesting study to determine what he called the private and public attitudes of high school and college students towards blacks and three physically disabled groups; stutterers, cerebral palsied and the blind. He tested a number of hypotheses including the idea that people who are prejudiced against blacks are also prejudiced against the physically handicapped, that those prejudiced against one physically handicapped group are also prejudiced against others and the major hypothesis that people are internally or actually more prejudiced against these groups than they will admit publicly. He gave two similar tests to his 312 subjects, 102 of them college students and 210 high school students. The questionnaire tests were given two weeks apart. The first test was a "projective" test designed to get at the "real" attitude of people and involved 10 incomplete statements about each of the four groups. The second test was a direct response questionnaire which asked them what they would do in a particular real-life situation. For example in Table 3.2 the first item in the projective test was, "When Mike heard that a blind person wanted to come to his school, he . . ." The student was told to answer this quickly because if was a ("disguised") test to see how quickly subjects could develop phrases or sentences. The comparable first item in the direct test given two weeks later was "When I heard that a blind person wanted to come to my school, I ..." Students were told to take their time on this test as the college or school wanted a measure of their personal and social attitudes. Responses were scored as either positive or negative. They were given negative scores if the response indicated in some way apprehension, dislike, withdrawal from, or fear of the minority person or handicapped person. As shown in Table. 3.2 there was more hidden or internal prejudice toward the blind than the students admitted in the direct questionnaire. In fact, 69% of the students who admitted some prejudicial response to the blind in the projective test, dropped it in their direct response. Much of the same pattern occurred with the other groups. Privately, 51% of the subjects were prejudiced against stutterers, but only 23% publicly. Fifty-five percent of the respondents showed less prejudice in their public attitudes toward stutterers. Privately 33% showed prejudice against the cerebral palsied, but only 12% did publicly, a decrease of 65%, and 47% showed private prejudices against blacks but this dropped 74% to 12% when stated as a public prejudice. Several other interesting findings were that those who were prejudiced against blacks tended to be prejudiced against handicapped people and those prejudiced against any one of the handicapped groups also tended to be prejudiced against the other two. This data supported the contention of the author that handicapped people are fundamentally a minority group like blacks. While public norms and legislation have discouraged both handicappism and racism, private attitudes hinder their full acceptance in many ways.[10]

Robert Scott spent two years investigating attitudes toward the blind and their behavior patterns, and agencies that serve them. He found that three different explanations existed in the literature to explain the attitudes of and behaviors of the blind. While each of the three explanations had merit they were inadequate in his view. He then goes on to develop his own thesis that the blind role is not given in nature but is learned through socialization processes that are common for the blind. We will look at his thesis in more depth after we review the three explanations which he finds somewhat true but inadequate taken singly or together. The first explanation is the "common sense explanation" which says the blind do think differently and have melancholic, reflective, humorless, frustrated personality characteristics because the handicap makes them this way. He finds this explanation flawed for three reasons. First it over magnifies the restrictions placed on the blind, especially those not totally blind. Secondly, research findings on numerous blind groups — veterans, the congenitally blind, the adventitiously blind, the detected blind served by

97

Table 3.2

Private and Public Attitudes Toward

the Blind Among 312 High School and College

Students

Questionnaire Item	Private Attitude % Negative	Public Attitude % Negative
Blind Person in Same School	20	3
Choose between schools with and without Blind	85	43
Meeting a blind person	25	3
Working next to a blind person	18	2
Blind student in the same class	26	5
Admit blind person to club	29	11
Friend stopped dating a blind student	28	7
Having a blind worker	46	14
Helping a blind student with his homework	9	1
Sibling marrying a blind person	24	6
	—	—
Percent of all responses Negative	31	9
N of Negative Reponses	968	296

Adapted from: Alexander Alexanian, "An Investigation Into Public and Private Attitudes Toward Various Handicapped Groups: Stutterers, Cerebral Palsied, and the Blind." Unpublished Ph.D. Dissertation, Boston University, 1967.

blindness agencies and the undetected blind unserved by
such agencies, show such personality uniformities are
lacking. The blind are diverse. Thirdly, those attitudes that the totally blind have are also shared by
the seriously visually impaired suggesting that their
behavior is learned and not simply a uniform response
to the condition of blindness.[11]

The second explanation is the "psychological
explanation" which assumes that blind people are diverse
but yet this diversity is patterned in predictable ways
because of the initial shock reaction to becoming blind
and the enduring limitations which sightlessness imposes
on their personalities. Blind people either adjust well
or poorly to these initial and enduring problems. Three
inadequacies are found in this theory also. First, not
all people go through a traumatic reaction as the theory
assumes. Secondly, it assumes that good adjustment to
blindness involves the blind accepting their blindness;
but in fact some well adjusted people continue to deny
their blindness. Thirdly, it assumes the individual's
reaction to his blindness is simply a personality response involving psychic processes. This assumption
excludes the important role that social stereotypes and
societal reactions have in influencing the response
patterns of the blind.

The third explanation Scott calls the "stereotype
explanation." Basically it is elsewhere called the
labeling theory. It argues that the stereotype of
helplessness that the sighted apply to the blind not
only influences how the blind see themselves but acts
as a self-fulfilling prophecy to limit an array of opportunities to them. This theory contains considerable
explanatory power for both those sighted and blind who
in fact do conform to the stereotype. Yet it has one
major weakness. It over-emphasizes the role of beliefs
and attitudes in determining behavior; conversely it
tends to neglect the heavy influence of special inter-
actional patterns that the blind have with the sighted
in both informal and formalized institutional roles in
determining behavioral outcomes. An example of the
stereotype emphasis in the literature on blindness is
Monbeck's fifteen attitudes toward the blind which we
reviewed earlier.

Scott's thesis is,

        The disability of blindness is a learned

social role. The various attitudes and patterns of behavior that characterize people
who are blind are not inherent in their condition but, rather are acquired through the
ordinary processes of social learning. Thus,
there is nothing inherent in the condition
of blindness that requires a person to be
docile, dependent, melancholy or helpless;
nor is there anything about it that should
lead him to become independent or assertive.
Blind men are made, and by the same processes that have made us all.[12]

Scott then goes on to show that the role of
blindness is learned in (1) childhood from the stereotypes widely shared of the blind in that society
including the blind who usually become blind long after
they learn about the "poor" blind, (2) unique face-to-
face interactions between those who can see and those
who cannot, and (3) a variety of service organizations
which help the blind from a "professional" perspective of
what blindness is all about. Each of these points needs
to be elaborated upon.

Before becoming blind most people have felt they
are normal. But what happens after they become blind?
Many go through a period of depression, particularly if
the onset of blindness is rapid rather than drawn out
over many years as is often the case with progressive
diseases which diminish vision slowly. Some continue
to define themselves as normal and try to refute the
stigma and personality dynamics attributed to them.
Many others, however, define themselves as blind and
take on some of the personality characteristics and
spoiled identity of the stigma attributed to them. In
either case, the effect is profound for most recognize
that others do not really accept them as equals. Should
they accept with graciousness the help offered to them
even though it is not needed or should they reject it
and be seen as hostile? They are often in a no-win
situation. If they accept, they reinforce the view of
their helplessness; if they refuse, they are interpreted
as ungrateful, hostile and distressed.

In face-to-face encounters the blind and sighted
are put into a situation where the usual norms of
reciprocity and ascribed equality are not frequently
assumed by the sighted and in fact are rather open to
situational contingencies. In comparison to encounters

between two sighted people, the encounter between a sighted and blind person have a number of factors that can make them awkward, ambiguous, strained and socially unfulfilling. Consider, for example, the sighted person's special problems in such an encounter: (1) Should he consider the person's dress as an identifying characteristic since the blind person may not have picked it out and may be unaware of color clashes or stains on it? (2) Since he cannot have eye contact with the person, should he concentrate on facial expressions and body movements as clues to the conversation or depend wholly on the blind person's voice? (3) If the blind person does not face him squarely when talking does this mean he is disinterested in the topic? (4) If the person engages in "blindisms" like tilting the body, moving his head, twitching the face, and exaggerated gestures (more usual among the congenitally blind), how should he interpret and react to this? (5) Since he may not know the degree of blindness or the capabilities of the person, should he offer help which could be embarrassing or not offer it and be considered rude?

The blind person has different problems in such face-to-face encounters: (1) Since he cannot see the person's dress, size, eyes, facial or motor behavior, he has even fewer clues to guide him in giving an identity to the speaker. He must depend almost solely on his voice. Should he depend solely on that voice even though people can better dissemble with their voices than with facial expressions? (2) Without eye contact, he cannot determine how the other person is reacting to him other than by words. (3) He may be unaware of his own appearance and the other person's reaction to his clothes, hair style, and possibly rolling or disfigured eyes. (4) If he should ask for help he confirms his dependency on the other person which makes for an asymmetrical power relationship in which one person needs the other more. On the other hand, if he does not ask for help but then falls, sits on the arm of the chair instead of the seat, drops cigarette ashes on himself rather than in an unlocated ashtray, he may make himself look bad while also making the other party feel guilty about not proffering assistance. Because of the uncertainties and the fact that sighted people have little contact with the blind, their encounters are often marked by strain, vague expectations of what the other will be like, and awkwardness in responding to incomplete clues of how

the other person is reacting.[13] Such encounters can
be very frustrating as the enclosed capsule, "Letter
From A Friend of A Blind Man" indicates.

Letter from a Friend of a Blind Man

"Dear Mr. Jerigan,

I am a fully sighted woman, age 23,
who is dating a blind man, age 23. You
may know him --- his name is Jim Smith.

When I first joined NFB (National
Federation of the Blind), I did so because I wanted to better understand the
concerns and problems that Jim had. I
knew there were problems and discrimi-
nations, but I never knew they were so
overt until just recently.

Both of us are college educated
and now hold very good jobs. Jim works
for the Social Security Commission and
I teach blind children. My philosophy
in teaching is that they are just children
and need the same things that all children
do. I believe that in order to teach them,
I must look at them first as children and
second as children who need special
training in certain areas. If I can't
do this, the only think I'll teach them
is how to be physically handicapped and
blind. Because of my job, I had begun
to understand why Jim was so angry with
public attitudes. I, too, have experienced anger toward people who (when they
see my children) shake their heads and
say, 'But he's so happy' as if the only
thing he's capable of doing is being
pleasant. My children are happy. They
also are smart, sweet, cranky, mean, irritable, etc. They're all the things
children are. They get discipline when
they need it and praise when they earn it.
They are not told how wonderful and brave
they are. They are praised for accomplishments and praised for trying as well. I
tell my children that I will never ask them
to do anything that I don't think they can

102

do. I expect them to achieve and they
expect achievement, too. I think this
is the only way a blind child can grow
up to be a worthwhile adult... All of
my children are proud of their accomplishments and they should be--they
worked hard for them, but I think it's
insulting to the child to go on and on
about how wonderful he is. To me it
implies that you think the child is
stupid to begin with and you never had
enough faith in him to think he could
do it in the first place.... I feel
anger toward parents who baby their
children and never permit them or make
them do anything. All children fall down,
fall out of swings, bump their heads, etc.,
and the children I teach have a right to
fall down too. I know it's hard for some
of these children to do certain things,
but they have to try. When you get these
children in a classroom, they're almost
impossible to teach. They have been made
to feel that they don't have to do anything, and they'll grow into adults who
think the world owes them a favor.
Another group of parents I detest are
the ones who are ashamed of their children.
These children are also hard to teach. They
feel that they're ugly and unloved. They
stay angry and hurt all the time because
they have been made to dislike themselves.
I believe that you have to learn to like
and accept yourself first before you can
expect anyone else to.... In my experience
I have come in contact with the pitying
reaction: 'Poor, pitiful little thing.
It must be awful to go through life like
that'; the brave and wonderful syndrome __
everything the child does is somehow beyond the realm of human expectations:
'My aren't you smart!' The child is always
described as 'special' and 'brave'; nobody
expects him to be able to do anything, and
when he does, praise is grossly out of
proportion. Rejection: the child is
ignored or avoided.

Jim and I have experienced a mixture of all three. Friday night, Jim and I had some people over for a cookout. I was in the kitchen fixing baked beans and deviled eggs. Jim came in and asked if there was something he could do. I asked him to slice the tomatoes. (I never meant to start a riot. I only wanted the stupid tomatoes cut up.) One of the other men came in the kitchen and said, 'But, he might cut his finger.' Jim told him that he had cut tomatoes before and was sure he could do it again. He did so and soon had a nice plateful. The other man, who stayed to watch, then took Jim by one arm and the plate of tomatoes in the other to show everybody what he had done. (A cerebral palsied child who has just learned to walk doesn't get that much praise.)

Jim then proceeded to walk out back and light the charcoal. The same man said, 'Are you going to let him do that?' I shrugged and said, 'Why not?' The man jumped up and ran out back. When he came back, all he could talk about was how remarkable Jim was.

Everyone calmed down and we began to eat. Then it started to rain. Jim got up and said to me, 'Are the car windows down?' They were, so Jim proceeded to run outside to roll them up - without his cane. The other man jumped up and grabbed Jim's cane. He said, 'Does Jim need this?' I said, 'No. Don't worry about him, He's fine.' Jim came back and we started to eat again. Jim wanted some more beans, so he went to the stove and got them. The comment then was, 'That is just wonderful.' What is so wonderful about dipping beans? Jim told me later (after they left), that he felt like taking a bow after everything he had done. I don't think he did anything out

of the ordinary, and neither does he. The
whole night he felt as if he were on exhibit, and I was experiencing a strong
desire to stand up and scream, 'He's not
stupid, and he's not a child. He's not
doing anything terrific, so shut up!'
It didn't end there. Later on that night,
Jim and I made a trip to the hospital
emergency room. He had got into some
poison ivy, and it had spread to his eyes.
The nurse on duty was horrible. She didn't
think he was remarkable - she thought him
to be blind, deaf, mute, stupid and incapable of doing anything. She asked me,
'What is his name? Where does he live?
Do his eyes itch?' I was offended and
said, 'I think he can answer his own
questions.' Jim calmly told her what she
wanted to know, but I could tell he was
mad. When he went in for treatment, a
man came over to me and said, 'You are so
wonderful to be kind to that poor man.'
I tried to explain that I felt lucky to
have a man like Jim. (And I am. He's
the best thing that ever happened to me.
When we're together, I feel happy and
secure and protected. I love him.)
After I finished trying to explain to
this man our relationship, he said, 'You
mean you're dating him? He's blind.'
Then I said something I should not have
said, 'Yes, he is blind, but he's more of
a man than you'll ever be.' Jim came out
of treatment then, and we left. . . .

    By Sunday, I was so overwhelmed with
all that had happened I couldn't even
think. . .

    I told him that I didn't think it was
fair, and that I loved him too much to
watch him put up with all that mess. Jim
is a sweet, loving,compassionate, intelligent, sexy, desirable man, and I love
him and it hurts for everybody else to

105

In her autobiography describing her experience of
slowly becoming blind, taking a leave of absence from
college to learn braille and mobility training with the
use of a cane, Deborah Zook, explains that the blind
often have trouble retaining their independence with
dignity:

Blind persons often find themselves in awkward situations. Some tend to demand perfection
of themselves. Others may react in the opposite
way and hardly ever try. Without proper sensory
and mobility training, a blind person may come
to feel he can never achieve dignity. He may
then use his blindness as an excuse for lack
of poise, sloppy dress, bad table manners,
and practically no social skills. It is easy
for him to forget that he can compete with
the sighted world in all these areas, although
he may need to make some allowances here and
there.

The two extremes of ultrasensitivity
about mistakes and not caring at all can be
equally dangerous. The happy medium is striving
for poise and awareness. [14]

Later Deborah Zook learned that "living independently" is an art. But gradually came to realize
that accepting help when it is needed is a much finer
art.[15] She believes that accepting help and even asking
for it when needed and politely refusing it when
unneeded can be done in such a way that the blind need
not lose their dignity or fundamental sense of autonomy.

The third source from which the blind role is
learned is what Scott calls the "blindness system." It

106

involves the public and private agencies which serve
the blind. Altogether around 900 such agencies exist
in the United States which offer a variety of services
which fall into five major categories:

(1) income maintenance and social support
(recreation, counseling and communication)
services:

(2) instrumental services, such as training in
use of braille, canes and seeing-eye dogs,
to make the blind more independent;

(3) rehabilitation and vocational counseling
and training services to enable the blind
to enter competitive employment if possible
or to work in sheltered workshops;

(4) educational, instrumental and rehabilitative
services for children either in special
schools or mainstreaming educational
programs; and

(5) special medical services for the blind
like vision enhancement, prevention of
blindness and eye treatment.

Discrimination exists in the provision of these
services through a process known as "creaming." While
income maintenance and social support services are
available to all blind, they are most continuously used
by the blind who are aged, unemployable and multiply
handicapped. Services for children are relatively
available to all blind children. However, "creaming"
is most apparent in the remaining three services-
instrumental services, rehabilitation and vocational
counseling and training services, and special medical
services. Only about one-quarter of all the blind use
these services. The blind who are most likely to use or
be selected to use these services are children and non-
aged adults whose employability is seen as high.

On the other hand, the less elite of the blind--the
aged adult judged as less employable or trainable and
the multiply handicapped are least likely to receive
these services. This type of "creaming" selection process involves judgments about the social worth of people.
Indirectly it involves socialization processes in
learning who is considered most eligible among the blind

for some services.[16]

Scott argues that socialization of the blind in the blindness system occurs in two phases: the recruitment phase during which some clients are screened out and later the rehabilitation phase for those who are screened into the agencies' service system. Most of those who come to blind agencies are not totally blind, but are legally blind--that is they have narrow tunnel vision or a visual acuity below 20/200. A visual acuity below 20/200 means the person has 10% or less of visual efficiency, but may be able to see well enough to move around and even read large print. Because of the administrative definition of blindness, many blindness system workers, opthalmologists and others try to convince people with borderline vision that they are "blind" with only residual vision. Many clients find it hard to redefine themselves as blind with all the associated stereotypes of maladjustment, helplessness, uselessness and sorrow that accompany the use of this powerful label. Some leave the blindness system before they are screened into it because they are not convinced they are really blind and they are fearful of the stigma associated with the label. However, most accept the definition that they are blind and accept the blindness system of agencies as the appropriate place to go for a wide range of professional services when in fact some of the agencies are not very "professional." [17]

Once accepted into the blindness system, most of the blind come with specific ideas about the few services they need. But at this point they get a rather rude awakening by even stronger labels from the workers in the blindness system. As Scott states:

> The personal conception that blinded persons have about the nature of their problems are in sharp contrast with beliefs that workers for the blind share about the problems of blindness. The latter regard blindness as one of the most severe handicaps, the effects of which are long-lasting, pervasive, and extremely difficult to ameliorate. They believe that if these problems are to be solved, blind persons must understand them and all their manifestations and willingly submit to a prolonged,

108

intensive, and comprehensive program
of psychological and restorative services. Effective socialization of
the client largely depends upon
changing his views about his problem.
In order to do this, the client's
views about the problems of blindness must be discredited. Workers
must convince him that simplistic
ideas about solving the problem of
blindness by means of one or a few
services are unrealistic. (Emphasis
added)[18]

The typical socialization of the blind in these
agencies involves a long diagnostic work-up of their
problems, learning to reject their own views of blindness for that of social workers, psychologists and
physicians and learning to be cooperative with these
workers who control rewards and punishments for being
"insightful" or "uncooperative."

Some blindness agencies tend to take a "restorative
approach" with regard to blindness--they believe blind
persons can be restored to a sufficiently high level of
independence that their life can be almost normal.
Others however take an "accommodative approach" which
assumes that many blind cannot make such a successful
adjustment. This approach involves supplying the blind
with more aids to recognize obstacles, giving them more
help (creating more dependence), over-emphasizing the
importance of trivial achievements, supplying them work
in sheltered workshops, and supplying them with nearly
all their social and recreational outlets. How blind
people respond to these socialization processes is
rather variable. At one extreme are the "true believers"
who end up seeing themselves as blind and acting the
way counselors want them to act. In the middle are the
"expedient blind" who rather tentatively act coopera-
tively with agency personnel in order to get through the
system. At the other extreme are the rejectors who
leave the blindness system. In terms of life style
there tend to be two types--the "professional blind"
and the "independent blind." The independent blind are
those who leave the blind agencies after rehabilitation
to return to or enter competitive outside employment
and return to their normal circle of friends and interests. The "professional blind," however, work
within the blindness system, sometimes in sheltered

workshops, and organize most of their vocational, social and recreational lives around fellow blind people
and the personnel who serve them.[19]

Many of the public and private agencies engaging in
work with the blind use an accommodative approach to
work with the blind. In contrast is the Veteran's
Administration program which emphasizes exclusively the
restorative approach. It sends all blinded veterans to
one of three rehabilitation centers for a predetermined
length of time at the end of which it is assumed they
will return to their home communities to lead independent lives. Because of this, because of the disability benefits they receive, because of the training and
educational benefits they receive as veterans, most do
become independently employed, better off financially
and involved in more non-blind community organizations.

These pieces of information, Scott concludes,

indicate in a very striking way how alternative
approaches to rehabilitation can produce radically
different socialization outcomes among blind people.
Organizational systems that are constructed so as
to discourage dependence in fact produce independent blind people; systems that foster dependency
by creating accommodated environments produce blind
people who cannot function outside them. There
is no more dramatic way than this to demonstrate
just how important a factor in the making of blind
men are the organized efforts of blindness workers
and blindness agencies.[20]

In his speech to the 1976 annual meeting of The
National Federation of the Blind, the blind president
of the organization made much the same point:

The Federation is based on the proposition that
the principal problem of blindness is not the
blindness itself but the mistaken notions and
ideas about blindness which are held by the
general public. We of the Federation believe that
the blind . . . tend to see themselves as others
see them. Accepting the mistaken public attitudes,
we help those attitudes become reality. Moreover,
we believe that the governmental and private service agencies are also victims of the same
misconceptions and stereotypes and that they make
their voluminous studies, plan their programs, and

custodialize their clients, not (as they claim)
from professional expertise and knowledge but
from ignorance and prejudice, absorbed from the
general culture. Finally, we believe that when
we as blind people accept the second-class role
assigned to us by the agencies and the public, we
do it because of social conditioning, not because
of correct information or necessity. We do it
because of fable, not fact.[21]

Some employers have a good attitude toward
employing the blind for work which they can do. However, in one study of "positive attitude" employers,
66% indicated a blind person could not work in their
business and 70% said they would not welcome one in
their company. High level managers were found to be
authoritarian in their personality structures, and exhibited prejudices toward all non-conforming disabled
workers including the blind.[22] Another research study
found that the top managers in firms without previous
experience in employing the blind were cautious, reserved and suspicious in hiring the blind. The public
image of blind workers performing only unskilled labor
reinforced their beliefs that blind workers would need
more supervision, major safety standards, affect attitudes of other workers and create new problems of
which they need no more.[23]

One blind person tells of her experience in replying
to a want ad in the Lakewood Colorado Sentinel:

I called to inquire about the job and was
told to come in Tuesday for an interview.
The ad indicated that the job was for
telephone ticket sales, but no other information was given. I arrived at the
office...and was told to speak with Joe
Chapman. Upon noting that I was blind,
he immediately said I could not take this
job because there were cards with names
and addresses on them, which I could not
read. I offered to get the cards brailled.
I offered to have a reader come and read
the cards. Each suggestion I made was
either ignored, or answered rudely. When
he began to see that my suggestions were
valid, he started making irrelevant excuses
such as "Many times these businessmen make

111

excuses, and you have to know what to say to them", and "I give directions at the beginning of each day, and you would have to digest them." I ask you, what does blindness or sight have to do with following directions-using one's ears and mind to listen and think? He later said that he didn't have time to spend with me individually. He never did say what he would have to do for me that he does not have to do with other employees. When I asked him what he does for the others (I was going to point out that he would do the same for me, no more, no less), he rudely said, 'That isn't any of your business.' He was even further demeaning by saying, 'Believe me, I understand; I've been down and out, too! He still clings to the old notion that all blind persons are down and out. After some discussion (I was trying to find out more about the job, explain my qualifications and capabilities, and make suggestions, and Mr. Chapman was interrupting), he finally told me to leave. When I would not, because I still had not been interviewed, he threatened to call the police. I had come down for an interview, and he would not grant me that right.[24]

No systematic reviews of the extent or kinds of discrimination the blind face have been made. The literature is primarily of examples of discrimination against the blind in a variety of contexts. These examples do illustrate, however, that the impairment of blindness is often met with patterned reactions typical of a dominant group against a minority group.

In the past blind children have often been separated from the sighted in education. To a certain extent this needs to be done for educational reasons such as teaching braille. Nor should handicapped children be dumped into regular classrooms where the teachers have no training to handle the special needs of handicapped children. But at the same time, integrating visually impaired children into some mainstream classes has a benefit not only to them but also to sighted children. They both grow up in a less protected environment which fosters understanding and acceptance of differences rather than an emphasis upon them.[25] In one church school, for example, the blind were separated from sighted students and put in a special class with the crippled and mentally retarded.[26] Under federal law schools receiving federal financial assistance are not to discriminate against the visually impaired. Yet some restrict blind students by fallacious attitudes about their lack of ability, their proneness to injuries, their need for additional supervision and their rejection by classmates. In mainstream physical education classes for example, blind students are sometimes excused from participation, giving them unearned marks, taking part in only passive and unchallenging activities, or handing out towels and equipment. Yet, many of them do well in physical education activities. They dive, scuba dive, wrestle, swim, sky dive, bowl and go hiking. "Each year about 25 blind and partially seeing wrestlers are among the top five placers in various state high school wrestling tournaments."[27]

Discrimination against the blind is not limited to employment or educational discrimination or even those interpersonal put-downs where a sighted person talks to the sighted person accompanying a blind person as if the blind person was an incompetent imbecile. Sometimes the blind are segregated into special housing projects. Sometimes the blind are assumed to be incapable of responsible parenthood. Kenneth Jernigan writes:

> The discriminations against us are not imaginary, but real--not exceptional but commonplace. It is illustrated. . . in two recent court cases. In one a mother was threatened by the loss of her child, on the grounds that, as the judge put it, "she is industrially blind, and doesn't have the ability to care for the child." In the other case, a married couple was declared unfit to adopt a male child because, in the words of the husband, 'it was felt that a boy could not relate to me because of my blindness.'

> It need only be added that hundreds of blind mothers are successfully caring for their offspring every day and that adoption of children by blind parents has occurred repeatedly with no problem.[28]

Lower Status

One of the characteristics of a minority group is
that they have lower status. The blind have had a
lower status throughout history. Often they see themselves as second class citizens because the rights
easily open to others are often denied to them. With
high rates of unemployment and concentration in less
skilled, low paying work when employed, they are
relatively powerless in an economic sense. Many carry
the stigma of being useless citizens who are on welfare.
Numerically, they are also weak. Constituting only
about one half of one percent of the U.S. population,
they have little political power. Scattered over the
entire country and predominantly old and undereducated,
they have little potential power at their disposal.

Group Self-Awareness

How the blind picture themselves depends extensively
on the learning they have been exposed to with regard
to the blind and their contact with the blindness
system--that unorganized network of programs and services made available to the blind. No blind person can
entirely escape the predominant attitudes of our society
toward blindness. But if blindness occurs before old
age, most will be exposed to and some indoctrinated
either into accommodative patterns or independent patterns of dealing with their blindness. The
accommodative pattern of reaction is marked by accepting definitions of themselves as blind, of remaining
segregated from the sighted for purposes of work, social
events and recreation and sometimes housing. The independence pattern of reaction is marked by definitions
of themselves as normal, useful people who have a vision
problem but can engage in competitive employment and
participate in all the usual institutions and organizations of sighted people. This two-fold typology of
two patterns of reactions is overly simple. There will
be degrees of both accommodative dependence and
independence.

One of the characteristics of some minority group
members is that they take on the attitudes of the dominant groups about themselves and other blind persons.
These reactions are more common among or essentially
part of the accommodative approach. According to
psychiatrist Robert Blank, this is seen among some
blind people in two ways. Fist is that of self-contempt

plus self hatred--identification with the aggressor's attitudes. A second way is that they often duplicate the stratification system of the larger social system which stigmatizes blindness within their own subsystem. Blank writes,

> In two schools for the blind I found the children stratified into three group "pecking orders": 1. the totally blind who constituted the bullied, exploited and scapegoated; 2. the dominant group who had enough vision to dominate the others, and who were feared and envied by the others; 3. and those who had very little and variable vision, and found themselves identifying alternatively with the other groups.[29]

Another reaction, typical of and part of the independence response, is the rejection pattern of attempting to "pass" into the dominant system of denying their blindness, refusing to get medical services which would constitute an admission of blindness, and refusing to associate with the other blind people and the whole blindness system of services.

The history of social service programs and special agencies providing services for the blind in the last two hundred years in both the United States and Europe reflect both of these approaches. Some agencies and programs have emphasized a separate system for the blind where they were segregated into different educational, work and housing programs and facilities. Other agencies have emphasized putting the blind on a parity with the seeing by providing special services and financial assistance when needed to integrate the blind into the mainstream of our educational, economic and social systems. The overall movement of federal legislation and service programs has been away from accommodation to independence, integration or mainstreaming. However, the resilience and pervasiveness of stigmatizing public attitudes about blindness and because of vested interests in some blindness service agencies, the movement has been slow.[30]

Most of the organizations which serve the blind have been founded by and continue to be run by the sighted. For example the American Association of Instructors of the Blind was established in 1853 to improve instruction for the blind. The American

Foundation for the Blind, Inc., was organized in 1921
to consult with local blind service agencies, lobby for
legislation, act as an educational forum on the needs
of the blind, and sell special aids to the blind from
Braille Scrabble to Braille thermometers and watches.
Today it has a central staff of 180 people. The
National Society for the Prevention of Blindness, Inc.,
founded in 1908, supports research, eye health care and
vision screening programs. In addition to these major
national organizations concerned with the blind are
many state and local groups.[31]

However, some organizations have been principally
established by the blind themselves. The first of
these in the United States was the American Blind
People's Higher Education and General Improvement Association founded in 1895 to push for more education
for the blind. It was reorganized in 1905 and renamed
The American Association of Workers for the Blind. The
major association of the blind today is the National
Federation of the Blind composed of 50 state and 350
local organizations of the blind. It monitors federal
policies affecting the blind and lobbies to change
policies and promote legislation on behalf of its
50,000 members. It evaluates programs serving the blind
and acts as a civil rights group to promote its goal of
"the complete integration of the blind into society on
a basis of equality." In the last decade the blind
have become more militant minded as a spinoff of the
1960 civil rights era. Blind people have gone to court
contesting their right to serve on juries, their right
to participate in contact sports in high school, their
right to be hired as teachers, their right to adopt
children. They want to be seen as persons not non-
seeing objects who are to be pitied.

Kenneth Jernigan, President of the National
Federation of the Blind, believes that a lot of progress
has been made in the last three decades in opening up
civil service jobs for the blind, in providing them
financial assistance, sheltered workshops, vocational
training programs, counseling, libraries, and a better
chance of dignity. He feels the National Federation of
the Blind has "helped us understand and made us believe
in ourselves, in each other, and in our collective
strength. It has also taught us to fight. In short, it
has brought us to see that we are (in every modern sense
of the word), a minority."[33]

The blind eminently qualify as a minority who suffer from a variety of handicappisms--stereotypes about their limitations and personality characteristics and discrimination in housing, education, medical care, employment and personal encounters. Many of them are easily identifiable. They suffer from the stigmatizing status of a person with a spoiled physical identity. However, they have been helped by many others for centuries in such ways that they have been socialized into needless dependency on society. Increasingly they are organizing to press for independence with dignity, for integration with equality.

Chapter 4

The Invisible Minority: The Hearing Impaired

Human beings have three distance sensory processes--
seeing, hearing and smelling. These sensory processes
can reach further out in the environment than the close
senses--taste or touch. Whenever one of the two major
distance sensory devices, seeing or hearing, does not
work well or at all, the other distance sensory process is elevated in importance in experiencing and
communicating with the environment. For the deaf then,
their eyes must function as their ears. The close
senses also become more important, especially the tac-
tile senses which can pick up vibrations to alert
persons to changes in their environment. In some ways
the loss of hearing is more important than the loss of
sight. Hearing is extremely important in learning about
the world through the spoken language and without spoken
language it is more difficult to acquire a mastery of
written language. The person who learns language before
he becomes deaf is at a decided advantage over the person either born deaf or who becomes deaf before spoken
language skills are developed. While some people who
are deaf from birth do learn to speak, it is a much
more difficult and tedious learning process than for
those who had no major hearing impairment for the first
seven to ten years of life. But just as those who are
blind can learn to read with their hands with braille,
those who cannot hear can be taught to communicate with
others through reading, writing, lip reading, (speechreading), speech and a variety of manual communication
systems which use the eyes. Before examining whether
the hearing impaired fulfill the four criteria of a
minority group--identifiability, perjorative treatment,
lower status and group awareness, we need to examine the
particular nature of sensory deprivation that comes
through hearing loss.

The Nature of Deafness[1]

Many classification systems have been developed to
deal with the nature of deafness for different purposes.
Four classification systems have been developed to deal
with the four significant aspects of deafness. These
four significant aspects are (1) age of onset of
hearing impairment, (2) degree of deafness, (3) the
source of the causal factor in hearing impairment, and

119

(4)   the physical location of the impairment.

Age of Onset is an important factor because unless
language is acquired and remembered in the normal
(hearing) way there are greater obstacles to overcome
in developing speech and reading skills and other communication skills. Since mental, social and even
physical development are profoundly influenced by
hearing communication with the world, the age at which
hearing impairment occurs heavily influences development
from that point on. Two major classifications regarding
the age of onset are (1) the congenitally deaf, who
are born deaf, and (2) the adventitiously deaf who are
born with hearing but sometime during their life span
they lose their ability to hear. As in the case of
vision impairment, with advancing age there are increasing numbers and an increasing percentage of people
who have some degree of hearing loss.

Degree of Deafness. The term hearing-impaired
covers the two major degrees of hearing loss. The first
is the term deaf--those who have no hearing. It involves a loss that may go beyond the comparable term
"legally blind" with regard to vision. Deafness involves a sense of hearing that is nonfunctional for the
ordinary pursuits of life. The second kind of hearing
loss is called hard of hearing. People who are hard of
hearing having some degree of hearing either with or
without a hearing aid but which is in some degree defective compared to those with normal hearing ability.
There are various degrees of residual hearing.

A brief digression is in order here to distinguish
between sound and hearing. Sound is the term used to
designate stimuli, usually airborne, which activate the
hearing mechanism. Sound has three primary physical
characteristics: frequency (the number of times in a
second vibrating particles complete a cycle), intensity
(the magnitude of the sound), and complexity (the mixture of frequency and intensity in a variety of patterns). In contrast, hearing is the psychological
experience of sensing sound. Hearing has three attributes which respectively refer to the three attributes
of experienced sound: pitch, loudness and timbre.
Timbre involves complex learning to be able to distinguish between the predictable rhythms, frequencies and
intensities of human speech or music and the irregular
sequences and conglomeration of frequencies and intensities designated as "noise." Audiologists are those

who conduct tests using audiometers and other devices to determine the degree of hearing impairment and whether the sound is being transmitted through the air or the bone surrounding the ear.

Finer distinctions about degrees of hearing impairment are made by audiologists than those given above. Distinctions are made about hearing loss with regard to loudness in terms of decibels (dB) and to pitch in terms of Hertz (Hz). Before listing several degrees of hearing impairment it is helpful to note degrees of loudness. The rustling of leaves is about 20 dB, average conversational speech is around 60 dB, live rock and roll music around 90 to 130 dB, the roar of a jet airplane taking off from several hundred feet around 140 dB, and bazooka fired at one foot 163 dB. "Slight" hearing impairment is a loss of 25 to 39 dB and would involve difficulty in hearing faint speech. "Mild to moderate" hearing impairment involves a dB loss of 40 to 54 and makes hearing a normal conversation difficult if the speaker is over four feet away. "Moderately severe" loss involves a dB loss of 55 to 69 which means a person usually cannot hear normal conversation. A "Severe" hearing loss includes the 70 to 89 dB range which means that a person cannot usually hear even shouted conversation. Children with such a degree of impairment are sometimes called "educationally deaf" because they cannot hear the voices of teachers. A loss of over 90 dB is a "profound loss" where any thing but very loud noises are not heard. Profound loss is deafness while moderately severe to severe loss is borderline deafness.

Another type of hearing loss is high frequency hearing loss. Human conversation usually varies between 250 Hertz and 4000 Hertz. Most vowels are heard at below 1000 Hz while consonants are usually above 1000 Hz. Significant numbers of people develop high frequency hearing loss which means that speech comes through garbled because they hear mostly vowels but not consonants. Such hearing losses are primarily due to overexposure to loud voices or presbycusis--a hearing loss that comes with age.

The source of the causal factor in hearing impairments is divided into two major sources with a further subdivision in one of them. The major distinction is between endogeneous causes and exogeneous causes. Endogeneous causes are hereditary ones while

121

exogeneous causes are all other factors which include pre and post natal diseases, injuries, maldevelopments and aging factors. Around one fourth of all hearing impairments appear to be due to heredity while three quarters is due to infections,noises and accidents. There are many diseases which lead to partial or complete loss of hearing: German measles (rubella), meningitis, pneumonia, scarlet fever, whooping cough, mumps, pertussis, influenza and other viral infections. Accidents as well as exposure to loud noise may also damage the highly sensitive mechanism called the ear and lead to hearing loss. Otorhinolaryngologists are medical specialists who are concerned with diagnosing the causes of ear, eye, nose and throat diseases and treating them. Otolaryngologists specialize in both ear and throat problems while otologists are ear specialists only. In some cases early treatment may be able to reverse the progression of an ear disease, especially if it is due to a controllable infection. Surgery may be able to repair some types of hearing loss.

There are two types of hearing loss, while exogeneous in nature, do not fit neatly under such causes as diseases, injuries or ear maldevelopments. One is feigned hearing loss or malingering. This involves a person who pretends not to hear but whose hearing equipment is in good condition. The other type, hysterical deafness, is not concerned with hysterical outbursts as the label suggests, but is a psychogenic disturbance where a person is unable to experience sound because of some mental disturbance. Hysterical deafness is often seen as an unconscious escape mechanism from some unpleasant or terrifying experience. There is no organic defect in the person's hearing equipment. Nor is there a conscious effort to avoid hearing as in feigned deafness. Hysterical deafness may come about as an escape from stress just as other psychosomatic disturbances such as memory loss, paralysis or ulcers may be produced by stress.

The physical location of the hearing impairment may be in any one or more of the three areas of that complex and sensitive mechanism called the ear: the outer ear, the middle ear, or the inner ear. There are three types of hearing impairment which are medically defined by their location in the outer, middle or inner ear and by the nature of the condition: conductive deafness, sensory neural deafness, and central deafness.

    Before describing the nature of these three types
of deafness, I will briefly digress to describe the
three parts of the ear and how the human hearing mechanism works. The outer ear includes the exterior ear
cup (Pinna) to catch the sound and the ear canal which
channels the sound inward. The middle ear begins with
the tympanic membrane (eardrum) and transforms acoustic
sound waves into mechanical energy by setting into
motion the three tiniest bones in the human body--the
malleus,incus and stapes. The middle ear is an air
filled cavity that is connected by the eustachian canal
to the back of the nasal cavity and which allows for
the adjustment of air pressure in the middle ear. The
inner ear is a sealed fluid-filled cavity made up of
two parts. One of these parts is the snail shaped tube
called the cochlea. It changes the mechanical vibrations of the last little bone, the stapes (as well
as vibrations from the surrounding boney structure),
into hydraulic energy or waves which move against rows
of thousands of microscopic hair cells inside the
cochlea. The movement of these hair cells converts
hydraulic energy into electrical energy which are con-
ducted by nerves to the brain. There electrical energy
is converted into "psychological" energy or the sensation of sound. The inner ear also contains the
semicircular canals which control a person's sense of
balance. If deafness or trauma injures the semicircular
canals as sometimes happens with hearing impairment,
the sense of balance will also be injured.

    The first type of deafness, conductive deafness,
occurs in the outer or middle ear as a result of the
blockage of sound or damage to the eardrum or the three
bones in the middle ear--the malleus (hammer), incus
(anvil) or the stapes (stirrup). People with conductive
hearing deafness are usually only hard of hearing and
not deaf. Injury to the outer or middle ear may be due
to maldevelopment, disease or trauma. Treatment of
conductive hearing loss is almost exclusively surgical.
Sensory-neural deafness occurs in the inner ear as a
result of maldevelopment, disease or trauma. Extended
exposure to high sound or noise levels may damage the
sensitive hair cells in the cochlea and lead to some
type of hearing loss whether it be a decline in high or
low frequency sound hearing or a decline in hearing of
loudness. Cures of sensory-neural deafness are infrequent, the best "cure" is prevention of disease,
accident and exposure to excessive sound. The third
type of deafness is not well understood but is called

<u>central</u> <u>deafness</u>. It involves a dysfunction in the
auditory nerve pathways that lead from the inner ear to
the brain. It involves both ears. The other type of
deafness, a non-organic one called <u>psychogenic</u> <u>deafness</u>
or <u>hysterical</u> <u>deafness</u>, is located in the personality
functioning of the individual which is seated in the
brain.

In medical diagnosis all or some of the factors
may be important. For example, sensory-neural deafness
may be due to either exogeneous or endogenous causes,
may be either congenital or adventitious, and partial or
complete. Such diagnoses will also have important rami-
fications for the medical and educational treatment of a
person with hearing problems.

Prevalence of Hearing Impairments

Exact statistics on the number of hearing impaired
are not available. In 1975 federal government personnel
estimated that 14,491,000 Americans had hearing impairments in one or both ears. This constituted 6.7% of
the American population. Of this 14,491,000 just over
45% or 6,548,842 had "significant" impairment in both
ears. And of the 14,491,000 an estimated 2.3% or
330,000 were totally deaf in both ears. This means
that about 1 out of every 651 Americans is totally
deaf, while 1 out of 33 has significant hearing loss in
both ears, and 1 out of 15 has some hearing impairment.
In 1970, among youth under age 22, there were 50,000
totally deaf and an additional 440,000 who were hard of
hearing.[2]

Through 1930 the Census Bureau took a census of the
deaf every 10 years, but stopped doing it because it got
such widely varying reports. Beginning in 1971 the
federal government gave one million dollars to New
York University's Deafness Research and Training Center
and the National Association for the Deaf to carry out
a new census of the deaf. It took four years to complete and came out with findings which yielded higher
estimates than those of the federal government. It
found 13,400,000 people with significant hearing loss
of whom 1,800,000 were classified as deaf. Their
findings indicate that hearing problems far outnumber
any other single chronic physical disability. They
also found the prevalence rate for those under twenty
was nearly twice what was expected. This indicated
that the prevocationally deaf was an enormously under-

served group. It found nearly six times as many deaf
people as the federal government had estimated.[3]

Audiologist Richard Carmen accepts the figure of
1,800,000 people as deaf but believes that instead of
14.5 million with hearing loss set by the federal government or the 13.4 million with hearing loss discovered
by the census of the deaf population, there are over 33
million with hearing disabilities. In Our Endangered
Hearing he argues that the numbered of hearing disabled
has climbed to 15 percent of the population. Our social
systems have grown increasingly noisy since the advent
of the industrial revolution. He argues that noise
pollution--jets and city traffic, jackhammers and rock
and roll bands, guns and high speed drills, firecrackers
and power mowers, is leading to an increasing amount of
hearing problems. In developing his "high" estimates,
he used a "conservative" 25% of 75 million industrial
workers or 18,750,000 workers with impaired hearing.
He notes that a 1975 federal government study of 19
major industries found that 36% of all production
workers experience hearing losses before the age of
sixty. Of the 21 million Americans over 65, he estimates that 28% of them (5.9 million) suffer from serious
hearing loss while 88% of them have some hearing loss,
with about half of this group having a serious hearing
handicap. In addition, about 10% of the population
under 18, or around 5 million, have impaired hearing.
The total number of hearing impaired people, nearly 34
million, exceeds the total population of 23 of the less
populous states. The United States Public Health Service concludes that hearing impairment is the nation's
greatest handicapping condition and affects greater
numbers of people than any other chronic condition.[4]

Communication Among The Deaf And With The Hearing

For the deaf and near deaf who cannot be significantly helped with hearing aids, a number of methods
have been develped to enable them to communicate with
each other and with the hearing. Controversies have
existed among deaf instructors, and often the deaf themselves, over which method of communication is better.
I will look at the controversy in more detail later.
But the three major categories of communication are the:
(1) oral, (2) manual, and (3) a combination of both
of these used simultaneously.[5]

125

Those who use the oral method contend that the deaf must learn to speak orally and be able to speech-read. To this end, they must first learn oral communication if born deaf or prelingually deaf. If they learn manual methods of communication this will delay, disrupt and probably make oral communication rather poor they contend. The major argument here is that if they are to move into and be a part of the hearing world they must learn to speechread and talk. They cannot rely on manual communication systems which less than one percent of the population uses. Long and arduous training is given to the prelingual deaf to enable them to shape vowels, consonants, and words with their throats, tongues, teeth, size of mouth opening and release of air. Even if such speech is used among the postlingual deaf it may become distorted, but probably more understandable than the speech of the prelingual deaf. The use of mirrors in such training is often vital to give the person some visual feedback for that auditory feedback missing since he cannot hear his own voice.[6]

The second method of communication is called the manual or silent communication. It is most likely to be taught in one or more of its forms to the congenitally deaf, profoundly deaf and those who attend schools for the deaf.

There are four modes of manual communication: (1) Sign Language, (2) Signed English, (3) Finger-spelling, and (4) Manual English. Sign language is a manual language in which gestures do the work of words (including numbers). It has its own morphology, syntax and semantics. The gestures stand more for broad concepts than they do for particular words. Signed English uses English syntax with a rapid succession of signs glossing the content words of English in an approximate way and glossing some function words. Both the signer and addressee in this mode must understand the English language because the words for the syntax of Signed English are independent from the syntax of sign language. It usually includes some fingerspelled words. Finger-spelling is a system of using hand positions and configurations for the twenty six letters of the alphabet. Much practice is needed in this method to maintain the speech of spoken language and even then it is rapidly tiring to both the signer and the receiver. Sometimes this method is needed for complex words and new words and therefore needs to be an adjunct to nearly any method of manual communication. Manual English

augments the signs for words with additional signs invented to stand for the more important morphemes of the
English language to indicate plural forms, past tense,
present participal, infinitive forms and suffixes. Of
course, if the deaf understand written English, communication can occur with or among them with written
English. But this process is slow, and usually a focus
in oral methods of communication.

The simultaneous method uses both signed English
and vocal English at the same time. Thus the message
sender also says vocally or with silent lip words what
he is simultaneously gesturing in signed English. The
message receiver usually uses both the signed English
and the mouth movements (and perhaps sound if he has
some residual hearing) of the sender to understand the
message. As an educational tool the combined or simultaneous method is often referred to as the "Rochester
Method."

If the focus is shifted away from methods of
communication to methods of instructing the deaf, until
about 1960 the two major schools of thought on instructional techniques were the "oralists" and the
"combined system." The oralists maintained that instruction in oral and written English was necessary and
that it would most likely be unsuccessful if combined
with some form of manual communication. The pure
oralists excluded the use of signing on the grounds that
it would prevent the acquisition of speech. This method
often has good results with the postlingually deaf but
less so if deafness occurs in even earlier years. Some
children taught under this method, especially the congenitally deaf, have had limited or no meaningful speech
acquisition and are educational failures. The combined
system emphasized manualism in the beginning years of its
history and excluded any form of articulation training.
More recently it has maintained its emphasis on various
forms of signing with some speech training being added.
Starting in 1960 a new philosophy of educating of the
early deaf developed which is usually labeled the
total communication approach. It is more child centered
and less oriented to philosophical and pedagogical strat-
egies of oralism versus manualism. It emphasizes
utilizing any techniques available to enable the deaf to
communicate. Inasmuch as about 40% of all lip movements
are ambiguous (e.g. paper and baby use the same lip
movements), speechreading has limits. Rather than exclusive training in one method, it utilizes a variety of

127

communication techniques that takes into consideration
the amount of residual hearing, age of onset and the
capabilities and interests of the deaf learner. "Total
communication" is different from the combined system in
one other important regard. It starts with children at
an early age whereas the manualism of the combined
system was often begun after a child failed in the oral
method and critical periods of learning had already been
passed. It tries to give due regard to both manual and
oral techniques of instruction and communication.[8]

Identifiability of the Hearing Impaired

At first glance, the hard of hearing and the deaf
are an invisible minority. They appear no different
than other people. This group of people is certainly
less identifiable than racial minorities, or the obese,
or facially disfigured, or those with obvious physical
handicaps. However there are a number of clues which
begin to make them visible when contacts are established
with them. These clues are not uniform for all the
hearing impaired because hearing loss varies widely in
terms of extent and whether it is accompanied by oral
and written speech deficiencies. Thus, the type of
hearing loss, age of onset, and the kind of training or
education the hearing impaired have experienced will
influence the degree to which a number of identifying
clues or symptoms are present and visible. The following identifying clues apply to a greater degree as
the hearing loss goes from minor loss to a complete one.
Major symptoms of hearing impairment are: lack of attention to casual conversations, frequent requests to
repeat what has been said or to talk louder, a tendency
to withdraw from social activities or a lack of interest
in them, peculiar speech patterns and intonations, frequent confusion over what has been said, constant
scanning of the environment and people's faces to be
aware of what is going on, frequent earaches and/or ear
discharges and/or complaints of ear difficulties, ig-
noring directions or questions, close observation of
people's faces--particularly the lips, disinterest in
music, spells of dizziness and head noises (tinnitus),
difficulties in reading and spelling, peculiar "lunging"
walking gaits and/or poor sense of balance, and of
course, the use of sign language or fingerspelling and
the wearing of hearing aids. Certainly not all of these
clues will be visible in any one person. And they may
require observation over an extended period of time to
be aware of them. Naturally, attendance at a school for

the deaf is another sign of deafness.[9]   Some of the
totally deaf are also mute--they do not speak.   Depending on when they became deaf, and the nature of
their education, some of the deaf are recognizable by
their simple levels of language and their difficulties
in phrasing and pronunciation, speaking and intonation
generally.   Others, however, who are totally deaf even
from birth, develop good speech skills and speechreading
skills that enable them to "pass" in the everyday world.
Thus, in some ways they are a silent minority.   It is
as if they lived in glass boxes where they cannot hear
but with training can learn to communicate with the
world through a variety of channels.[10]

Stereotypes of Discrimination Against the Deaf

The history of deafness is primarily the history of
deaf education.   Throughout most of recorded history
speech was assumed to be an innate or inborn ability
rather than learned.   Therefore until the 1500's, the
deaf were assumed to be dumb.   A low intelligence was
believed to accompany deafness.   Little thought was
given to their capacity to reason for without language
in what symbolic mode could they reason?   The philosophical and scientific prejudices of the time took it
for granted that it was impossible for deaf mutes either
to learn to speak or to understand language.   Some
people still inappropriately refer to the "deaf and
dumb" when they mean deaf mutes.   As David Wright, deaf
since age seven, so capably explains about congenital or
early childhood deafness:

> At this time of life it is a calamity worse
> than blindness, because the consequences
> strikes at the roots of intellectual develop-
> ment.   Loss of hearing involves loss of the
> only means by which a child acquires lang-
> uage.....   For the blind can at least hear,
> and so pick up speech and language like other
> children.   But the deaf child, left to his
> own resources, must grow up not only unable
> to speak but denied even a concept of lang-
> uage, that indispensable instrument of
> thinking and reasoning.   Not only is he
> unable to communicate with others, he cannot
> even communicate with himself--he has no
> language with which to think about what he
> sees and experiences.   Thus, unable to re-
> ceive or transmit any but the most elementary

communications by means of signs, with
his reasoning faculty atrophied or badly
hampered for lack of a vehicle, a deaf-
born person may grow up indistinguishable
from an idiot. His case is worse, for his
case is not a defective but a trapped and
frustrated intelligence.[11]

Thus, until around the 16th century the deaf were
categorized with infants as having no speech ability
and abandoned to a hopeless condition. The scientific
leaders of the time assumed that the dumbness of the
deaf-born was always a concomitant disability <u>rather
than a result of deafness</u> as was later discovered.

Throughout history their abandonment often meant
uncouthness, animality, an inability to either compre-
hend or be comprehended. This neither inspired sympathy
or trust. The ancient Greeks and Romans often destroyed
malformed or crippled children by age three while the
Jews, Egyptians and Persians allowed them to live but
little was done for them. In the Talmud deaf mutes
were held incapable of owning property since their
legal status was like that of children. This legal
position became part of Roman and Spanish law wherein
deaf mutes were treated as legally insane, could not own
property or make contracts or wills. They were without
rights or obligations. However, if the deaf could speak
they had some rights. The legal status of the deaf,
according to David Wright, was probably the precipi-
tating factor which led to efforts to teach them to
read, write and speak.[12]

While there were rare isolated reports of the congenitally deaf being trained to paint or even speak
before the fifteenth century, the innovative efforts
toward this end came as a result of events in Spain.
With the treasures of the new world flowing back to
Spain in the 1500s, the rich in this highly stratified
society of rich and poor wanted to leave their estates
to their heirs. But because of an aristrocratic ex-
clusiveness and frequent intermarriages among the
wealthy some congenitally deaf children were born who
could be sole heirs of great estates. But Spanish law
followed Roman law in this regard. The speaking deaf
could inherit estates and enter into contracts while
deaf mutes were excluded from these rights. The relatives of two deaf and dumb brothers, Francisco and
Pedro de Valaseo, secured the services of a Benedictine

Monk, Pedro Ponce de Leon, to teach these brothers to
read, write and speak. Ponce de Leon had earlier suc-
cesses in enabling deaf and dumb men to learn to speak
so that they could go to confession and carry out other
communicative functions. Ponce de Leon was able to
teach these deaf brothers to speak so they could assume
military duties and the other privileges and duties of
people of their class. Ponce de Leon was born in 1520
and died in 1584. While his methods of instructing the
deaf to speak were supposedly written down, a monastery
fire reportedly burned them. Nonetheless, his techniques were carried on and used by others who worked
with him.[13] One of these was Juan Pablo Bonet who
published in 1620 a treastise on the education of the
deaf. This work became a great turning point in deaf
education because it developed a system of associating
letters in the alphabet with phonetic elements and it
showed the technique of teaching deaf mutes language
and speech which in many fundamental ways is still in
use in the United States. First pupils learned a one-
handed manual alphabet which was associated with a
printed one. Next, pupils were taught to pronounce
letters, beginning with vowels, then syllables, then
words, and then sentences in a series of grammatical
steps. Pupils learned to read, write, and speak
simultaneously so that they would reinforce one another.
Some of these basic ideas go back earlier to an Italian
physician and astronomer, Girolama Cardano, who argued,
contrary to the wisdom of his times, that writing is
associated with speech, and speech with thought, and
therefore that written characters could be connected to
ideas without the intervention of sound. However,
Cardano did not teach the deaf to communicate.[14]

Cardano's theory and Ponce de Leon's practice which
showed the deaf could be taught to speak were revolu-
tionary and were carried to other countries, or perhaps
in some cases developed independently, where about a
century later they were adopted. However it was nearly
two centuries later before the education of the deaf was
widely undertaken. The development of deaf education in
England, Germany and France essentially went through
three stages in about a century. In the first stage
educated men developed the theory of deaf education and
quite frequently developed new or more complex manual
communication systems. Sometimes these theorists worked
with a few deaf pupils themselves primarily in order to
determine the soundness of their ideas and instructional
techniques. In the second phase professional deaf

teachers were developed who frequently became full time
instructors of the deaf whose families could afford
their fees. This meant that few of the deaf in the 16th
and 17th centuries were educated in communication skills
because of the cost. Furthermore many of these teachers
were quite secretive about their particular techniques
because they were their livelihood and they did not
want others to know about them. Some private schools
were established for the deaf and run by a family or
dynasty. The first private school in England was
started in 1760 while Pereira was offering individual
instruction to deaf mutes in France in the 1740s. The
third phase, the extension of deaf education to a
greater number of people including the poor, was begun
by the greatest figure in the history of deaf education,
a French priest, Abbe Charles Michel de l'Epee.
De l'Epee developed a sign language based partly on the
natural signs, the "mother-tongue", of the deaf born.
He "evolved a combination of mime and arbritary signs,
obeying grammatical laws, systematized into a visual
equivalent of spoken language." In this communication
system, "nouns and verbs were mimed--gestured ideographs
as it were--while grammatical inflections and parts of
speech like prepositions and the definite article were
shown by arbitrary or invented gestures."[15] While
de l'Epee emphasized silent communication, he did not
disregard the teaching of speechreading or speech.
However he could teach large numbers, up to sixty in a
class, the silent communication system in a period of
several years. In contrast the teaching of reading,
writing and particularly oral speech to the deaf-born
or childhood deaf was much more time consuming, required
much more individual instruction in pronunciation and
oral skills and was therefore much more expensive.
De l'Epee's development of sign language and his charitable extension of manual communication classes to the
poor and to teachers from many other countries in the
1760s not only extended deaf education to all classes
but gave rise to two rival systems in deaf education.[16]

The advocates of these two rival systems, the
"oral" and the "silent", were to battle for the next
hundred years about the relative merits of these two
forms of communication and education. In fact, remnants
of their controversy remain today. The merits of the
silent (manual, or later 'combined') system is that it
is easy to teach, takes less time to learn, and can be
used best with those born deaf or who became so early
in life (prelingual deaf). It is more economical

educationally, more easily adaptable by those of limited
ability or some forms of multiply handicapped deaf. It
has inherent advantages for communication within the
deaf community since much speechreading is inherently
ambiguous, even more so among the deaf with poor pronunciation skills; and many deaf people speak little.
The oralists maintained, however, that if the deaf person is going to enter the hearing world he must
communicate with it on its terms and not be dependent on
his manual systems not known in that world. While ad-
mitting that acquisition of the oral language is a more
complex and arduous task, and perhaps beyond the capa-
bility of some, the oralists believe it opens up normal
reading and daily communication with the hearing that
is vitally necessary for everyday integration into the
total hearing community. They contend that the use of
a manual system not only makes the deaf more identifiable but subjects them to differential treatment. Using
a sign language, they believe, is socially stigmatizing.
Furthermore the emphasis on manual systems impedes the
development of speechreading, learning oral communication skills, and inhibits entrance into advanced
training and institutions of higher education which presume oral communication. But many of the manualists,
or orally combined system advocates, point out that few
of the orally taught reach a proficiency of reading and
oral communication that allows them to successfully
enter the hearing world. They believe that since so few
become skilled in oral skills, they need a variety of
other communication skills including manual systems. In
the last two decades the total communication approach
emphasizes combining the merits involved in both
systems.[17]

A detailed history of the evolution of deaf education in the United States, Great Britain and the
continent would be too long for our purposes. But it is
of interest to note that for a period of time, from
about 1800 to 1850 the silent (manual) method of instruction gained ascendancy world wide. Part of this
was due to the secrecy of the oralists about their techniques in teaching the deaf to speak. The first school
for deaf mutes opened in the U. S. in 1817 under private
philanthropic support with Thomas Gallaudet as its principal and teacher using the silent system he had studied
abroad. The various asylums established in the U. S.
before 1850 usually segregated their pupils from mainstream education and emphasized vocational education so
that the students could earn a living after schooling

was completed. However, pure oralism had been kept alive in Germany and eventually spread to France, England and the United States. Eventually it became the dominant method in most schools for the deaf abroad by 1880. Helen Keller became the most famous pupil of one of the pure oral method schools established in the U. S.--the Horace Mann School at Boston. However, in the United States, the ascendancy of the silent method lasted until after the turn of the century when Alexander Graham Bell, who became wealthy after inventing the telephone in 1867, promoted the oralist method of instruction as superior. Bell had been a teacher of the deaf in several schools which promoted oralism.

In the present century many advances have been made in different fields to promote the education of the deaf. Audiometers have been developed to determine rather precisely the amount of and location of hearing loss. This has meant not only better medical diagnosis of the cause of impairment but the proper placement of the impaired that depends on their degree of hearing loss. Hearing bells or horns had been used for centuries, but electronic breakthroughs led to the first hearing-aids being produced in 1932. With the development of transistors, 1954 marked the introduction of small hearing-aids that even small children could wear to augment various levels of residual hearing. Psychological studies of the hearing impaired have come to recognize the important role that speech and communication play in the emotional, intellectual and social development of children. These findings have helped pave the way for improved methods of instruction. Sociologists have come to recognize that those who have no language skills, or only silent ones, tend to become segregated into their own communities and cut off from the social intercourse and everyday activities of the hearing world. This has had implications for educational mainstreaming. Governments have enlarged their commitments to research on deafness and for the education of the deaf from special pre-school classes through post-secondary technical training schools and colleges such as Gallaudet College, in Washington, D. C.

One of the continuing issues with regard to the deaf is how to (1) give them the best education possible in light of their handicap while simultaneously (2) attempting to integrate them into the mainstream of society. An emphasis on either one of them tends to

undermine the fulfillment of the other. To get the
best education including speaking and speechreading
skills, the severely or profoundly hearing impaired
need specially educated teachers who can instruct them
in these skills and who are aware of their special
needs. Because there are few deaf people in many communities this means segregating them into either special
and separate classes or into separate schools, often
residential ones. Such schools can also more easily
afford the special equipment that may be quite useful
in their education. In these schools, the slower pace
they must follow in learning to read, write and talk
means they will not face the discouragement and sense
of failure they would likely experience in a normal
classroom where they would fall behind in reading,
writing and speech skills of their age mates. But in
these special schools a "protected climate" develops in
which teachers sensitive to their needs will be there
to help them. However this may falsely make them think
that all adults in the "outside" world will be like
their teachers. This may result in a special socialization of the deaf that does not adequately prepare them
for participation in the workaday world. At the same
time, to attempt to mainstream the deaf (not so true
for the lesser hearing impaired) will subject them to
untrained teachers, early failure and social differentness in oral skills. This approach also creates
problems of not always providing the best education for
them.

The attitudes toward the deaf have largely para-
lelled the level of education provided for them. When
no education was provided they were seen as deaf and
dumb. As education was seen as feasible and increasingly widely undertaken in the last four centuries,
their potential as thinking, intelligent human beings
was slowly disseminated. As Furth comments,

> The history of the deaf has yet to be
> written. We know little about them in
> the past, and what we do know reflects
> more the hearing person's prejudices and
> unenlightened attitudes than the actual
> life and feelings of the deaf themselves.
> Because deafness is an invisible dis-
> ability manifesting itself mainly in
> failure to communicate, hearing people
> cannot readily understand the effects
> of this handicap, and even scientific

135

investigators are faced with a serious
and unfamiliar obstacle.[18]

While seeing blind can communicate with the blind,
hearing people often have trouble communicating with the
deaf. It is not that they don't know what to say because of the handicap. It is because they do not know
if they will be heard at all or how well they will be
heard. Conversely, some of the deaf have little lip-
reading ability and low levels of language proficiency.
While their teachers in school may be able to understand their frequently abnormal speech patterns, many
in the hearing world will have difficulty in doing so.

Inasmuch as the hearing impaired frequently become educationally retarded because of the centrality
of speech in learning and their slower acquisition of
these skills, fewer of them go on to college. In some
cases, congenital deafness is not detected early so
that special education is delayed. In other instances
hard of hearing children whose progress in school is
behind their age mates are believed to be retarded when
in fact the reason for the poor performance is deafness.
But some do make it to college, especially Gallaudet
College in Washington, D. C. This school is funded by
the federal government and is the only school in the
country exclusively for the deaf and the multiply handicapped deaf which has the power to confer college
degrees. In 1969 this school also opened a federally
funded "Model Secondary School for the Deaf" to act as
an exemplar for the nation in testing new curriculum
materials and teaching techniques. It was started
partly because only about 8% of all deaf secondary
school graduates go on to college compared to about half
of all other high school graduates. Part of the reason
this is true is because there is a deficiency of secondary schools for the deaf and educational progress for
deaf students is often slower than for hearing students.
Teachers in the MSSD program use any combination of
communication techniques that will be useful for a given
student--lip reading, sign language, gestures, finger
spelling and audio aids for students with residual hearing. This comprehensive approach, called "total
communication", no longer accepts the position of the
pure oralists or pure silent communication advocates
who contended that if more than one method of communication is used one method will become dominant and
debilitate the others. Many of the students get involved part time in commercial firms to first gain

experience in the hearing world before going to work for pay. In 1973, five of the school's 120 high school students worked in computer operations at NASA's Goddard Space Flight Center. Elmer Terry, computer center chief, says "MSSD students learn the operation quickly, they are dedicated, and they are dependable."[19] This kind of outcome buttresses the findings that the deaf have the same range of intelligence as do hearing people. It helps destroy one of the older stereotypes that was perpetuated and reinforced by psychologists in the early twentieth century. This stereotype was the belief that deaf people are usually of lower intelligence than the hearing.[20]

Many writers about the deaf note that the deaf are more likely to be employed in manual trades where contact with the public is less likely and oral skills less needed. These same writers often point out that more of the deaf are unemployed; but a few go on to high skill occupations or the professions. Undoubtedly this is due to one or more of the following three factors. One is the fact that few of the deaf are likely to go on to college--1.7% in 1960 compared to about 40% of hearing students. This in turn results from the fact that without extensive reading and education, the deaf experience a serious educational lag despite their normal intelligence. In 1965 and 1966 for example, 30% of all deaf students of school age or older were functionally illiterate, 60% of the seniors were reading at a grade level of 5.3 or below and only 5% of the seniors achieved a tenth grade level of reading. And most of these higher achievers were either hard of hearing or became deaf postlingually.[21] A third factor in their low levels of achievement and employment is that the public and employers often assume that the deaf's impairment is a greater handicap than it is in fact. As with the blind or other physically handicapped, employers have worries about safety, unemployment compensation and insurance costs, additional costs for training and supervision, and their basic acceptability to other employees or customers.[22]

But some people who are deaf do make it through college and into a profession. One of these is Dr. James Marsters who became a dentist. He attended New York City Public Schools because his family treated him as a normal child. They did not pity or overprotect him as is too often the case with devastating results on self-confidence. Nor did they reject him and

137

not talk to him. They talked to him from an early age
so that he could associate lip motions with objects and
events. At an early age a speech pathologist made him
aware of speech vibrations by having him touch the
throat and cheeks of both the doctor and himself as
they made sounds. He became a magician in high school
in order to attract attention and also became an eagle
scout. At age fifteen he entered the Wright Oral School
for the Deaf in New York to overcome his slovenly
speech, poor pronunciation and nasal accent. Constant
criticism and merciless work helped him improve his intonation, pronunciation and accent. Periodically he
needs to work on these so that he does not fall back
into a pattern of a "lazy" soft palate and a flat tongue.
He feels there are many erroneous opinions about the
deaf. He comments, "I was told from my earliest childhood that I couldn't talk, but I do. I was told I
couldn't drive, fly, go to college, become a doctor,
but I have done all of these." He developed a large
orthodontist practice in Pasadena, and engages in
fencing, boxing, swimming, tennis and teaches at the
Dental School of the University of Southern California.[23]

The hearing impaired face a number of barriers to
everyday social life because their disability excludes
them from the things people talk about or experience in
everyday affairs, like radio, or television, or music.
Many of today's entertainment mediums either center on
the aesthetics of hearing, most noticeably music in its
many variations, or utilize sound and voice to carry the
message of the play, the movie, the TV show or the game.

Most of the hard of hearing and deaf get little
from most television programs. Yet television has become a central mode of news, education and entertainment.
The average person watches TV over 6 hours a day and
has enjoyed non-silent films since 1927. But for the
hearing impaired these major technological developments
have had little impact. These mediums were geared for
hearers, not the deaf. This situation is beginning to
change through several technological developments called
"captioning." Captioning takes two forms. In "open
captioning" the spoken conversations or abbreviations of
it appear at the bottom of the T. V. screen. These
captions are superimposed on the film or TV scene, are
occasionally hard to read because of the background
pattern, and are sometimes annoying to the hearing audience. "Closed captioning" avoids these problems on
television but requires that the program be captioned

ahead of time and that the television reception unit
have a special decoding unit which must be turned on
for any captioned program. If a deaf person has such a
decoder (it costs about $200.00), it can be turned on
and if the program has been captioned, he will get the
subtitles at the top of the screen. If he turns off the
decoder the captions disappear. In evaluating the importance of captioning for the hearing impaired,
Galladuet College personnel surveyed 1,400 hearing impaired T.V. viewers. They found that 90% would not have
been able to understand these programs without this
special visual service and that 94% said they could pur-
chase such a decoder. This is a major technological
breakthrough for the hearing impaired. At the same
time, relatively little television programming is available with either open or closed captioning. In 1977
only about eight hours a week of television programming
was captioned and much of that on Public Broadcasting
Service television stations. Part of this is due to
its newness and part to the cost of captioning. While
the costs of closed-captioning encoding equipment is not
high, $25,000 to $50,000, the process of closed captioning is quite time consuming because it involves many
steps to translate the audio portion of the program into
captions which must be closely timed to parallel the
video portions of the program. Furthermore captioning
must take into consideration nuances of the language
that some deaf readers would misunderstand because the
average deaf person has a fourth-to-sixth grade reading
ability. While news is spoken at about 165 to 185 words
per minute, the captions should not exceed about 120
words a minute for the average deaf viewer who also
wants to periodically glance at the picture. This means
that the audio content of the program has to be somewhat abbreviated and sometimes specially located on the
screen to indicate which of several personalities is
saying what.[24] To open up the world of television for
the hearing impaired will take additional breakthroughs
so that live programs can be instantly captioned rather
than delayed about five hours as is now the case with
captioned news. Live news cannot be captioned ahead of
time as are movies, documentaries and other pre-recorded
programs. A few programs are captioned live. This involves a person using sign language to immediately
translate the audio portion into sign language. The
signal sender is located in one of the corners of the
screen.

The Office of Education has also received federal funds since 1958 to caption over 450 theatrical films and 800 educational films. The theatrical films can be obtained from a central captioned-film lending library in Indianapolis. The captioned educational films are available from 60 different distribution centers which make them available to schools and classes for the deaf. This too is but a small beginning to lower the barriers the deaf experience in a hearing world. Only a fraction of available films have been captioned.[25]

Other technological developments that will aid the hearing impaired are occurring. Alarm clocks are being made with vibrations. The telephone is useless to the deaf unless they have a teletypewriter. This expensive tool uses a special typewriter to both send and receive messages over the telephone. One firm is developing a "ticklebelt" which translates the sounds shown on a computer visual screen into a rippling sensation across the stomach from an electronic device attached around the waist. Visual screen computers also are being used to provide drill and practice in visual memorization, a skill essential to reading.[26] And doorbells can be wired to lights located at strategic visual points.

The deaf experience other problems in a hearing world. What happens to the deaf in criminal proceedings against them? If they cannot hear what is being said in a courtroom, they cannot adequately or fairly converse with their attorney. For some time groups advocating the rights of the hearing impaired have lobbied at the state level for laws that would require the presence of a qualified interpreter at all such legal proceedings where there is a hearing impaired person. New Department of Justice regulations require that interpreters be made available to deaf persons who have been arrested or are undergoing treatment in the judicial system.[27]

The rights of the deaf are the rights of all other people: the right to prevention of a disability if at all possible, the right to an education in the least restrictive environment, the right to work, the right to choices. As in the case with the other physically handicapped persons, the rights of the deaf are frequently interfered with or not protected or implemented as they might be. No systematic studies have been

140

carried out in this regard, but a number of different case studies attest to the problems the hearing impaired face.

One area where this is true and that affects all people is the increasing crescendo of noise pollution. The amount of sound we are exposed to from the high whine of hair dryers, motorcycles, subways and air conditioners to the rock and roll bands which play at 90 to 120 decibels may have long term affects on human hearing capacity. For example the Occupational Safety and Health Administration provides what it considers to be safe limits of noise exposure within allowable time limits. A person could safely take eight hours of 90 decibels (dB), four hours at 95 (dB) or thirty minutes of 110 dB. Beyond these time limits the risks of hearing damage increase. Any exposure to 120 dB may be damaging, yet this is the level at which some amplified bands play. Audiologist Richard Carmen says that even these estimates may be too liberal because extended exposures to loud sounds may fatigue the delicate microscopic hair follicles of the inner ear. If exposed frequently, hearing impairments will show up in time. He points out that many industrial and construction workers are exposed day long to levels of noise (90 dB) intense enough to cause damage to the ears. About one fourth of all such workers have a hearing loss. The situation is even worse in the military for those working around jets, and the rifles, bazookas and howitzers of the infantry. One study revealed that 60% of the men with such military jobs suffered permanent hearing loss with 10 or more years of service. People in some jobs are increasingly turning to ear protectors even though some of them are poorly made and worthless. That hearing is a major problem is seen in the fact that it is estimated that over 600,000 hearing aids are sold annually in the United States. Research on the effects of prolonged exposure to loud sound (noise is unwanted sound) indicates that it has both short and long range effects on people psychologically and physiologically. Psychologically it has been shown to precipitate a number of emotions and disturbances: annoyance, nervousness, fear, frustration, stress, anger, fatigue, tension and aggression. It has been shown to result in a number of debilitating physiological effects in addition to hearing loss: increased pulse rate and heart rate, high blood pressure and a complex array of changes in blood chemistry and adreno-cortical activity in the central nervous system. These reactions are part of the

human response to excessive stress which in the long
run lead to a variety of medical disorders. High noise
levels thus may lead to more job errors, sickness days
and lower productivity. And significant hearing loss
not only increases unemployment compensation and health
insurance costs, but severely damages the occupational,
social and personal lives of those affected. Yet,
little is being done by local, state and federal Environmental Protection Agencies while the situation
is getting worse.[28] Carmen warns:

> In the past 20 years, the loudest noises to
> which man has been exposed have been getting
> louder by one decibel per year. We could say
> that in 20 more years, if noise is allowed to
> increase, the problem will be out of control.
> But the fact is that noise is out of control
> NOW! "Sociocusis" is a hearing loss attri-
> butable to environmental noise. We will
> become more and more familiar with this term
> in the future and, if in fact noise is al-
> lowed to increase at the steady rate it has
> been for the past 20 years, we can say that
> nobody will have "normal" hearing, as we know
> it, over the age of 10 by the year 2000.[29]

The overall low educational status of the deaf
population is both disconcerting to those who know the
importance of education and training and not subject
to easy criticism because of its difficulty. Over half
of the adult deaf population has not completed high
school. Of those who have, 72% were reading below the
eighth grade level, 50% under the mid-fourth grade level
with only 28% at or above the eighth grade level at time
of graduation. In fact only 10% were above the eighth
grade level and less than 2% go on to college.[30]
Despite the fact that deaf education has been occurring
for over one hundred and fifty years, in the U.S., the
educational achievement levels are abyssmally low compared to hearing students. A number of explanations
are available for this situation. One is the difficulty
of such education. Such education has also been hampered by contending manual and oral philosophies of
teaching rather than sound research. Quality education
has also been hampered by underfunding, some poor
teachers, and its delay for some children because of its
inaccessibility, remoteness, and socially isolating
effects. These explanations all point to hidden forms
of discrimination in the education of the hearing im-

paired. And, of course, they have life-long effects on the employment opportunities and life choices of the hearing impaired.

Reactions to the Deaf Experience

How people who are hearing impaired respond to their handicap is highly variable. It is influenced by the extent of hearing loss, the age at which it occurs, the kinds of reactions they receive from parents, friends and institutional personnel, the kinds of education available to them and which they may or may not have taken advantage of, and the kinds of personality skills they have developed as a result of all their experiences. The predominant pattern has been for the totally or near deaf to be segregated into special schools, private or public, for their education. The hard of hearing have more likely been mainstreamed. Separate education, while often better, has its limitations in preparing the deaf for entrance into the hearing world. The shock of release from a sheltered sympathetic environment to the handicapping attitudes of society may be great. One teacher of a group of deaf teenagers sequestered in a special school for the deaf tells of one experience of exposing these impending high school graduates to the nonhandicapped:

I taught an "honors" English class which consisted of the school's most talented and best-prepared students. As the year proceeded, I became increasingly disturbed by what I felt was a false sense of superiority in these youth. Although they could barely read fourth-grade material, they were so far ahead of the other students in the school that they had acquired a feeling of confidence and assurance I feared would be destroyed mercilessly after graduation. So I planned a visit to a local public high school class whose teacher I knew. When I just mentioned my plans to the students, the silence was, if you will, deafening. I could feel the fear throughout the room. One student after another asked tentative, probing questions about the class they were to visit: how old were the students, what grade were they in, what books were they reading. Simple, quite normal questions, but revealing their apprehensions.

On the day of the visit, these normally
loquacious kids were abnormally catatonic.
No one said a thing as we drove to the school.
When we entered and stood at the back of the
classroom, the kids' bodies were rigid, their
eyes filled with fear. I tried repeatedly to
get them to say something, even hello, in vain.
They hugged the back wall as though they needed
it to stand. Finally, I asked the public school
students to come back, talk a little, share their
materials, and mingle with my students, but that
too was a disaster.

So I gave up and we returned.[31]

While this example may not be typical, it does reflect the fact that the deaf have often built up
attitudes about themselves that they are inferior and
limited in important ways because of their handicap.
Undoubtedly some of this is due to the labeling processes to which they are exposed by some parents,
agemates and the laborious testing to which they are
subjected by doctors, audiologists, psychologists and
educators. Once labeled as having a learning problem,
many children are expected not to learn much because
they have been labeled as such. One piece of research
shows this well. Two groups of teachers were shown the
same film of a fourth-grade boy carrying out various
activities. The first group was told he was normal
while the second was told he was learning disabled. The
second group identified significantly more "problems"
in his behavior and saw him as having less academic potential than did the first group.[32]

According to Ballantyne, four different modes of
adaptation tend to typify most of the young people who
leave the segregated school of the deaf for the hearing
world. A small group consisting primarily of those with
"useful" hearing are able to integrate successfully with
the hearing community. A second group aspires to be
accepted by the hearing community but also reconizes
that their deafness sets them apart as marginal to the
hearing world. They ask their hearing friends to accept
them as deaf persons. While they do seek interests
where hearing is not a significant factor, their participation in the hearing community's activities remain
rather marginal. This group is the largest. The third
group also aspires to be a part of the hearing community
but finds it is rejected by them just as they reject

144

participation in the deaf community. This smaller group is the most marginal because it rejects the social community of the deaf even while it is rejected by the hearing community. This group is the most isolated. The fourth group knows it is rejected by the hearing community, feels ill at ease in it and tends to withdraw into the deaf community for its social and recreational purposes. This group is also most likely the profoundly deaf.[33]

The adult who becomes deafened or hard of hearing later in life often has a different and more isolating experience, especially if the deafness occurs gradually at about the period of usual work retirement. While commanding speech and relatively able to communicate to others, this person will probably not get schooling on how to read lips and learn one or more systems of manual communication. Having not been in the deaf community before and isolated from those having silent means of communication other than reading and writing, he will experience greater stress in trying to listen to others carefully and filling in what he has missed. Slowly such a person's self esteem and confidence may deteriorate, he may become more irritable as he loses contact with his social environment; he may have to change jobs--perhaps to one of lesser status and income if hearing is important in it; and he may increasingly isolate himself to become a recluse. For the suddenly deafened adult, the rapid adjustments that must be made to a huge sea of silence may be even more depressing and socially alienating.[34]

At the same time, some deaf people make a remarkable response to their disability and the discrediting attitudes of society. One example is that of David Wright whose thinking is excerpted into an accompanying boxed quote. Most of the people who write about the deaf and deaf experiences are hearing people.

145

Reflections on Deafness

David Wright became deaf at the age
of seven as a result of scarlet fever.
With the help of oral teachers he became
fluent in both oral and written English.
After graduating from Oxford he became a
poet and writer. In his book Deafness,
part of which is autobiographical, he re-
counts some of his experiences and
reflections on deafness:

The use of language as gesture, as
reassuring noise rather than an instrument
of specific communication, is largely denied the deaf.

. . .

So far as cripples are concerned pity
is no virtue. It is a sentiment that de-
ceives its bestower and disparages its
recipient. Hellen Keller hated it, and
she was blind as well as deaf. Its acceptance not only humiliates, but
actually blunts the tools needed to beat
the disability. To accept pity means
taking the first step toward self-pity,
thence to the finding, and finally the
manufacture, of excuses. The end product
of self-exculpation is the failed human
being, the victim.

. ...

The deaf do not, because they cannot,
deal in nuances--particularly the verbal
nuances--of personal relationships. Their
dealings are direct... They have a naivete,
and also a plain honesty of intent, that
often makes the polite wrappings-up of
ordinary people, seem by contrast, hypo-
critical.

. . .

146

> Deafness is of course very much of
> a nuisance and its disadvantages are severe.
> The blind and deaf Hellen Keller said that
> she found deafness worse than blindness.
> I wouldn't agree, though in combination
> the deafness must obviously weigh more
> heavily. Among the minor but none the
> less oppressive afflictions that deaf-
> ness entails I would note the continual
> drain of energy.
>
> It is after all only a few hundred
> years since the first attempts were made
> to rescue the deaf-born from their in-
> visible intellectual dungeon by providing
> them with keys of language. But now that
> the education of the deaf and technolog-
> ical developments in electronics are
> advancing hand in hand, intelligence
> that would otherwise be bound and gagged
> in languageless silence are being freed.
> This is one of the unequivocally val-
> uable and encouraging aspects of progress
> in the present century.[35]

A number of exceptions to this exist, one of
which, The Deaf Experience, is an anthology of literature either by or about the deaf. It is interesting
to compare the literary writings in this anthology of
the hearing and the deaf. The literary writers about
the deaf in the nineteenth century emphasized their
differentness which was not quite tolerable. They
created characters who had a rather untarnished natural
nobility to them in spite of their handicaps. The
hearing in these stories treated the deaf as liberals
do minorities today. The deaf were treated as saint-
like--patient but dedicated, reconciled to overcoming
an almost accepted fate. But if the deaf did not act
in a saintly way as expected, the idealization changed
to contempt. It was as if the hearing were saying, "In
spite of your deafness I'll accept you, but only if you
are perfect." In the twentieth century, the literary
writers about the deaf use them more often, no longer
see them as outsiders to society but rather as one of
many minorities who are caught in the absurdities and

demands of a technological society. These writers see them as more accepted and tolerated. In contrast to this the deaf writers often emphasize defiance of society and their handicaps. Pride is taken in facing the unfair handicaps that come to some and learning how to dominate them. It involves steering between the extreme choices of being victimized by society or victimizing it by playing dishonestly on the sympathy and pity of others.[36]

The deaf and hard of hearing have an impairment which limits social interaction with the hearing world unless they are in that small minority who learn to speak relatively normally and speechread well. Those who do so tend to be either postlingually deaf or only hard of hearing or both. The deaf by-and-large are an interacting group held together by manual languages, social and athletic clubs, and separate schools and organizations for them. If deaf children are born to deaf parents (only 10% are), they will be integrated into the deaf community immediately. However, most deaf children are born to hearing parents which means their socialization into the deaf community is delayed until they go to either separate classes for the deaf or residential schools for them. This usually occurs anytime between 5 and 13. The transmission of deaf culture largely takes place among other deaf children for few deaf children get a deaf teacher until they reach high school. Schools for the deaf form a nation-wide network which transmit the language and subcultural norms of the deaf community. In most cases they learn a sign language which ties them tightly together for it is their major source of communication among themselves in their early years. The deaf have endogomous marriage patterns. For example a survey of New York State's deaf population found that only 5 percent of the women born deaf and 9 percent of those who become deaf early in life married hearing men. Most get much of their social and organizational life by joining local, state and national organizations for the deaf.[37]

Relatively few of the hearing impaired develop a militancy about their rights. A few do press for educational reforms or institute civil suits against employers whose noisy workplaces damaged their hearing. But most accept their lower status and discriminatory acts.

One exception to this usual placid acceptance of

discrimination was Ronald Nomeland. He graduated from
the Minnesota School for the Deaf after which he graduated from Gallaudet College. Subsequently he got a
masters degree in educational technology from the
University of Maryland, a masters degree in administration from California State University at Northridge and
a Ph.D. in education from Syracuse University. Nomeland
had been deaf since birth and communicates only in sign
language. When the principal's position opened up at
his old school, the Minnesota School for the Deaf (MSD),
he applied for the job along with 27 other candidates.
He was among the 10 finalists for the job, but lost out
to a hearing candidate who had only a master's degree.
Nomeland then filed a suit of job discrimination against
MSD under the Minnesota Human Rights Act, the Federal
Rehabilitation Act of 1973 and the Education of the
Handicapped Act of 1975, all of which forbid discrimination against the handicapped and which all forbid
prospective employers from inquiring about the nature
of the disability. During the process of interviewing
him he was asked how he would answer the telephone and
communicate with parents and staff members who did not
know sign language, his only method of communication
with the hearing, outside of writing. The National
Association for the Deaf and the Center for Law and the
Deaf in Washington supported him in his case. The
Director of the National Association for the Deaf noted
that of the 8 residential schools for the deaf in the
United States, only two have deaf superintendents and
only 5 have earned doctorates. The Director said
"Schools for the deaf should be in the vanguard in
hiring deaf students who can serve as models for their
students." One teacher of the deaf, Edward Gobble,
commented, "it is widely assumed that deaf applicants
must be overqualified--twice or thrice--over hearing
applicants to get a fair shot at promotions."[38]

   While there are many local, state and national
organizations which serve the deaf, most of these are
run by advocates for the deaf rather than the deaf
themselves. They often provide separate athletic or
social outlets for the deaf. The American Athletic
Association for the Deaf, founded in 1945, now has
seven regional groups and a national membership of over
13,500. It fosters athletic competition among the deaf
and runs state, regional and national tournaments in
basketball and softball. In the same vein the International Committee of the Silent Sports has 42 member
countries which promote international sports competition
for the deaf patterned after the summer and winter

149

International Olympic Games. There is a United States Deaf Skiers Association. The Junior National Association for the Deaf has 5000 teenage members in 70 local groups which works toward goals of independent living, self-determination, community service and maximizing the development of individual potential. Perhaps the most important organization for the deaf is the National Association of the Deaf which serves a multiplicity of purposes for its members: their legal defense, protection of their civil rights, lobbying for legislation and programs to aid them, research programs on hearing impairment, acting as a clearinghouse on deaf information, assistance to other deaf agencies and the publication of a magazine and a newspaper.[39]

The National Fraternal Society of the Deaf was begun in 1901 by young deaf adults who could not buy life insurance from other firms. This society of 13,500 members, divided in 120 U. S. and Canadian divisions, still sells life and other forms of insurance to its members as well as promoting the rights of its members to drive cars (who, incidentally have fewer accidents than the hearing), eliminating employment discrimination, promoting good deaf education and carrying on a number of charitable activities for the deaf.

In summary it is obvious by the evidence that the deaf are a minority group. Although superficially invisible in the terms of physical characteristics, even limited contact with the hearing impaired makes them noticeable in their lack of normal hearing. They display a variety of behaviors which indicate they have a hearing deficiency including for many manual forms of signing to communicate with the hearing world or among themselves. For most of recorded history the deaf were assumed to be dumb rather than mute, an alterable condition. As oral and manual techniques of communicating with and instructing the deaf were developed and promoted, some of the barriers to their inclusion in the mainstream of society have been eroded although still noticeable. They still face barriers in education, employment, recreation and social life not only due to their hearing problems but because of the handicapping stereotypes of society. To a large extent they form an endogamous group with low levels of educational achievement, high levels of unemployment but low levels of occupational status and low levels of income. To a considerable extent they are aware of the discrimination and attitudes toward them. They have depended extensively on benefactors to help them deal with their hearing impairments and society's restrictions. But gradually they are becoming more involved in self-help groups aimed at insuring their constitutional rights and opening up channels of opportunity for them.

Chapter 5

The Littlest Minority: Dwarfs and Midgets

Mankind has had a long fascination with those who
are statistically abnormal in size: giants and dwarfs,
human skeletons and the hugely obese.   Before the advent
of photography in 1839 they had to be seen to be believed.   Before the advent of television such people
got most of their public exposure in circuses and side
shows as "freaks" and "human curiosities."   Perhaps
with high levels of education, greater awareness of the
world beyond our own communities and more humanitarian
motives with regard to the physically abnormal, such
physical aberrations are now less likely to be put on
public display.   This does not necessarily make any of
these groups less of a minority.   It may only mean we
are more subtle in the discrimination and interest we
display toward them.   But the short of stature have provided an enduring fascination for mankind for thousands
of years.   Hy Roth and Robert Cromie's illustrated history book on dwarfism, The Little People, makes for
fascinating reading and viewing as it contains hundreds
of photographs of the tiniest adults.   This book also
tells about their work, their lives, their romances and
their problems in recorded history.

Identifiability of Little People

On the human scale of normal height, dwarfs are
small in stature.   But that's not enough.   Dwarfs are
operationally defined as people under four feet eleven
inches in stature although a few writers use the figure
of four feet six inches.   The shortest one to survive
to adulthood was around 18 inches tall (Nusa Adele Ber
of Yonkers, NY).   A number of midgets had such small
sizes their dimensions are rather unbelievable.   Lucia
Zarate from Mexico was 20 inches tall and weighed under
five pounds at age 12.   Her arms were reportedly 8
inches long and her waist 14 inches around when she was
killed in a blizzard in the United States in 1890.   The
most famous midget in history was 25 inches tall.
Although born as Charles Stratton, he was called General
Tom Thumb for publicity purposes by his manager, P. T.
Barnum.[1]

The range in size of dwarfs from 18 inches to 4

feet, 11 inches makes them readily identifiable. In history and myth and literature they are pictured as human curiosities because of their rare diminutive sizes.

Types, Causes and Prevalence of Dwarfism

The over-all term used for people of abnormally short stature is dwarfism. However, for centuries observers noted that some dwarfs had limbs and heads proportionate to the size of their torso while others had normal size torsos and heads but stubby limbs. In 1878 Parrot coined the term"achondroplasia" to distinguish short persons whose limbs were disproportionate to their body size. In today's medical world those with short stature and disproportionate in form are called dwarfs. In contrast, midgets are those who have bodies, heads, and limbs proportionate in size, and thus like normal people except in height. Since 1929 the dwarf group has been medically subdivided into two groups--short limb dwarfs and short trunk dwarfs.[2]

Most little people are dwarfs rather than midgets. But as true among normal people, there is a large variation in stature and degrees of disproportion among little people. Thus, it is a complex task of medical classification to determine which classification is most appropriate for each little person. While this may be important for medical purposes in establishing the cause and possible treatment of little people, it is largely irrelevant for our purposes. In any case, of all little people, around 70-80% are dwarfs while around 20-30% are proportional midgets.

There are no accurate figures on the extent of dwarfism and the estimates vary widely from about 5,000 to 100,000 little people in the United States. Most estimates however tend to converge around 20,000 or 25,000 in the United States. This makes them a tiny minority--perhaps around only 1 person in 8,000 to 10,000 is born with a dwarfing condition. If there are 20,000 dwarfs in the United States as estimated by their own organization, Little People of America, around 5,000 of them would be midgets. The midgets are born tiny and grow very slowly and rarely exceed a height of 40 inches. Midgets usually stop growing in childhood and may reach their full stature by age 10 to 13. In contrast, most dwarfs are born nearer to the size of a normal baby. However, during the growth period they grow only about one quarter an inch a year while normal children are growing an average around two inches a year. Dwarfs usually reach a fixed height of 40 to 54 inches. Incidentally, pygmies who average around 56 inches tall and always inherit their small size, are not classified as dwarfs. In extremely rare cases, some dwarfs experience a burst of growth beyond the normal growth period, and usually in their twenties or thirties. Adam Rainer of Austria had the most dramatic growth spurt known to medicine. At age 21 he was only three feet ten inches but zoomed to seven feet two inches by age 32.[3]

The causes of dwarfism are highly complex and somewhat variable depending on whether the person is a midget or true dwarf. Dr. Joseph Bailey, an M.D., says there are "about" 150 conditions which can lead to proportionate short statures and over 115 for a wide variety of disproportionate short statures and they may not all be found yet. Some of the causes are dominant or recessive hereditary genes toward shortness, bone and skeletal disorders, inborn errors of metabolism, endocrine dysfunctions, chromosomal mutations and disorders, malnutrition and disease of the visceral organs. Even social deprivation may inhibit growth. The dwarfs in particular may be afflicted with a number of conditions which impair movement, normal functioning and attractiveness. Some dwarfs must live with facial deformities, joint laxity, curvature of the spine, or other spine anomalies, severe arthritis, rigidity of joints including the spinal column, limbs of uneven length, clubfoot, hearing loss, respiratory problems, deformities in the ear and nasal bridges, and angular deformities in all the limbs and joints, particularly in the hips, knees and feet. Many dwarfs then must contend with more than shortness. They must contend with other impairments and medical disorders which frequently accompany shortness and which are impairments in and of themselves.[4]

Midgets actually come in four varieties. True midgets are normal born children whose body growth stops somewhere from infancy to the pre-adolescent years. They are like normal stature people in most ways. They constitute a majority of all midgets. When proportionate dwarfism exists from birth we have primordial midgets. They are not started out as normal children like true midgets and they may continue to grow, although at a slow rate. Often they are the smallest midgets. Infantile midgets are intellectually normal

155

but neither develop secondary sex characteristics (like facial hair on the male's face or breasts and hip development for females) or erotic desires. Hypermetabolic midgets have metabolic rates that run about one and one-half times faster than that of normal people. While most midgets have a normal life span, these vigorous midgets age quickly and often die by their thirties.[5]

Some dwarfism, perhaps as much as 10%, is due to the underproduction of the Human Growth Hormone by the Pituitary Gland. Some dwarfism, perhaps a 10% to 15%, is due to thyroid gland deficiencies. In many instances these types of dwarfism, if detected early, can be treated successfully with appropriate hormones. Dwarfism is much more prevalent than giantism. One of the causes of giantism is an overproduction of the Human Growth Hormone. Robert Pershing Wadlaw, born in 1918 in Alton, Illinois, became the world's tallest human as a result of an overactive Pituitary Gland. While Wadlaw was a normal 8 and 1/2 pounds at birth, at six months he weighed thirty pounds. When he was only 8 years old, his 6'2" frame weighed 195 pounds. Three years later he was 6'11" and weighed 248 pounds. At 18 he was declared the world's tallest man at 8'3½". When he died at age 22 from an infection, he was just a fraction of an inch under 9' tall, weighed 491 pounds and took a custom made shoe of size 39.[6]

The Treatment of Dwarfs in Historical Perspective.

The medical and genetic origins of dwarfism are not fully understood even today. Thus, in looking back at them in history, they were often viewed as marvels, freaks and human curiosities whose origin were as likely to be seen as mysterious or supernatural as a natural but rare occurrence. No matter what the assumed cause of their condition, there has always been an intense curiosity about such little people. People not only wanted to see them physically, but to hear their voices (often high pitched and shrill) and to have their curiosities answered about their personal, social and sexual lives. Usually there seems to have been more fascination with midgets than other dwarfs. This is so for four likely reasons. (1) Midgets are rarer than dwarfs. While no precise statistics are available, maybe 1 out of 10,000 persons is a disproportionate little person while perhaps only 1 out of 50,000 is a proportionate little person (a midget). (2) Midgets

are usually smaller than other dwarfs. Since midgets
run from 18 inches to about 40 inches and dwarfs from
about 40 to 54 inches, on a scale of human size midgets
present the biggest contrast. (3) Midgets, being proportionate, are usually more attractive and blessed with
soft skin. In contrast, dwarfs have distorted figures
with stumpy arms and legs or other orthopedic aberrations. Not infrequently their heads are somewhat
distorted too by round flat faces and snubby noses.
(4) When the last two factors are combined we have
midgets who appear as miniature adults, or, disproportionate dwarfs who have not only been cut down in size
but deformed in comparison to normal human symmetry.
Midgets were more likely to be adored, while disproportionate dwarfs were more likely to be shuttered
at in negative terms. Midgets usually appear younger
than their age, other dwarfs appear older and more
gnarled. For over a thousand years myth and folklore
have painted pictures of imaginary little people that
often get in the way of knowing what little people are
really like. As Fiedler comments, "Every child knows
what a Dwarf is long before he has met one, and it
therefore remains hard for all of us ever really to see
one past the images first encountered in stories our
mothers told us." The images of little people in fairy
tales use such names for little people as elf, fairy,
goblin, troll, leprechaun, midget, sprite, gremlin,
brownie, pixy, gnome, sylph, Lilliputian, munchkin, and
hobbit. Some of these have positive connotations, other
evil ones. These images often carry over to little
people themselves.[7]

Before about 1400 the major accounts of short
stature people are those who became noteworthy in some
way. A few became princes and kings while most apparently led humbler and forgotten lives, and most
older accounts do not give people's measurements which
mean that some who became recognized may have been short
in stature but not necessarily shorter than 4 feet 11
inches. Some noteable short people and probably dwarfs
in ancient times were Aesop, Pepin (715-768) who was
King of the Franks and Ladislas I (1260-1333) King of
Poland. Other famous short persons safe from today's
measurement were Neubuchadrezzar, King of Babylon;
Croesus, King of Lydia; Charles III, ruler of fourteenth
century Sicily and Naples; and Bertolda, adviser to
Albion, King of the Lombards in the 800s. Ancient art-
work sometimes showed short adults in servant roles.[8]

From about 1400 to 1700 the most notable social and occupational role for dwarfs was in the service of Kings, Queens and other persons of high status. Some were clowns, or court jesters or fools, servants or sometimes artisians for their wealthy or powerful patrons. Kings collected sizeable numbers of them to be their entertainers and servants. For example, in 1572 the Emperor of Germany presented three dwarfs for the use of Charles IX of France when he visited him. Queen Henrietta Marie, wife of King Charles I of England played matchmaker for two dwarfs in their court around 1635. Richard Gibson, an artist in the King's court was 3'10" tall when he married Anne Shepard, the same height and who was in the Queen's retinue. They had nine children, all of normal size, of whom five lived to adulthood. Peter the Great, the Russian Czar, married his dwarf, Valalkoff to a female dwarf in 1710. The invitations to this affair were delivered by richly clad dwarfs while the guests at this wedding included 72 dwarfs.[9]

The third era in the treatment of the dwarf was in their exhibition for money. This appears to have begun as early as 1581 when English author John Stow reported seeing "two Dutchman of strange stature" shown together. One was a crippled giant at 7 feet 7 inches tall alongside a crippled 3 foot dwarf. This early beginning of publicly exhibiting all sorts of freaks appeared to increase over the next several centuries and perhaps reached its zenith around 1850 to 1900. Since that time the public display of Siamese twins, giants, dwarfs, fat women, thin men and wild men of Borneo has slowly declined in western societies. But before the advent of photography and television, large numbers of people visited fairs, circuses, carnivals and dime museums where strange creatures, bizarre persons and strange inventions were shown for pay. Furthermore, such adventures were lines of work for dwarfs who found it most difficult to compete with ordinary-size persons in the area of physical labor. In fact, some dwarfs and their managers profited quite handsomely from shows that traveled the countryside to display these phenomenal persons. The agents of such dwarfs used many clever names to draw attention to the size of these little people: Miss Minnie, General Shade, Tom Thumb, General Mite, Admiral Dot, Lilliputian Opera Company, Aztec Dwarfs, Princess Winnie Wee, Baron Littlefinger, Princess Wee Wee, Lady Little, Commodore Foote, Mrs. Short, Anita the Doll Lady, and the Little Russian.[10]

During this era of showmanship and vaudeville acts by groups of dwarfs, the master of promotion was Phineas T. Barnum. While hundreds of other promoters here and abroad did the same thing, he did it best. When he was 32 in 1842, Barnum heard of a 5 year old midget by the name of Charles S. Stratton. He interviewed the shy little boy and offered his parents a four week contract of three dollars a week and all expenses. Barnum called him General Tom Thumb and advertised him as 11 years old, 16 pounds and 25 inches tall. Patrons flocked to see this midget at Barnum's American Museum in New York City. At the end of a month he re-signed the mother and child to a year long contract at $7 a week, all expenses and a $50 bonus at the end of the year. Before the year was up the weekly wage was increased to $25 and in the following year to $50 with a European trip option. With a lot of publicity Barnum took Tom Thumb to England and Europe for three years. By clever staging and invitations Tom Thumb was visited by royalty and even got an audience with the Queen. Money poured in as the publicity of his adventures preceded him around the continent and upon his return to the United States in 1847.

Tom Thumb and Barnum became equal partners and both became wealthy with additional tours. In 1848 they parted. Until about 1855 Tom Thumb only did occasional tours spending many of these years looking after his investments from his home in Bridgeport, Connecticut. In his late twenties Tom grew several inches so that he now stood 37 inches tall. In 1862 he visited Barnum's Philadelphia Museum where he met a 32 inch beauty, Mercy Lavinia Warren Bump, recently under contract to Barnum. This famous pair was married in 1863 at an ostentatious wedding at Grace Episcopal Church in New York City. Parents flowed in to them from many famous people and one from President Lincoln who received the Thumbs at the White House during their honeymoon. The wedding was such an important social occasion that some would-be-guests offered as much as fifty dollars for an invitation. While Tom Thumb and Lavinia Bump became the best known midgets, hundreds of others were on tour or exhibition in the United States during the 1700s, 1800s and 1900s.[11] At the same time, most other dwarfs became recluses from the staring eyes of others. They led lives of isolation, unemployment and poverty.

In more recent times show business as a source of employment has decreased for dwarfs. But some are still found in circuses, nightclubs and the movies. There are dwarf wrestlers, dwarf bands, and dwarf comics. Billy Barty, a dwarf movie actor, founded Little People of America, the dwarf's civil rights group, in 1957. Perhaps the dwarf best known to contemporary Americans is Paris-born Herve Villechaize. Villechaize broke into acting as "Knick Knock" in The Man with the Golden Gun and now plays opposite Ricardo Montalbain in television's Fantasy Island.

No surveys have been done on the employment status or social status of dwarfs in contemporary American Society. While many have become successful in a variety of occupations, there are cases of discrimination against them. At the same time that some doors are closed to them because of the physical limitations they have in doing physically hard work, others are open to them because of their small size. They have been stunt men for child actors or employed in watch and clock making and repairing because of the excellent adaptation they can make to intricate tasks. They have appeared as Munchkins in the Wizard of Oz. A midget Frenchman, Richebourg, dressed in a baby's outfit and carried secret documents as a spy during the French Revolution. During World War II a number of little persons were honored by Franklin Roosevelt for their work inside aircraft wings and other small places that men of larger stature could not enter. Dwarfs have been employed to enter other small or tight places--to clean jet engines and work inside Saturn rocket boosters. But by and large they are treated according to their size and assumed mentality. They are the size of children so they are assumed to be weak and rather naive, like children. People "talk down" to them both literally and figuratively.

Unlike most people, their relatively small size becomes a central life focus for them. According to Edward Sagarin,

> "When you meet a dwarf, you will hear the
> story of a lifetime of travail, of staring
> eyes, rejection by friends, and sometimes
> even family, of difficulties in obtaining
> employment, of being addressed as though
> retarded; of being humiliated as a child and,
> in later life, being shunned by adults."[12]

160

The story of Burton Gutterman, 4'3½" may be typical of some dwarfs who find they get the run-around when it comes to employment. Gutterman applied for a job as a policeman in Boston. Even though he scored 90 on the entrance exam, 30 points above what is required, and passed the markmanship and physical exams, they told him they didn't want him on the force because he was too small. He feels that life has not been fair to him.[13] At age 26 in 1980 he remains unemployed and on welfare because he cannot find work. He has had brief job stints as a door-to-door salesman, an assistant in an alcoholic center and running an upward mobility program for the U.S. Customs Service. After being unable to get a job for two years with state government, he decided to dramatize his plight by running for a "state government representative's" job in Massachusetts. He has been selling pencils at 15 cents each at the state house to raise money for his campaign. A large sign on his chest states "Governor King and his high paid professionals offer me welfare not work--living with a broken promise." Gutterman comments on his candidacy, "It's a way of expressing my moral indignation of not having a job. I've been given the runaround so many times, I don't know which way I'm going. I've decided to run for office and this is my first fund-raising event.[14]

Charles Bedow is 4'6" at age 45. While he weighed 9 pounds at birth, he grew slowly being only two feet tall at age 5 and three feet tall at age 10. He has the head and torso of a bigger person but with small and short arms. His parents split up when he was age six. Since neither wanted custody of him, he shuffled from relative to relative until age 18 when he ran away. He says he had no dates in high school and not many friends. He comments "When you're the only dwarf in sixteen counties, whom do you date?" He had other problems--it's tough to find size one loafers in a shoe store. "It took me more than six months to find a job. I applied to more places than you have fingers and toes, and everyone felt my brain must be as stunted as my body."[15]

Reports have been made that dwarfs have been turned down as laboratory research scientists because they couldn't reach the laboratory counters or as teachers because it was assumed they couldn't maintain control over and discipline of a class. Frequently however they are used in public relations jobs where they will be remembered for their differences.[16] Depending somewhat on their size, dwarfs face a number of architectural

161

problems. Eight inch curbs and steps for a three foot dwarf with short legs may be the equivalent of two foot steps for a six footer. Bathroom urinals or stools, elevator buttons for the 76th floor, water fountains, and coin slots in pay telephones may all be out of reach. In the same vein most have difficulty in getting clothes that fit them; often they have to go to expensive tailors for custom made clothes. And should they order children's portions at a restaurant and reinforce their childlike stereotype? For the very short of stature the architecture of furniture, counter tops, and refrigerators may make daily living somewhat problematic.

Heavy pedestrian traffic is a menace to dwarfs. A 4'5" dwarf comments "You have to get against the wall during rush hour to protect yourself. People literally are not aware of you and they can knock you down. It can be a frightening thing.[17] Four foot John Louis Roventini who called out "Phil-lip Mor-rees" in a shrill voice for over two decades had a clause in his contract which forbade him to ride on subways during rush hours.[18]

Ken Brown is a black dwarf born in 1940 in Charleston, South Carolina. After age four months, he grew very slowly. He didn't enroll in school until age nine and didn't graduate until he was 21. While he has had a few odd jobs, at the last report he was unemployed and on welfare. He feels he has trouble being recognized as an adult.

Edward Darmstadt is typical of dwarfs who want to drive automobiles. They need extension pedals and seat elevators. At 4'7" Darmstadt tells of one encounter he had with another motorist at a Chicago intersection. Both arrived at the intersection at the same time and simultaneously started, then stopped, then started and stopped again. The other man jumped out of his car in a rage and dared Eddie to step out and fight. Eddie looked out and saw a lot of people standing at the corner. Eddie says, "I figure he's not going to slug me in front of witnesses. So I got out and looked up at him. He just stood there, looking down at me, and his wife yelled at him from their car, "okay big mouth! What are you gonna do now?" The man quickly returned to his car and drove away.[19]

There are four critical stages in the social lives of dwarfs. How they are treated and respond at the earlier of these three stages will influence subsequent adjustments. The first stage is in the pre-school years. If the parents either overprotect them or reject them, this will likely be damaging to their future development. If they learn to play upon their dwarfness to gain pity or special privileges, they may be establishing personality deficiencies that will last a lifetime.

This may stunt their maturation and make their size a more central life focus than it should be. They may become self-centered egotists and take a (overly) fierce pride in their size and the accomplishments of famous little people with whom they equate themselves. On the other hand, if they are treated as inadequate and insufficient in more than physical stature, this will damage their ego and probably establish social patterns of avoidance and withdrawal. Since research on the personality growth patterns of dwarfs is deficient, the inferences above are made on the basis of what happens to other minority groups which are both physically different in some way and handicapped by social attitudes.

The second critical stage in the development of dwarfs is upon entrance to school. Their diminutive size may earn them special attention from teachers who take on a protective parental role. At the same time they will be exposed to teasing and physical abuse from larger peers. Learning to fend for themselves is the critical problem at this stage. Perhaps the third stage, the adolescent and teenage years, are the most critical in their social development. Their physical stature will exclude them from contact and team sports like football, basketball and field hockey as well as limit or exclude their participation in other sports. A three inch hand has real trouble with a bowling ball and table tennis tops may be at eye level. Since normal physical size is so important in interpersonal attraction, they will normally be excluded from dating and the social life of these developmental years.

The fourth critical stage is young adulthood when people begin their first jobs, marry and have children. They usually experience barriers or hazards in these three central life activities. The very diminutive and the grossly malformed will experience the greater problems in getting a job. Because of the widespread geographical dispersion of dwarfs and their rarity, finding a mate of the right size in and of itself is a difficult task. No recent research on the marital patterns of dwarfs has been undertaken. But those found in a 1934 survey of 233 midgets in the United States may still hold true. This survey by Bodin and Hershey found that only 22% of the midget population married in comparison to a normal rate of 90%. Of those who married, 56% married other midgets while 44% married normal size adults. In marriages between midgets, only 11% were without children, but 59% of the marriages between midgets and normals were fruitless, and disproportionately end in divorce. Some midgets are not only worried about having dwarf children but also fear pregnancy itself because delivery by Caesarean section is often necessary.[20] In any case, large numbers of dwarfs do not marry and many who do marry do not have children for a number of reasons.

Across the centuries the treatment of dwarfs has generally run the gamut of behaviors exhibited toward other minorities. Some have excluded them from entrance into the activities of the larger society. Others have exploited them by displaying them for charge to those curious about the size and shape of nature's freaks. Some have been their benefactors by trying to find them jobs and meaningful social lives. Hitler had them sent to the gas chambers because they were a deviation from healthy-sized adults. Contemporary American society shows a declining interest in physical anomalies and a growing tolerance and place for little people. But employment discrimination and social exclusion appear to remain pervasive.

Individual and Group Reaction to Dwarfism.

How do dwarfs and midgets react to their own statures and the handicapping attitudes and practices of society? For the most part they have wanted to be accepted into society--to assimilate into the large people's world. To do this they have adopted several techniques of label repudiation and label evasion throughout history. We will turn to their techniques shortly. Failing to achieve full integration (which is normally the case), they may (1) exploit their small stature in social performance work roles, and (2) adapt patterns of withdrawal, and (3) develop groups to either try to change society or provide them with fuller social lives or both. In fact, all of these options have been

164

pursued by some dwarfs and midgets.

As a result of biomedical research, new hope has been opened up for a small percentage of dwarfs that they can join the big world by growing bigger. Research has shown that if dwarfism is due to an underactive pituitary which produces insufficient Human Growth Hormones (HGH), and if this condition is detected early enough and treated, short stature may be overcome. The problem is in getting enough HGH from the pituitaries of recently deceased people, identifying the people who need it and getting it to them. Pituitary HGH is very scarce. About 5 milligrams of this precious hormone can be extracted from a single tiny pituitary gland. But this is only enough for one week's treatment consisting of three shots. Literally thousands of cadaver's pituitary glands are needed for the normal growth period of a single person. To help in this collection effort, the National Institute of Arthritis, Metabolism and Digestive Diseases established the National Pituitary Agency in 1963 to collect these glands from hospitals doing autopsies. In 1970, for example, this agency collected 78,000 glands. This agency works with the Human Growth Foundation, founded in 1965 by families of children with growth problems. This foundation carries on education programs, research, and aids in the collection of pituitary glands. It is estimated that less than 10% of all dwarfs can benefit from this treatment due to the nature of their dwarfism. But it can be of aid to others of that stature even though they are above dwarf sizes of four feet ten inches. But by 1971 only 400 children had benefited from HGH shots out of an estimated 7,000 to 10,000 youngsters headed for very short stature. In a study of 29 boys and 21 girls ranging in age from 2 to 17 years, it was found that before undertaking HGH treatment they were only growing an average of 1.4 inches a year. But after treatment was initiated, 46 of the 50 children grew an average of 3.5 inches a year with no success with 4 of them.[21]

But most dwarfs have little hope of escaping their short stature by medical or surgical means. Rather, they must deal with a double label or stigma; being children and freaks. To do this they engage in what Truzzi calls disidentification techniques but which I prefer to call label repudiation and label evasion. People may react to labels applied to them in nine different ways according to Rogers and Buffalo: (1) acquiescence, (2) repudiation, (3) flight,

165

(4) channeling (into advantages), (5) evasion, (6) modification, (7) reinterpretation, (8) redefinition and (9) alteration. Label repudiation involves "actively rejecting the label while label evasion involves rejecting it and taking positive steps to avoid the negative label."[22]

In label repudiation and label evasion dwarfs engage in a number of behaviors to show (1) they are adults and not children, and (2) that they are normal human beings and not some freak. For example they may dress quite formally to show they are not casually attired as children or even other adults. This puts them in the business world of adult activities and responsibilities. The males may grow beards and mustaches, use hats and canes, carry attache cases, smoke cigars and brag about their sexual exploits with midget or full-sized women to show they are not children but men with normal desires and responsibilities. Tiny women too may dress in high fashion and wear elaborate hairdos and extensive makeup to repudiate a child-like status. At additional cost they may order adult portions of food or avoid buying children's clothes to emphasize their older status. They may forthrightly reject help offered to them in crossing streets or mounting stairs to show they are independent adults and not helpless dependent children. In addition midgets sometimes reject being called dwarfs who are more "freakishly" misshapen. "Like most minority groups, midgets have accepted the dominant groups as their reference point in the creation of their values," Truzzi points out. He adds, "Thus, midgets see themselves as merely small persons" and not as aesthetically grotesque dwarfs.[23]

Truzzi perceptively points out that "calling a midget a dwarf is considered an insult by most midgets. It seems to be largely because of the fact that midgets seldom have much to do with dwarfs or the professions of dwarfs. Thus, midgets are very seldom found in circuses as clowns, as professional wrestlers, or in other jobs which often falsely advertise themselves as midget exhibitions but in fact include only the disproportioned dwarf. On the other hand, many dwarfs prefer to be referred to as midgets even though they are not technically such."[24]

However, because of their need for a livelihood some dwarfs and midgets engage in various types of show business which plays on their size-from serious acting

166

to being elfs at Christmas time in department stores.
This response is called label channeling where they try
to make an asset out of a freakish label. At the same
time they may engage in label reinterpretation. While
viewing adults may look upon dwarfs and midgets as
curiosities, the dwarfs and midgets emphasize their talents as singers, clowns, dancers and musicians. Thus
they look upon themselves as capable adult entertainers
who have more to offer the world than a Lilliputian
size. But this often creates an internal conflict in
dwarfs and even more so for midgets. Their agents
often want them to appear as caricatures of adults, as
precocious children. "But the audience has always responded to these performers--many of whom are truly
exceptional in their abilities--as midgets first and
performers only second."[25]

Because of this value conflict most midgets and
dwarfs choose non-exhibitionist work roles if they are
open to them. Many midgets react negatively to show
business; and their self-help group, Little People of
America, points out that less than one percent of all
little people go into some type of show business. In
this way they try to emphasize their nonfreakish adult
statures.

Some dwarfs engage in label flight by decreasing
their contact with the normal size world. They withdraw from situations where their height is discussed,
they are teased, or they are at a serious disadvantage
because of it. Thus they rarely go to dances with
normal sized people and abstain from contact sports
with normal sized people. Many little people abstain
from joining any groups including those designed by and
for them either because they are isolated or do not want
to be associated with freaks. They want to join the
big people's world.

A number of these processes were involved in the
creation of Little People of America in 1957. This
group has a membership of over 3000. Membership in it
is limited to people 4'11" and under. The children of
their members are called "Little Littles." Billy
Barty, the founder of it, reports there are comparable
organizations in many countries which go by different
names. Billy Barty, a three foot nine inch actor
started in vaudeville acting as a child but feels that
the dramatic roles suitable for little people are quite
limited. Little People of America (LPA) has a number of

167

stated purposes including providing fellowship and providing moral support for its membership. It provides
a forum for the exchange of ideas and solutions to the
unique problems of little people through newsletters,
national conventions and twelve regional groups. It
acts as an information clearinghouse on employment opportunities, housing, clothes, shoes, life insurance,
education, and adoption opportunities and procedures.
It operates a speaker's bureau. It sponsors sports
competition and a variety of social activities. The
motto of the organization, "Think Big," emphasizes their
adult world orientation. In 1968 it established a
foundation to raise funds for scholarships and the
ordinary expenses of needy dwarfs. In addition, this
organization promotes the civil rights of little people
and works in conjunction with other organizations of
handicapped people to promote the removal of architectural barriers and social barriers.

According to Edward Sagarin's analysis of LPA,
most of its members are achondroplastic (disproportionate) dwarfs. Midgets are frequently ambivalent
about joining the organization because they want to
disassociate themselves with the freakish characteristics of dwarfs and some see the LPA as primarily
serving the unhappy and maladjusted dwarf. The "Think
Big" slogan emphasizes what many members of LPA do not
do. They see themselves as a maligned group and often
need mutual support and fellowship to reaffirm their
basic humanity. Its adoption service mainly serves
normal size people who have given birth to a disproportionate dwarf that is unwanted by the parents.
This reflects the continuing stigma that accompanies
a spoiled physical identity.[27]

While LPA has a number of stated purposes, the
behavior of many of its members suggests that its major
function is primarily social--especially oriented to
finding a suitable mate. Alvin Adams contends that 95
percent of the members never had any social life before
they joined LPA.[28] According to Weinberg most of its
members are single who go to the regional and national
meetings in hopes of finding a suitable mate that will
fill a void in their empty social life. The most
enthusiastic members of LPA are those who found a mate
through it. And three quarters of the LPA members who
are married made initial contacts with their mate
through LPA.[29] As Truzzi comments, "Dwarfs live in a
world in which their possibilities for social contact

are limited. They are deeply restricted in finding partners for sex, love and marriage...." While many handicaps and diseases, particularly stimatizing ones, limit people in their selection of partners, the dwarf man is further limited by the general social insistence that the male must be at least as tall as, and preferably taller than, the female. "This places the achondroplastic male in a double bind; he can seldom find a normally sized female to court, both because of his condition and his desire to avoid the Mutt-and-Jeff caricature."30

Furthermore, little people adopt the same attitudes about beauty and attractiveness held by the dominant society. Sagarin tells about John, a handsome midget of 35, who attends LPA meetings to look for a mate. He is lonely. Most of his friends are married and now go their separate ways. While he lunches with men at work, they never invite him to their homes. He watches television, reads, and broods over his bleak future most evenings. When asked why LPA will not likely give him an opportunity to meet a mate, he responded, "Because most of them are achondroplastics, and I guess I'm prejudiced. I shouldn't be, but I am. I don't want to go out with a girl like that. I'm uncomfortable with them." Yet he continued to go to LPA meetings in hopes of meeting a short girl like himself.31

After attending some of the district meetings of an LPA branch, Sagarin concluded that many of the members were caught in a contradiction: they want to meet one another but the structure, goals and processes of the meetings are rather purposeless and boring. Such groups are not designed as social clubs, but that is their main function. The members share few common hobbies, vocations and interests. About all they share is a small size whose very problems they wish to avoid. Many come looking for dates or mates but end up disappointed. Small size alone makes it difficult to maintain an organization. However, national conventions are more task oriented although they involve fellowship as well.32

The LPA, organized as a self-help group, has certainly made some headway in bringing to public attention the oppression and plight of little people. Yet most little people do not join it. For many it functions as a social outlet with a low prospect of changing the structure and stereotypes of a dominant group which so

169

vastly outnumbers it. As Fiedler comments, "Individual Dwarfs may have been highly visible in the bad old days of their oppression, but as an organized group they fade into invisibility beside other stigmatized minorities like blacks, Indians, and Jews or afflicted ones like heart disease victims, cancer cases and sufferers from muscular dystrophy."[33]

The Special Status of the Dwarf

I have tried to point out in this chapter that little people come in a variety of shapes and sizes. There is the proportioned midget and the disproportioned dwarf plus many variations of each. But in literature, mythology and historical treatment these conditions have often been treated as of the same nature. Both are smaller in stature, especially midgets, which gives normal sized people a sense of physical superiority in terms of strength. But only dwarfs, and then in varying degrees, are misshapen by statistical and social standards of human symmetry. This brings an additional stigma to them as freaks, a repugnance toward them as malformed beings. The following comment by Fielder illustrates this double image which is based more on myth than on contacts with little people which so few people experience:

> Looking back over their five thousand years of recorded history, it seems to me that the Dwarfs are, in a real sense, the Jews of the Freaks: the most favored, the most successful, the most conspicuous and articulate; but by the same token, the most feared and reviled, not only in gossip and the popular press, but in enduring works of art, the Great Books and Great Paintings of the West. They have been, in short, a "Chosen People," which is to say, a people with no choice; but they have begun, like the children of Israel, to choose at least to choose. How appropriate, then, that they, who began their escape from oppression via the back doors of the great courts of Europe and have prospered in show business in America, take the lead now in organizing for mutual defense, consciousness-raising, and social action.[34]

170

Dwarfs and midgets, tiny in size and numbers are in the process of reinterpreting themselves as a minority group with physical characteristics different from larger people. They want to recast their deviant physical statures into the world of functioning normal adults. They want to redefine themselves as oppressed by society rather than inherently limited blemishes of nature. By becoming a minority group, the onus is put on society for the personal tribulations and limited opportunities they experience. And certainly the formulations of social scientists, who write about them as oppressed minorities rather than physical misfits, helps them in their cause. While some of them have successfully integrated into the world of larger adults, many of them lead isolated lives fearful of big people who still seem threatened or amused by little people.

Chapter 6

The Ugly Minority: The Facially Disfigured

The facially disfigured, the ugly or unsightly if
you will, are not like the other physically handicapped
groups discussed in this book in one significant way.
With few exceptions in the "pure" cases, they have no
physical impairment which limits their performance or
productivity. They are like the other physically handicapped groups, however, in that they are handicapped by
society. While the physically impaired may be handicapped by both their disability and the attitudes and
behaviors of people toward them, the facially disfigured
suffer only from the latter. This difference points up
an interesting facet of society. In our rational bureaucratic society we usually assume that productivity
and performance are what count in evaluating people in
many human activities like work and sports and religion.
But at the same time personal appearance is given great
importance. While it is true that this personal appearance is more important in interpersonal encounters
as a basis of attraction, it underlays judgments in
many commercial or business transactions. The importance of attractiveness reaches its zenith in the high
fashion industry, the movies and a number of related
enterprises in publishing where facial beauty, size and
body symmetry are the entrance requirements. It is more
important for women because of sexist standards with regard to attractiveness. Conversely, as people decrease
in attractiveness, barriers are erected to social acceptance and success. Of special importance is facial
attractiveness or ugliness. While people do communicate with the whole body, the face is the center of
emotion and communication. When there is some defect
in the face it tends to become the center of focus
rather than the emotions which the face is capable of
displaying. The defect becomes an anchor point, the
center of attention, rather than the whole face.
Research on facial expressions indicate that they can
express six emotions - surprise, fear, disgust, anger,
happiness and sadness.[1] However, some types of facial
disfigurement, like nerve paralysis or gross deformities can prohibit the face from being used as a normal
center of communication. Because the human face is so
central in human interaction, deformities in it can
greatly inhibit normal interactions. When normal human
interactions are impeded, the consequences on personality development and one's entire lifestyle are often

highly injurious for the afflicted person.

Case Studies of Facial Disfiguration

Because most people give little conscious thought
about facial deformities, several case histories of
persons either born with a defect or one occurring later
in life will point up the nature of the interaction between disfigured and normal people and some of the
problems this yields for both.

Tommy Jonson was born with a congenital malformation of his left ear. Instead of having a normal
ear, there was only a small ear lobe and a small piece
of cartilage covered by skin about the size of a dime.
This gave his head an asymmetrical appearance. His
parents did not seem unduly upset about his missing ear
when he was born. He first asked about his missing ear
when he was four and in the next several years sometimes
complained that "All the kids laugh at me about my ear
and I don't like it." He seemed fairly happy as a child
but in nursery school starting at age four he often
showed aggressiveness toward both younger and older
children. While he had a strong desire for companion-
ship, he was unable to form lasting relationships with
children about his own age, partly because of an unwarranted aggression toward them. During his early
years his family moved frequently. Increasingly he got
into difficulty at nursery school and kindergarten where
he was frequently mean to other children. He was not
liked by the parents in the neighborhood in which he
lived because of his aggressiveness. But sometimes
other children blamed him for other acts of mischief he
did not commit. He became the scapegoat for a number
of incidents. Finally his kindergarten teacher said
she would not tolerate his disruption of her class and
Tommy reported to his mother that the other children
were glad he was not in school any more. By this time
his parents felt that many of Tommy's problems were
connected to his ear defect. They noticed he never
looked in a mirror, wore a cap pulled over his ears
even in hot weather and resented the teasing he got
from other children. His parents felt he was jealous
of his older brother who had no such imperfect ear and
Tommy also felt that his parents liked his older brother
better.

Starting at age 6 he had four operations to develop a prosthetic ear. During the early stages of

174

this he had mixed reactions to the new ear because it didn't stick out more, his brother said it "doesn't look like much of an ear," and he had to wear conspicuous bandages over it. But after the last operation, Tommy seemed to mature more rapidly, gained self-confidence and was able to relate to his age mates better because they no longer teased him. He got along better in school, with his parents, and older and younger brothers. People no longer stopped the family out of curiosity to ask questions about Tommy's ear. His scholastic performance at school improved and he became a good class participant after he got a good ear. This case study reveals how a facial defect can influence the development of a child and his relation to all those around him. It also reveals that reconstructive plastic surgery can have a highly positive impact on changing a person's self-conception about himself, how he is reacted to by others and thus his relationship to them.[2]

Elaine Gorin did not get plastic surgery until she was 38. Since about age 14 she has had a conspicuously malformed jaw and a long convex nose. As the oldest child in a large family, her father had hoped she would be a boy. But with the later birth of male siblings, he seemed less sad about this. However, as the oldest in a large family she was often given heavy housekeeping and child care assignments by a whining mother who had little affection for her. Her father wanted the house kept quiet. He dominated the family and on occasion slapped Elaine when she complained. This may have broken her jaw and precipitated the beginning malformation of her jaw starting at about age 14. Her mother noticed her misshapen jaw at 14 at which time she had several teeth extracted. This procedure also may have broken her jaw. She was ill at this time for a while but by age 18 her jaw was noticeably distorted. Her teeth were maloccluded with a very noticeable deviation of the chin to the left with the left side of her upper jaw and especially lower jaw undeveloped. Elaine was rather withdrawn as was her father and partly as a result of his preference for boys and her own appearance, she was a tomboy during adolescence. She never felt interested in most social activities and felt unattractive to boys even though she was a petite woman with attractive red hair and brown eyes. She did not finish high school on time and experienced difficulties in work and schooling because of her appearance. She once overheard a conversation on a bus in which a woman said, "Look at the ugly face"

and wondered aloud "why nature had played such a
freakish trick" on her. She was once rejected for a
secretarial job and nurses' training because of her
appearance. She did take a job as a typist before she
finished high school because of the family's economic
plight. After being turned down for a nursing career
because she lacked a high school diploma and her appearances, she quit her job as a typist after four
years. At age nineteen she took a job with an
engineering firm where she worked for seven years.
During this time she dated an engineer but her stern
father forbade the proposed marriage. By attending
night school she got a high school diploma but was
again turned down for nurses' training because of her
ugliness. She considered getting plastic surgery when
she was 27, but was told that she could not be helped.
With the help of a doctor she got into nurses' school
at the age of 33, graduated from it three years later,
and became a private duty nurse where she would have
limited contact with the public. She often felt excluded from social contacts by acquaintances. When she
was 38, friends told her that new developments in
plastic surgery might apply to her. She made an ap-
pointment with a plastic surgery clinic where she was
interviewed by the staff and a plan of different surgical procedures worked out. In the first stage her
mouth was wired shut and corrections made in the left
side of her jaw. In the second stage excess bone was
taken from the right side of the jaw to make her face
more symmetrical. She was delighted with the results
but had serious doubts whether she would marry or be
socially successful. She thought her problems might be
her lack of social attributes rather than her deformed
face. A third operation involved correction of her
nose and further work on her jaw while the fourth
surgery involved a chin bonegraft. After the operation
her friends told her she looked younger, that she looked
"terrific" and that she seemed happier. While the results of the surgery were not perfect, she felt much
better about her appearance although at times she remained tense, sensitive and distant, personality
patterns that had developed over a twenty year period.
She felt happier and was pleased that people were
friendlier and more complimentary to her. After a
period of confusion, she began to participate in more
social affairs, became more aggressive, and fourteen
months after the last operation she was married. The
results of the surgical procedures were described as
"tremendous." They eventually transformed her social

life even though she had pursued her vocational goals slowly but successfully in spite of the handicap.[3] This case study indicates that a facial deformity and its correction can have major social consequences for a person. Of course, how a person reacts to a facial deformity will be influenced by many factors: sex, age of onset, personality patterns developed prior to or as a result of the defect, and the attitudes of parents, friends, employers and the public in general.

Nature and Origins of Facial Disfigurations

There is extensive variation among cultures as to what is considered beautiful. In some African societies scarification of the face, body, and limbs has been seen as enhancing beauty. In East Central Africa women commonly extended the lips with disks until they became as large as coffee cup saucers. In other societies weights have been hung on earlobes to elongate them. The New Britain Arowe mothers flattened their infants' heads to give them a sugarloaf shape. Papuans and other primitive societies inserted sticks in the nasal septum while many societies have engaged in color tattooing of the face and other parts of the body. In other societies the two front top teeth have been removed, or the teeth blackened or filed to points, or the ears and noses enhanced by rings following piercing. To many these "primitive" practices make people uglier rather than beautiful. Beauty is relative to culture.

But within any given society or subdivisions within it such as racial or ethnic groups, the range of what is considered beautiful is less relative and subject to narrower standards of normality. At the one end of this continuum will be the very handsome and beautiful who have improved marketability and social attractiveness. At the other end will be varying degrees of ugly people who have lessened marketability and social unattractiveness. In our society and throughout Western history the face has been the most central element of beauty. Not only is the face the conveyor of verbal and nonverbal messages, its structure, shape, and color have been viewed as a window to the inner person. In myth and fairy tales and real life, the good looking person has been assumed, until proven otherwise, to be good. In contrast, ugliness on the outside has been assumed to represent something evil or immoral inside the person. While people can disassemble or mask some of their feelings in their

177

face, an "honest" face is assumed to stand for an honest inner person. With the rise of the mass media in our society, advertising has contributed even more to the emphasis on appearance, especially facial appearance. Impression management and the importance of appearance has given rise to and been stimulated by a multi-billion dollar cosmetic industry to exploit this concern. Wrinkle removers, blemish removers, lipsticks, eye shadow, hair dyes, shampoos and bleaches, and smoothing creams are sold to an anxious public concerned with unblemished smooth skin of just the right shade to enhance one's clothes, eye color and hair color as well as symbolize the inner person. A whole range of occupations from cosmetologists, barbers and beauticians to orthodontists and plastic surgeons have developed techniques to enhance or restore human beauty.

For those at the ugly end of the scale, the beauty aids and restoration techniques are often of critical value because of social attitudes toward facial deformity. Facial deformity may come in many forms. There are those born with no ears, or huge rabbit ears which stick out at right angles from the head. There are those who are born with tiny heads, huge heads, or pointed heads, tiny noses or huge noses, noses too concave or too convex, eyes close together or far apart or uneven. There are those with extremely receding chins or overly prominent protruding chins. Some have low hairlines and others irregular ones. Some are born with cleft palates and hair lips. Some people have their skin ravaged by pock marks, chemical burns, cancer, stabbings or automobile accidents. The course of a bone disease may require surgery to save the life of a person but leaves that person's face badly damaged. Some are born with teeth badly aligned or destroyed by an accident. The origins then of facial deformities are congenital (present at birth) or adventitious (acquired after birth). Congenital deformities may occur from hereditary defects or those that result from pre-natal diseases of the mother. They may be apparent at birth or show up during early or later developmental stages. The adventitious deformities are those that come from either diseases which affect the face or skull or from accidents.

A wide variety of cranio-facial anomalies are both congenital and hereditary. Some can be repaired early in life such as cleft lip or palate, a condition affecting one child in 700. But many are relatively permanent and fundamentally irreparable. Hydrocephalus involves excessive fluid in the skull with concomitant enlargement of the head and intellectual impairment unless surgery is performed early to shunt the excess cerebrospinal fluid into the blood stream. Cretenism due to hypothyroidism is characterized by a large protruding tongue, mental retardation, a large abdomen but a dwarfish stature. Down's syndrome (mongolism) is characterized by a broad face, flat or stubby nose, open mouth, mental retardation and oblique eye openings. A pituitary disorder that develops in adulthood, Romberg's disease, leads to atrophy of bone, skin and muscles of the face giving it the appearance of having been pushed in. Apert's syndrome is characterized by an abnormally high skull and bulging widely-set eyes. Acrocephaly involves a high pointed skull. A face with a froglike appearance from the front, with a broad, convex, "hooked" nose, a protrusion of the lower jaw, and irregular teeth settings mark, Crouzon's disease. Hurler's disease or gargoylism is typlified by heavy ugly faces with the bridge of the nose depressed. Treacher-Collins Syndrome involves underdevelopment of the cheek bones and a notching of the lower eyelids yielding flat-looking cheeks. Grieg's disease or hypertelorism involves a deformity in the front part of the skull marked by a low forehead, flattened nose at the bridge, wide separation of the eyes and a divergent strabismus.[4] Some are born with deep red blotches of skin coloration called "port-wine stains" that are rarely susceptible to successful treatment.

The prevalence of various types of malformed or disfigured faces is unknown. It is probably underestimated by the public because such people are reluctant to appear in public due to the stigmatizing questions and looks usually directed at them. In addition to the congenital conditions are a wide range of acquired disfigurements that come from hundreds of thousands of traffic and industrial accidents annually. Other sources of disfigurement are assaults, fires, war casualties, sports casualties and a number of diseases such as skin cancer which frequently attack the exposed head and face. The number who have facial disfigurements run into the millions. And with a growing emphasis on youth and beauty in our society and the commercialization of cosmetic surgery, even the effects of aging are seen as a form of disfigurement to some. Sagging skin, fleshy jowls and puffy lower eyelids are increasingly becoming the basis for cosmetic surgeons to restore the aging face to a more youthful appearance.

Identifiability of the Facially Disfigurement

Assume for a moment that the facial beauty of persons could be rated on a scale from 1 to 10 with 10 being perfect beauty. The scale points of 1 to 3 would be varying degrees of ugliness, while 4 to 7 would be those of average appearance—by far the large majority of the population. In fact, in one study plastic surgeons and an interdisciplinary team evaluated clients who came to them for plastic surgery along a four point scale that would include our 0 to 3 ratings. The scale point of 3 was a "slight" deviation involving a rather inconspicuous deformity that might require attention to be focused on it before it was really noticed. A "2" they described as "moderate" deformity which is noticeable and may elicit remarks or staring or teasing but not a violent negative reaction. A "1" categorized as a "marked" deformity which was likely to evoke strong reactions from others such as repulsion, avoidance, pity, curiosity and excessive staring. A "0" was categorized as "gross" disfigurement that brought strong reactions of repulsion, horror, pity and disgust. Of the 74 patients who came to them during a 29 month period, 23% had a slight deformity, 28% a moderate one, 31% a marked one, and 18% a gross disfigurement. These figures are not necessarily representative of the facially disfigured, but are presented to show judgments by others about it. Self views of disfigurement do not necessarily correspond to other's views. In fact, those with either slight or moderate deformities are likely to exaggerate the severity of the condition.[5]

The identifiability of the facially disfigured is somewhat relative in several ways. First, it is relative to one's culture or society as we have already seen. A number of primitive societies had standards of beauty fundamentally incompatible with ours. Second, within any given society or in the history of that society there may be some individual or group variations in defining ugliness and its counterpart, beauty. Just as plump bodies and faces were seen as beautiful several centuries ago, now thinner bodies and faces are seen as more beautiful. While beauty is in the eye of the beholder, the beholder is socialized in a system of shared values that define rather exactly whose appearance is unaesthetic. The rating scale of beauty to ugliness given above would probably be applied fairly uniformly to a sample of pictures by most American citizens. In fact, an interesting study to test the cultural uniformity in reactions to physical disability was undertaken a few years ago with 640 children who were 10 to 11 years of age. The study showed that even at this early age there was high agreement on the rating of handicaps. The 640 subjects were racially and culturally diverse and included some handicapped as well as non-handicapped children. The subjects were given six drawings of children the same sex as themselves and asked to pick the ones they liked best. It was removed and then they were asked to pick the one they liked second best. It was removed and the procedure continued. The nearly uniform rank order choices were as follows: Rank 1 - a child with no physical handicap; Rank 2 - a child with crutches and a brace on the left leg; Rank 3 - a child sitting in a wheelchair; Rank 4 - a child with a left hand missing; Rank 5 - a child with a facial disfigurement on the left side of his mouth; and Rank 6 - an obese child. In addition to the high uniformity of these ratings, several other things are highly interesting. The two lowest rankings, facial disfigurement and obesity, received the lowest ratings even though they do not necessarily suggest an impairment. That is, they deviated from normality in appearance, not in function. The other interesting finding is that the children who were handicapped rated the pictures in the same pattern as the non-handicapped. This supports the position of minority group theorists that minority group members usually take on the attitudes of the dominant groups toward themselves.[6]

A third way in which the identifiability of the ugly is relative is the degree to which they either try to visually hide the disfigurement or withdraw from public contacts to minimize exposure. They may try to hide some deformities by long hair over the forehead, neck and ears or by beards or mustaches if they are males. High neck sweaters, dark glasses, or bandages may be used to conceal some markings. But many try to hide their disfigurement by reducing contacts with the public.

Social Reactions to the Facially Disfigured

The facially disfigured are reacted to much the same way as other minority groups, with one difference. The difference is the degree of disfigurement. As the disfigurement becomes more severe, the negativity of the response becomes stronger. One sociologist who has spent many years counseling and doing research at plastic surgery clinics, Frances Cooke Macgregor, summarizes reactions to the facially deformed very well:

> "We live in a society that places high value on both a certain conformity and physical attractiveness. In our culture the way one looks makes a difference in the responses one gets. A person who is 'ugly' is devalued and set apart. If one happens to look different, one is likely to receive differential treatment and in turn to begin to feel different. To be disfigured, therefore, as studies have shown, is to be an object of staring, curiosity, pity, rejection, ridicule, remarks and discrimination. These reactions and attitudes are frequently more damaging to the individual's self image than the reflection in the mirror. Such persons find it an ordeal to move about in public. Their anonymity is attacked, strangers question them, or they are shunned altogether. In addition to these humiliations, major obstacles confront them in the efforts to make friends, attract members of the opposite sex, marry, or find employment. As a consequence, such persons frequently develop personality problems or emotional and behavioral disorders that, in many instances, are more serious than the physical defect itself. These may range from feelings of inferiority, shame, self-consciousness, anger, hypersensitivity, anxiety, and paranoid complaints to complete withdrawal, antisocial behavior, and psychotic states."[7]

If a child is born with a facial anomaly, parental and social reactions are frequently different than if it is acquired at a later date. Parents show a variety of responses to the bad news including shocked disbelief, grief, anger or guilt. Guilt reactions are high among those who interpret the deformity as a physical retribution for some moral deviation they have committed earlier or some unhealthy practice they have engaged in during or even before pregnancy. They may be angry at themselves for their attributed causal role in the defect or have a diffused anger about this unfortunate turn of events. Some of these guilt reactions go back many centuries to folk beliefs and superstitions which impute deformity to the sins of the father as "punishment for some wrongdoing, incestuous parentage, or maternal impressions. These are rooted in fear of the physically atypical or the malformed and go back to the beginning of history when 'evil spirits' or 'the wrath of the gods' was believed responsible for physical anomalies."[8] Such folk beliefs include the idea that malformities are due to such things as: thinking evil thoughts or having an accident during pregnancy, petting a rabbit during pregnancy, having an 'evil eye' cast upon the pregnant woman, an unfaithful husband, a family curse or being born during an eclipse of the moon.

Grief reactions are common in any loss including the partial loss of a child who is seen as abnormal or less than 'whole' or perfect. Disbelief often results in rejection, usually only temporary, unless the infant is multiply handicapped. These initial reactions often influence the treatment of the child during the developmental years. While parents usually report they try to treat a disfigured child as they do their own children or any child, their actual behavior often belies this. They may try to hide the child from public view. They may be either too lax in discipline or overly authoritarian with a child who is different. Edith Lauer reports that, "Usually the afflicted child was treated either with more consideration or with less warmth and approval, and sometimes with outright hostility." Siblings often had the same reactions but not always parallel with either of the parents.[9] There were many family variations on how they were treated differently. Some families tried to make the child not feel different. But this did not always work because their underlying sentiments differed from what they said or did. Families who said they tried not to show too much sympathy in order not to make the children more self-conscious often had no real sympathy for the facially deformed child. They might point out that there were other children worse off which indirectly showed their disapproval of the condition and the resentment they had toward the child because of it.

Reactions to facial defects by teachers or significant others often center on the defect as the cause of all a person's problems when in fact it may be only one of the developmental problems the person faces. For example the vocational advisor to a 19-year old girl insisted that the girl's only problem was due to her asymmetrical face even though the psychologists saw her personality problems as stemming primarily from an impoverished and unhappy family life. The advisor was of the opinion that anyone with a facial defect would have a "terribly difficult time." She added to it by advising the student not to pursue a career she wanted because she believed she would be automatically rejected because of her misshappened face.[10]

As I have mentioned, people who are ugly are often treated disparingly. The reactions often vary by the social context—whether it is on a public street in a large city, or at a small church in a rural area, or at the doctor's office, or in school. Some people stare, others turn away with disgust. Some people ask out of curiosity about the origin of the condition but in the process often embarrass the person as they unthoughtfully invade their privacy. Yet, if people know the origin of the condition it may change their reaction to the facially deformed person. If the origin has a socially acceptable explanation the disfigured person has fewer problems of rejection. Since deformity is often associated with immorality the person is better off if he can say that the scars on his face are due to an industrial accident rather than a barroom brawl or chemicals thrown on his face by a "hit man" from the Mafia. One woman who developed a large tumor in her lower right jaw had it surgically removed; but this left a deep indentation in her jaw. She became quite depressed and withdrew from all social contacts outside of work. Three years later at age 51 reconstructive surgery was undertaken to restore her jaws by bone grafts. However, she temporarily had wires protruding from her mouth which were holding her jaws and teeth in place while the graft was taking. Despite the fact that her face was more conspicuous than ever, her spirits were elevated and she was no longer afraid to meet strangers. She no longer felt embarrassed because she knew that soon she would be normal in appearance. She did not tell people she had had cancer; rather she told them she had been in an accident and was undergoing an operation to reconstruct her jawbone. She was no longer viewed with pity or having a horrible disease; rather she was reacted to as she saw herself—on the road to recovery.[11] Some patients however have difficulty in convincing others of the true origin of their condition. Macgregor tells of an interesting case to illustrate this point:

A 56-year old seaman had incurred a partial avulsion a part torn away of the end of his nose when he was attacked and robbed. The lacerations were sutured but required time for healing before plastic surgery could be undertaken. It was necessary for the patient to resume his work in the interim, and he went to sea with a crew he had never seen before. The men asked him what kind of disease he had and inferred that it was cancer. When he told them he had been the victim of a hold-up, they did not believe him, and he was forced to produce a medical certificate to prove it. "The fellows then apologized, and from then on, I was accepted."[12]

A series of stereotypes exist about the facially defective. One of the most common is that ugly people are retarded. Perhaps this is due to the fact that more of the retarded have multiple handicaps and congenital facial malformations than is true of the intellectually normal population. Another stereotype is that ugly people are wicked, or criminal, or diseased. For example, a group of non-disfigured individuals were shown the picture of a 38-year-old, successful male real estate broker who ten years earlier had his face grossly disfigured by chemical burns which later developed into cancer. With no clues given about him, the subjects were asked to first suggest the cause of the problem and then his life based on the photograph only. The responses about the causes or other reactions were: "A war casualty?"; "Is this syphilis or a physical injury?; Inevitable that the man must be sick in the head too"; "Probably a gangster;" "Horrible"; "Grotesque, inhuman, sad"; "A leper"; "Looks like an accident"; "In a fire or explosion." Some of the comments were: "He would have a hard time initially because he is so ugly. He couldn't do anything that would require personal contact. I don't think anyone would hire him." "Such an extreme kind of deformity must have a terrible effect on practically all people... would tend toward isolating himself as much as possible both from society and the gaze of other people." "Oh God! I wonder how he remained alive at this point . . . Naturally he lives in seclusion . . . Seems to me he would want to destroy himself."[13]

The photograph of a 30 year old junior executive in a chemical corporation was also shown to respondents. This man had a superior intelligence but was classified as having a "marked" congenital deformity: "low, narrow forehead; a prominent, convex nose; receding, pointed chin; narrow deep-set eyes; large buck teeth; and lop-ears;" facial contours that were "asymmetrical and incongrous." Of 60 respondents 59 reacted negatively to his photograph. Half classified him as "mentally inferior" while 27 of the respondents used such terms as "lethargic," "dazed," "weak," or "dull," to describe him. Some typical comments indicated they thought he was "mean," "nasty," a "follower in a gang," "a dope addict," "like a maniac," "repulsive," and "an imbecile."[14] While first impressions may not be accurate, they may be important.

Particular facial anomalies frequently have special character or personality traits associated with them. For example people with low foreheads are often pictured as dumb while those with high foreheads are "brains." Receding chins are associated with weak, passive, milk toast personalities. People with rough, big features are often seen as tough and crude—the opposite of the refined personality manners associated with people with "fine" features. People with large noses or ears are frequently the butt of jokes about having ski snoots or elephant ears. Such stereotypes operate on the assumption that the outer features of a person are an accurate portrayal of their inner personality or character.[15] Because of how they are treated, the facially crippled often begin to see themselves in the same light. A patient with a grossly deformed face reported "When I parked my car in front of a jewelry store, two cops came up and asked me for my identification card. They thought I was a gangster." Another person with a facial malformation reported, "I avoid restaurants as people may think I have a disease and won't want to eat after me." A patient with a harelip and cleft palate said, "children would make fun of the way I talked and looked and said I wasn't normal." A patient with a marked deformity following radical surgery for cancer observed, "People seem to think I've changed because my face has."[16]

Being facially different to the point of noticeable unattractiveness lowers the status of a person. Frequently he or she is seen as less than a whole person. While the disfigurement may in no way be

dysfunctional to the person in terms of potential productivity or performance, it is regarded so by others.
Society handicaps these individuals in every area of
life: getting an education, getting medical treatment,
getting a job and promotions, opportunities for friendship and marriage, restrictions in social activities and
recreation. A deviant face implies to many a deviant
mentality, a deviant personality, and deviant life
style. These handicapping attitudes and social
restrictions are deeply embedded in our society with
the result that many of those facially crippled become
psychological and social cripples. External labels may
become internal labels.

Preoperative and Postoperative Individual Reactions to Facial Disfigurement

        In this section of the chapter I will look at how
the facially crippled react to their deformity before
any surgery is undertaken for corrective purposes. In
addition we will look at how they react following
plastic surgery (which is frequently successful in varying degrees.) One feature about the analysis of the
facially deformed as a minority group is distinctive.
Most minority groups including the physically handicapped, blind and deaf have developed, in some degree,
self-help groups to heighten their own consciousness
about discrimination or improve their social standing by
lowering discriminatory barriers by means of a variety
of tactics. I have found no such groups among the ugly.
Their responses are individual ones. They do not seek
a political solution to their problem. They have not
lobbied for inclusion as a handicapped group in legislation even though societal responses to them are
handicapping. They have not participated in demonstrations or sit-ins because employers discriminate
against them. They do not form enclaves where they
can have social contacts and recreation among themselves
without the stares and jibes of others. Their solution
seems to be primarily twofold: to either get surgical
help to reclaim or restore their appearance to the best
possible or to isolate themselves as far as possible.
In both cases their attitudes toward deformity are those
of the dominant group: deformity is unsightly. Either
it should be kept out of sight or corrected so that any
deviations that remain are within the limits of the
socially tolerable. We will later look at why the
facially disfigured have not resorted to group formation
to deal with their problems.

As individuals the facially disfigured use three patterns of reaction to the stigmatizing attitudes of society. While each facially maimed person may on occasion use any of the three types of response depending on the circumstances and social setting, they often adopt one of the responses as their fundamental one. The three responses are avoidance, overt aggression, and deliberate attempts to deal with embarrassing situations. There are variations on each of these three responses that reflect the nature of the encounter between the disfigured and non-disfigured as well as personality variations of the participants.[17]

Probably one of the most frequently used response patterns to the staring, curious questioning and comments of others is some tactic of avoidance. It ranges from near total seclusion, to avoidance of some situations, say eating at restaurants, to simply pretending not to be aware of negative comments or obtrusive stares. If the ugly travel in mass transportation vehicles they may try to sit in secluded corners, or sit in such a way that their deformity is toward a wall and away from the direct gaze of others. They may use clothing such as large hats or glasses to obscure their deformity or hide behind newspapers. Knowing how others react to ugliness, they try to keep others from intruding into their life space or by not intruding into the life space of others. Of course, such avoidance tactics tend to isolate people and narrow their options for a full social life.

The case of Tom M. illustrates the avoidance pattern. Tom suffered a birth injury which paralyzed the right side of his face. When not talking his defect was less noticeable, involving primarily a left eyelid which drooped slightly and which did not close completely when he blinked. But his deformity became conspicuous when he spoke. He literally talked out of the side of his mouth because of his facial paralysis. Otherwise he was good looking, intelligent, well-dressed and well-mannered. His parents noticed his problems in infancy because hs "screwed up" one side of his face when he talked or laughed or cried. They took him to many doctors all of whom said that nothing could be done to help him because the muscles and nerves in the left side of his face had atrophied. In elementary school he was made even more aware of his condition when teachers would stop him in the middle of a response and ask him what was the matter with his face. They would say to

him, "Try to control it and don't talk on one side of
your mouth like that." He was embarrassed by such public investigations and wished that his teachers would
ask him about his condition after class. Because of
the kind of attention paid to him, he became very self-
conscious. He shied away from other children and
returned home immediately after school. He only played
with children from a neighborhood family that had a
child with a clubfoot. In neither case was the deformity mentioned. In high school he stayed away from
social activities and dances and class participation
because he hated the teasing of other students. He did
go out for baseball, but often left the game when members of the opposing team tried to upset him by calling
him "crooked mouth." After high school he tried to
become a policeman like his father and grandfather.
But he failed the physical. A friend told him later
the doctor failed him on the physical because of the
deformity. Six times he tried to get a job at a department store where he was always rejected until a
friend intervened on his behalf. He was given a job in
the packing department where he would be out of public
view. But at this job as at subsequent ones, he found
difficulties. He reported "The fellows made my life
miserable. They would tell jokes and make faces the
way I do when I talk. Or they would say, 'are you
trying to be tough, talking out of the side of your
face?'" Tom did marry the only girl he ever dated. He
was apprehensive about having children for fear that
they might have a facial defect like his. But none of
the three children did. He had difficulty getting and
holding other jobs because of responses to his face.
He felt, "I always have to go for jobs where they'll
take anybody." He was fearful of asking for promotions
because he knew he'd be turned down and such situations
were anxiety provoking to him which in turn made his
facial contortions worse when he talked. While his
wife was quite social, Tom was the reverse because of
his face. He rarely left the house for anything but
work because he knew people were repulsed by his appearance and whispered behind his back. This was
upsetting to him as was the fact that when people did
talk to him they "unconsciously drew up their mouths in
imitation" of his. He said people "don't realize that
it's not my fault that I look this way, and one crack
about my face stops me cold. I will go home and brood
for two months and draw into a shell. I get cross and
snap at the kids and my wife and won't talk to any of
them." The psychologist at the plastic surgery clinic

189

where he came for help, but where none was available because of the uncorrectable permanency of his condition, assesses his condition as follows:[18]

> While Tom made a relatively good adjustment
> to his life situation and was able to marry and
> support a family, he was crippled psychologically.
> His feelings of inadequacy and his periods of
> depression were caused less by his deformity
> than by the anticipated and actual reactions of
> others in his appearance. Being given derogatory
> nicknames by his peers, offered jobs where he
> would have a minimum of social contact, and
> characterized as 'tough' accentuated behavior
> patterns of a negative nature. Not only did
> his own feelings of frustration and deep
> hostility prevent him from developing more
> favorable aspects of emotional life, but his
> personality distortions were in turn projected
> upon his environment. His periods of depression,
> short temper, and refusal to enter into social
> activities distressed his wife and children
> and disrupted the family harmony.[19]

This particular case study not only illustrates the avoidance pattern of reaction, it illustrates the psychological crippling effect of a nondysfunctional impairment. It is not surprising that some facially disfigured people experience mental illness and a few commit suicide because of the damaging effects of stigmatizing processes.

The second pattern of response to prejudice and discrimination is <u>overt aggression</u>. This pattern reflects a more aggressive and less inhibited personality type of response to staring and negative comments. Such respondents stare back and talk back to those who attempt to invade their privacy or impugn their looks or character. By staring back at gazers they can often get them to avert their eyes from them. One disfigured woman reported that "when people stare at me, I sometimes get so mad I say, 'Take a good look.'"

One male who had a residual harelip defect reported he tried to humiliate anybody who made some negative comment about them in front of others. By making a whole group ashamed of victimizing him he was able to stop embarrassing comments. One of the things deformed people have to contend with are questions about the origin of their deformity. While these questions may not be ill intended they do make the person self conscious that he is defectively different. Sometimes the question is answered directly and without hostility; but flippant or defiant responses remind the questioner that it is none of his business. One grossly disfigured male has a series of one-liners which he uses to stop further invasion of his personality: "I stepped on my face going up the stairs," "I was in the war; I put my head up when I should have put it down," "I was in an accident," "I was in a ring wrestling with a bear," or "I got it for sticking my nose somewhere where I shouldn't."[20] This pattern of response is non-accepting of the lower status given the disfigured. Rather than seeing themselves as the locus of the problem, these disfigured people see the source located in the prejudiced attitudes of others. It is a defiant assertion of their rights as a person. They feel they are more than the face they present to the public. At the same time this technique widens social barriers. In addition to the initial barrier to satisfying interaction, the deformed face, it adds another — unfriendly or hostile responses.

The third pattern of response involves <u>deliberate attempts to deal with embarrassing situations</u>. This approach often seems to be more reflective because it anticipates how others are likely to react to ugliness and takes the initiative in minimizing embarrassing questions, remarks and stares. One tactic is for the disfigured person to barrage the non-disfigured with a series of questions about their interests and lives— to focus on the other person rather than their own apperance. By doing so they show their interests are in other people or ideas and not their own superficial appearances. Another tactic is to explain the source of the defect before others ask - "I was burned" or "I was in a bad car accident." Such short statements often keep others from further encroachment by continued questions. Or a facetious remark like, "I ran into a tiger," or "Please excuse my leprosy," humorously casts appearances into a minor affair which relieves tension and suggests to others they take the situation lightly because the bearer of the defect does. Techniques of charm, humor and manifestations of overt friendliness by the facially ugly may neutralize shock by anticipating it and taking counter steps to deal with it. One businessman who knows that his gross facial disfigurement is often shocking to people uses a different

191

technique. Recognizing that shocks to such surprising encounters require a few seconds of adjustment, he attempts to position himself at a distance from an approaching new contact that will give that person time to adjust before the conversation begins.[21]

These three general patterns of response characterize those who either have an uncorrected or uncorrectable facial deformity. Research generally indicates that if reconstructive plastic surgery can sufficiently repair such a defect so that the person becomes average in appearance or has only "slight" deformities that are only noticeable with inspection, such people can assimilate into the general population. In other words, they can drop various defensive patterns of response used when they were disfigured. However, if the defect is of long duration or existed during the years of personality formation, erasing the facial defect may not totally eradicate the crippling psychological effects it leaves on people. If a person is made fun of and shunned for twenty years and has developed defensive patterns of avoidance and overt aggression, he may not be able to alter his personality or life style to fit a new socially acceptable face. This is not to say the person cannot make some positive adjustments. But the changes come slowly and haltingly and incompletely; career channels and social opportunities once closed may not open up at all or in the same way had the facial deformity never been present.

The case of Charlotte B. illustrates the devastating effects of a gross disfigurement. At the same time her case illustrates such effects in midlife when her personality was well formed and the changes that reconstructive surgery can bring about to such a person are very dramatic. At age 36 Charlotte suffered from chronic inflammation of the mucous membranes in her forehead (suppurative frontal sinuitis). Radical surgery was undertaken which involved the removal of a large portion of the frontal bone in her forehead. This resulted in a deep and conspicuous depression in the middle of her forehead and a noticeable scar across her nose. Upon seeing herself in the mirror following the surgery, she was so upset that she cried for two days. She felt so repulsive she did not allow her friends into her hospital room to visit her. When she returned to her secretarial job her self-confidence was further undermined by stares and questions in the office, elevator, the streets and buses. Formerly sociable and outgoing, she now refused to go anywhere because of the constant staring and questioning. She avoided eye contact with people to stymie conversations. Increasingly she wept, became depressed and begun taking barbiturates to control her anxiety. After a few months recovery from the disfiguring operation and the accompanying swelling, she was eligible for plastic surgery. However, she needed extra money for this surgery. When she applied for waitressing jobs to supplement her regular income, she was always turned down because of her most displeasing appearance. She became semi-hysterical in her self pity. Her grooming habits declined. She became increasingly fearful she might lose her job because she could no longer concentrate. Finally Charlotte underwent reconstruction of her forehead bone using grafts removed from her ilium. The results were highly successful. In three weeks her face returned to normal except for a slight scar. Her expression became radiant, and her drab, untidy appearance was immediately remedied. "I've been a different person since this operation. It's as though I had gone to sleep and awakened as somebody else. I look in the mirrors and grin from ear to ear and spend hours looking at myself," she said. "Before, I couldn't bear to see myself. Everyone is amazed at the physical and mental change in me and I feel relieved of a great weight." She reported going out again, not crying any more, and being "glad to get up in the mornings."[22]

Not all cases of plastic surgery have such dramatic results. Those who have had a facial defect from birth may not respond in the same way. Carolyn Jones and Herbert Greene compared their personal perspectives on the effects of having a big nose made smaller (rhinoplasty) and substantial weight loss respectively. They both noticed after their changes that they tended to get mad at the people who were never very friendly to them before their changes but became friendly once they changed. They were mad because they had not accepted them for what they were but for the way they appeared. They speak:

> "My cross was a big nose. Very long and
> very unattractive. Let's say I wasn't over-
> whelmed with boyfriends. But after my nose job,
> the guys were all over me, opening doors, sending
> flowers, and my telephone was ringing off the
> wall."

"That must have made you feel good."

"It made me feel terrible. I wanted people to like me for me, and not because my nose was fixed. Why should my smaller nose make such a big difference? I got so wild that I wanted to scream at everybody sending flowers: Where were you when I needed one rose?"

Carolyn then went on to observe,

"But when I got my nose fixed, I became a much better looking human being. Attractive, if you will, and being attractive, I attracted. But I didn't know how to deal with that. I had a new nose, but I was the old me. I resented everybody who noticed the change for the better. Because it made me feel that they hadn't seen anything worthwhile in me before. I'd have given anything if I could have grown my old nose back. But when strangers began to pay attention too, I had nothing to feel angry about. After all, they didn't reject me when my nose was long. So I got a big clue. I needed to cut out all the junk that stood in the way of accepting myself — all the junk that had been there with the old nose."[23]

The kind of internal psyche reassessment described above becomes more formalized with some plastic surgeons and clinics. Individual and group therapy and discussions about the nature of the surgery itself and the expectations that accompany it are often undertaken. People need to be aware of their motives for undertaking plastic surgery and false expectations of what it may do for them physically and socially.

In all three of her books on the psychsocial aspects of reparative or corrective surgery, Frances Macgregor reports that most subjects benefit appreciably from such surgery. Most subjects are "highly pleased" with the results, a few are "fairly pleased" and occasionally a few are displeased. Follow up interviews with corrective surgery patients found that many of them showed immediate and marked improvements in their social lives and emotional adjustments. Subjects reported being more spontaneous and outgoing with a marked decrease or elimination of negative reactions to them. Without feelings of shame, inferiority and social inadequacy, they became less self-conscious and began taking a new interest in other people. As social distance between themselves and others declined, they became more friendly and outgoing with people responding to them in a reciprocal, friendly, normal way. Their less inhibited social attitudes were often accompanied by a more erect and proud body posture, and more attention to grooming and clothes. And quite importantly, energies formerly invested in defensive social manners and preoccupation with their deformities were rechanneled into more important and satisfying endeavors like work, friendship and community service. Of course there were exceptions—people who used these deformities as excuses for failure or who had more severe underlying personality problems and as in all surgery, some cases did not have successful outcomes due to excessively optimistic expectations, or poor surgical performance or complications.

Frances Cooks Macgregor reports on an interesting study of 89 people who had "nose jobs"(rhinoplasties). These people were intensively interviewed both before and after surgery about their backgrounds, their motives for surgery and their feelings about the surgical outcomes. An analysis of their motives for surgery— often hidden—revealed two major categories: the "changers" and the "fixers." The "changers" were those who felt they had an "ethnic" nose and wanted to have it altered to avoid discrimination, teasing and stereotyping. Most prominent among the ethnic groups were Greeks and Armenian Jews who had armenoid noses—those characterized as long, convex, downward sloping, with depressed tips and thick flared wings. They felt they could be "more American," more beautiful, and could get dates and better jobs if they did not have a "Jewish" nose. The other group was the "fixers" who had ugly noses—too big, too long, twisted, bulbous, hinged, hooked, convex or disproportionate. They wanted to overcome the tough or immoral personality characteristics associated with an ugly nose. They felt cosmetic repair jobs would enable them to avoid the teasing epithets they had known for a lifetime—Little Moose, Banana Nose, Pinnocchio, Tomato Nose, Beak, Hawk, Pug, Hook Nose and Ski Snoot. After the operations they usually reported that they liked themselves better and that things went better for them.[24]

Group Awareness and Plastic Surgery

One of the intriguing questions that remains is why
have not the facially disfigured formed self-help groups
like most other minorities? The answers described below are primarily speculative and subject to further
research. However, before I attempt to answer that
question, I will digress briefly into the nature of
plastic surgery and medical practice. This discussion
will help lay the groundwork for understanding why the
facially disfigured, who are not otherwise physically
or mentally impaired, are discriminated against but
have not organized to protest their situation.

Plastic surgery began in ancient India as efforts
to repair the amputations of ears, noses and other
bodily parts which were frequent forms of punishment for
criminals and adulterers. In this century plastic surgery has witnessed an explosive growth due to major
technological advancements in surgical techniques and a
rising demand for its services as it became more effective and as attitudes changed about "vanity" surgery.

Plastic surgery is a generic term which covers
both reconstructive surgery and cosmetic surgery. While
both subfields use many of the same surgical procedures,
they are distinguished by the purposes for which they
are undertaken. Reconstructive surgery is undertaken to
overcome congenital malformations or adventitiously acquired disfigurements as a result of accidents, diseases
which ravage the body, other surgical interventions
which leave the patient physically mutilated or scarred.
On the beauty-ugliness scale of 10 to 0 mentioned earlier, reconstructive surgery is generally aimed at
moving people in the 0 to 2 range up the scale to a
"better" appearance. This might involve moving a 0,
"grossly deformed," up to a 2 - a "moderate" disfigurement. Or it might involve moving a 1, "marked"
deformity to a 4 if surgically feasible. In contrast,
cosmetic surgery involves trying to "improve" the appearance of a normal person who has no major disfigurement. The person may be a rather "homely" 3 or 4 who,
with a chin augmentation, could be moved to a 6 or 7.
Or perhaps an attractive 7 could be moved to a "9"
with a rhinoplasty that reduces a large convex nose
into one with just the right size and slant to make her
beautiful. Cosmetic surgery, sometimes called "vanity
surgery," tries to improve upon nature for those people
born in the 3 to 9 category but less than the perfect
10. While the amount of surgery that could be

classified as reconstructive has grown in the last quarter of a century, the rapid explosion has occurred in cosmetic surgery. In 1949 only about 15,000 cosmetic operations were undertaken; the annual count in the U.S. today is over one million.[26]

Three major interrelated factors appear to be behind the greater demand for cosmetic surgery. One is the development of new surgical techniques that can alter nearly any part of the body: hair implants, ear repair, eye debagging, eyebrow lifts, nose repair, scar removal, face lifts, throat and jowl lifts, dermabrasion for some wrinkles and scars, breast augmentation or reduction or alteration, chin or jaw reduction or augmentation, eyelid lifts, removal of fat stretch marks on the stomach, upper arms, buttocks or thighs, skin repair, and vein removal.

A second factor is a change in public attitudes toward vanity surgery. Twenty five years ago most men and women who had cosmetic surgery tried to hide the fact if they had resorted to surgery to improve upon nature. Men particularly were seen as vain to want such corrections, but no longer. Now most men and women who undertake such surgery to remove the markings of age or to make themselves more beautiful openly admit why they have done it—to be more attractive and youthful in appearance. A number of movie stars report their lives transformed by such changes. With the advent of the television the emphasis on appearance can more easily be sold to the public. One book trying to push more cosmetic surgery points out it is not limited to movie stars and the jet-setters but everyday people.[27]

The third factor is the commercialization of the beauty industry. Just as the thinning industry has sold people on thinness to promote its wares, the beauty industry has impressed upon the public the importance of appearance and youthful looks to sell its wares. Many magazines carry articles telling people the cosmetic steps they can take to become a better person on the outside with the suggestion that if they have the right nail polish or nose size they will be better inside. This is the message of many television commercials also. Within this development has been the commercialization and sometimes deprofessionalization of cosmetic surgery. Dozens of books written by doctors have titles like that of James O. Stallings, M.D.: A New You: How Plastic Surgery Can Change Your Life or Kurt J. Wagner,

M.D. and Gerald Imber, M.D., <u>Beauty by Design</u>.[28]

Many cosmetic surgeons are now calling themselves "aesthetic surgeons" for they are trying to create demand for their expensive services by promising beauty, improvement, and more rewarding lives. Some authors have criticized these developments. For example Colette Dowling in <u>The Skin Game</u> argues that many doctors are promoting unnecessary cosmetic surgery for their own gains while Kendall H. Moore and Sally Thompson in <u>The Surgical Beauty Racket</u> contend many patients are being damaged by the complications which often follow plastic surgery and by the lack of skill and integrity of some plastic surgeons.[29]

Each of these three forces has stimulated the development of the other and are in the process of heightening the importance of attractiveness in society. The elevation of the importance of attractiveness has been an indirect factor in why the ugly have not seen themselves as a minority group. They have been swept along in the tide of public opinion that believes looks are vitally important even though ugliness is no barrier to achievement in and of itself. This group has been partially created and exploited by the commercializers of attractiveness. The ugly by and large accept their lesser status and all the barriers that society erects to their participation in the mainstream of life. Many choose the seclusion and self-depreciation route which simultaneously reduces contacts among them and inhibits group formation.

In addition to the role this indirect factor plays in inhibiting group awareness and formation is how the ugly are treated under legislation. While it is a social handicap because of people's reactions to it, it is not a physical or mental handicap per se. It is not a neurological disorder or a learning disability or an orthopedic limitation or a hearing or visual impairment or any other health condition which limits functioning. Because they suffer from no dysfunctional limitation they have not thought of themselves nor have others thought of them as physically impaired. However the Rehabilitation Act of 1973 as amended and as implemented by regulations of the Department of Health, Education and Welfare now broadly defines a handicapped individual as any individual who "(A) has a physical or mental impairment which substantially limits one or more of such person's major life activities, (B) has a record of such impairment, or (C) is regarded as having such an impairment."[30] This last phrase is quite ambiguous for it does not say whose judgment is relevant or useable in determining a handicap. Nevertheless, this 1977 amendment does make it possible to include the facially disfigured among the handicapped. But to date the ugly have not organized to protest their discriminatory treatment under their recent legal inclusion among the handicapped. This may be true for yet another reason. Most of the federal legislation has been undertaken to provide educational or rehabilitation funds and services to the handicapped. But the facially disfigured do not need such special services as a rule. Rather they need either social acceptance or plastic surgery. For over 80 percent of the population the cost of cosmetic surgery is borne by private commercial or non-profit insurance. Somewhere over ten percent of the population would be covered by the federal government's health insurance for the poor called Medicaid. Thus the decision on who needs cosmetic surgery is rarely a government decision. It is a decision made by the patient, his doctor and the insurance company. Thus, any protest about the lack of insurance coverage for aesthetic surgery must be directed to the insurers in the private sector rather than to government. This factor may also help to explain why the facially disfigured have not formed self-help groups to deal with their condition and their unequal treatment.

In summary, the facially disfigured are a minority group. They are readily identifiable by facial features which depart from normal appearances in varying degrees of ugliness. Because of a growing emphasis on the importance of appearance and high agreement on what is beautiful, this group's identifiability remains high. The facially disfigured are treated differently partly because by culture standards their appearances are seen as disgusting or repulsive. Furthermore, ugliness is often stereotyped as reflecting upon the inner person's intelligence or character—the ugly are frequently seen as dumb, weak, brutal or immoral depending on the nature of the deformity. The facially maimed experience discrimination in a wide variety of public encounters and economic and educational institutions. Their status is lower not only because of a variety of barriers to employment and promotion but also due to the stigma attached to ugliness in a society that increasingly rewards and promotes attractiveness. The commercialization of personal attractiveness makes changes in the

acceptance of the disfigured unlikely. The facially
maimed are highly aware of their deviant appearances.
Some respond mainly by avoidance of interpersonal encounters, others by overt aggressiveness to those who
stare at them and mistreat them and others by more
positive attempts to deal with their damaged identities.
Many resort to cosmetic surgery in an attempt to become
relatively normal in appearance. However, unlike most
minority groups, those with deviant faces do not
organize to protest their social treatment. Their
seclusion, the strength of the norms supporting attractiveness, their lack of an actual dysfunctional
impairment, and the medical solution to their disfigurement which is located in the private sector of the
economy all inhibit the development of self-help groups
to assist people with damaged faces.

Chapter 7

The Growing Minority: Fat People

Many books have been written about fat people and even more about dieting to become thinner or thin. These books often allude to the social problems fat people experience without adopting a sociological framework of analysis. Most of the literature on fat people treats the problem as a medical problem or a psychological problem. In many cases it is both of these. But it is also an interpersonal and institutional problem that lends itself well to sociological analysis because both the definition of obesity and the complex responses that average-weight persons make to the obese and the obese to themselves are deeply social in nature.

This chapter is not primarily about the nature of obesity, its origins, its medical treatment, or dieting, although all of these matters will be touched on. It is primarily about societal definitions of obesity and how thinness has been established as both an aesthetic ideal and a health ideal. With those ideals have come negative evaluations of fat people, the development of a whole set of economic institutions to cater to those overweight or fearful of becoming so, and many forms of discrimination against those defined as overweight. Relatively little has been written about them from a sociological perspective, especially that perspective called minority group theory. Yet, fat people easily meet the four characteristics of a minority group. They are identifiable, stereotyped and discriminated against, carry a stigmatized status, and are so highly aware of their stigma that in the last three decades they have organized to either pass into the dominant group or resist what they believe are unfair and injurious practices directed toward them.

Identifiability and Definitions of Obesity

In writing about fat people there is no term available to describe them that does not carry pejorative connotations. A lot of synonyms have been used in this regard--ample, plump, overweight, huge, fat, obese--to cite only a few. The simplest term to use is the one that is both most common and also used by self-help groups of large people--fat. Most behavioral minorities are not readily identifiable. But the fat minority is unique in this regard. They are readily identifiable

either because of their excessive eating behavior or
genetic or medical conditions which bring on obesity.

But what does it mean to be fat? There is no
agreed upon definition mainly because there are two
different sets of criteria that are used in defining
features — aesthetic and medical. The aesthetic criteria are more relative to time, place, history and
personality. The terms "fat and ugly" are frequently,
but not always, used together to connote the unattractiveness of being fat. Aesthetic criteria of what is
proportionate and pleasing to the eye vary by society
and even overtime in any one society. In many African
and Eastern societies being overweight was a sign of
success, symbol of economic surplus and conspicuous
consumption that placed one above those merely sub-
sisting. The nudes painted by the master painters in
the seventeenth and eighteenth centuries were quite
plump by today's standards, but were considered the
hallmarks of beauty at that time. Today they would
have to shed many pounds to be eligible for consideration for being a Playboy centerfold or a movie idol.
They would have to shed even more pounds, become skinny,
to reach the high fashion industry's idea of thinness
and beauty. Thus, our personal conceptions of what is
normal weight and what is overweight are a matter of
acculturation to a large extent.

The medical criteria of fatness are somewhat more
objective. However they rest on two different but related criteria. One of the criteria is based on a norm
of weight for adults according to their body build and
height. If a person is around 10% to 20% over the
weight of this norm he is said to be overweight, obese
(this word is used more by physicians), or fat. If the
person is about 25% or more overweight he is said to be
"very fat" or very obese. This criterion can be applied
in the present.. A number of other techniques have been
used to measure obesity such as the "pinch test" to see
if a person has more than a one-half inch of fat under
a double skinfold, or the denismetric method which com-
pares a person's weight to his displacement of water
(fat is lighter than bone or muscle). The second
medical criterion has to do with the consequences of
being overweight. This criterion treats obesity as a
disease because it is often related to or seen as either
a cause or contributing factor to other diseases. Thus,
seriously overweight people are more prone to gallblad-
der problems, strokes, diabetes, heart disease,

hypertension, and damage to weight bearing joints which can be further aggravated by gout or arthritis. Obese women are more prone to menstrual disorders and endometrial cancer. Because of these factors fat people average shorter lives than normal people. In addition to these organic disorders are eating disorders, particularly the phenomena of gorging, which the American Psychiatric Association labels a "feeding disturbance" under the category of "Special Symptoms."[1] Overweight people are also more prone to a variety of accidents. "For example, compared to the population as a whole, 31 percent more overweight men and 20 percent more overweight women die in automobile accidents."[2]

The "appropriate" weight for adults according to body build has been established by life insurance companies based on actuarial statistics of longevity and blood pressure by type of body build. These tables try to take into account wide human variations in physique. Following the work of Dr. William H. Sheldon, human physiques are classified into three categories: ectomorphs, mesomorphs, and endomorphs. Ectomorphs are characterized by an elongated skeleton, long slender limbs, hands, feet, toes and fingers. These small-framed people are often interpreted as skinny. Mesomorphs are the average-frame people with well-proportioned bodies and tending toward muscular physiques. Endomorphs are the opposite of the ectomorphs. They have large frames even though their bones often seem small in comparison to their rotund body shape. Endomorphs tend toward short limbs, hippiness, rounded shapes and barrel chests. These three body types are covered in Table 7.1, originally developed by the Metropolitan Life Insurance Company.[2] Underweight people are said to be 10 - 20 pounds under the "desirable" weight. It is estimated only two to three percent of the population is underweight.[4]

Table 7.1

Desirable weight in pounds for men and women age
25 and over by height and frame type in indoor clothing.

Height in shoes	Small Frame	Medium Frame	Large Frame
Men (1-inch heels)			
5'2"	112-120	118-129	126-141
3"	115-123	121-133	129-144
4"	118-126	124-136	132-148
5"	121-129	127-139	135-152
6"	124-133	130-143	138-156
7"	128-137	134-147	142-161
8"	132-141	138-152	147-166
9"	136-145	142-156	151-170
10"	140-150	146-160	156-174
11"	144-154	150-165	159-179
6'0"	148-158	154-170	164-184
1"	152-162	158-176	168-189
2"	156-167	162-180	173-194
3"	160-171	167-185	178-199
4"	164-175	172-190	182-204
Women (2-inch heels)			
4'10"	92-98	96-107	104-119
11"	94-101	98-110	106-122
5' 0"	96-104	101-113	109-125
1"	99-107	104-116	112-128
2"	102-110	107-119	115-131
3"	105-113	110-122	118-134
4"	108-116	113-126	121-138
5"	111-114	116-130	125-142
6"	114-123	120-135	129-146
7"	118-127	124-139	133-150
8"	122-131	128-143	137-154
9"	126-135	132-147	141-158
10"	130-140	136-151	145-167
11"	134-144	140-155	149-168
6' 0"	138-148	144-159	153-173

Source: Developed by the Metropolitan Life Insurance
Company and found in W. W.Bauer (ed.), Today's
Health Guide, Chicago: American Medical
Association, 1965, p. 143.

There seems to be no exact definition of overweight. But one authority says, "an individual is considered to be overweight if he is 10 percent about his ideal weight and obese if he is 20 percent or more above his ideal weight."[5]

Fatness is much more prevalent than being under-weight. Only about two to three percent of the population is underweight. Precise data on the number of people overweight is lacking. Martha Demmick estimates that 25-35% of the U.S. adult population is at least 10% overweight and that 15-20% of all teenagers are overweight. One study found that among those 20-74 years of age, 14% of the males and 24% of the females were 20% or more overweight--that is obese. Of those over forty years of age, 30% of the men and 40% of the women are estimated to be overweight. Other authorities often come up with similar estimates--that around 35% of the adult population is overweight and that the percent is often higher as people get older. Older people are somewhat prone to being overweight because they often consume as much food or richer food as when they were younger but tend to use up less energy because their metabolism slows down and they exercise less.[6]

The Causes of Obesity

Obesity has been studied by many disciplines and yet many aspects of it are not well understood. There are two levels of explanation of obesity. The Level One explanation is primarily a description of energy intake and output in the body. The Level Two explanation attempts to identify the kinds of factors which contribute to obesity and the role of each. Level Two explanations are more complex because they look at a variety of factors and their interplay in human experiences.

The Level One explanation is that obesity occurs when people consume more food than they expend in energy. The extra energy they take in is stored in fatty tissue as a surplus over what they are utilizing. One pound of fat tissue is equivalent to 3,500 calories. If a person consumes 500 more calories a day than he is using, he will gain a pound a week; if he consumes 500 less calories a day than what he is dissipating in energy output he will loose one pound a week. However, food input cannot simply be weighed to determine its caloric content. Fat contains 9 calories per gram in comparison to about 4 calories per gram for proteins and carbohydrates. Thus, obesity is not simply a product of eating a lot. It is also influenced by what is eaten in terms of caloric content and how much is used up in the round of daily activities of a particular person.[7] Most fad diets are built on rather simplistic ideas of eating less, or eating some foods and not others in order to lose weight.

Level Two explanations involve looking at a host of factors like genetic influences, metabolic influences, central nervous system disorders, environmental factors, psychological and sociological factors. However to separate out which factors are at work and their relative importance in any given case is very difficult and beyond science at this point. For example, one of the stereotypes is that fat people have fat children. This tends to be true even though there are many exceptions. In a study of Boston area families, Mayer reports that only 7% of the children of nonoverweight parents were fat but that this jumped to 40% if one of the parents was overweight and 80% if both parents were heavy. While this could be attributed to either social factors or hereditary factors, he argues that it is hereditary because adopted children of overweight persons are much less likely to become overweight. He reports similar findings from a large scale study in London where natural children inherited both body type and tendencies to obesity from parents.[8] Other studies however indicate that a range of cultural and childrearing habits with regard to eating tend to precipitate fatness running in families. If parents eat quickly before satiation signals reach the brain, they may not only indulge in overeating themselves but provide a model of fast and extensive eating for their children. If parents use food, especially high calorie sweets, as a reward system for their children, they may be initiating a pattern of self-reward with food that could become a lifetime pattern. If the parents come from an ethnic group that has a pattern of high caloric intake this too is a social pattern.[9]

If fat people tend to have fat children do fat babies tend to grow up to be fat adults? The answer is yes. One group of researchers did a retrospective study of 145 subjects who were divided into three groups by their birthweights. The light babies were those below the 25th percentile of all of them, the average babies between the 25th and 75th percentile and the heavy

babies those weighing at the 90th percentile or above.
By the time these babies, born between 1945 and 1955,
had reached the age bracket of 20 to 30, only 14% of
the light and average babies were overweight compared
to 36% of those who were classified as heavy babies.
The weight of their parents had a moderate correlation
with the weight of these young adults. At the same time
it is worth noting that a majority of the heavy babies
did not become obese adults.[10] Thus, while heredity may
play some role in obesity, how much of a role it plays
or the mechanisms by which it works are not well understood. Normal people have around 30 to 40 million fat
cells which are distributed between the skin and muscles
but tend to gather around the abdomen, heart, kidneys
and other vital organs. People who are obese from
childhood usually develop around 80 - 120 million of
these cells. Once these fat cells develop there appears to be little chance for eliminating them. But
people who become obese in adulthood have about the
same number of fat cells as normal weight people but
these fat cells are larger. Why this is the case is
not understood.[11]

Certainly one source of influence in the development of fatness is metabolism. In a small percentage
of the cases of obesity there are metabolic disturbances
such as malfunctioning thyroid glands that can cause
obesity as well as a series of other endocrine and central nervous system disorders which cause it. Some
people appear to have metabolic differences in how they
process, store and use calorie energy. Some thin
people eat large quantities of food and gain no weight
while some overweight people eat less but cannot shed
their fat. Why this is the case is not fully understood.[12]

Cultural and social influences appear to have a
noticeable relationship to obesity. But the meaning
and intepretation of this data is not totally clear.
For example there is a relationship between socioeconomic status and obesity. A study of samples of
people in both London and New York revealed that lower
class people of both sexes were more likely to be obese.
In London "72 percent of the lower class women were
overweight, 49% of the middle-class and only 34% of the
upper-class... The same pattern was observed in New
York, where it was even stronger; there obesity was six
times more prevalent among lower-class women than among
upper-class women."[13] The same pattern, but less pro-

nounced occurred among men. While social class may influence eating patterns, diet and weight control
attempts, it is also possible that weight has some influence on class determination inasmuch as obese people
are often discriminated against in the labor market.
In the United States as one moves up the socioeconomic
scale, black women get leaner but black men get fatter.[14]

Other cultural factors appear to be at work, but
exactly how they operate is unknown. For example,
Kolata reports that Americans of English, Scotch and
Irish descent tend to be thinner, but obesity increases
as you move eastward across Europe among American de-
scendants.[15] Anne Biller reports that people who came
from colder climates tend to be fatter. She reasons
that in climates with long winters and short summers the
fattest may have been the fittest to survive. It may
be that some ethnic or racial groups have a propensity
to fatness because in the evolutionary process those
who survived had more such genes.[16]

Family and cultural life styles of activity play
an important role in the control of obesity. In our
industrial civilization the work week has not only become shorter but much of the work less demanding.
Sedentary activities predominate in an affluent society
where the caloric intake is high and food and drink
often accompany social gatherings. Unless people are
into heavy calorie-consuming physical exercise routines
like jogging and swimming, it is easy to consume more
calories than one spends.

There is extensive and often contradictory literature on the psychological roots of overeating and
obesity. Some investigators report that the personality
traits and self identity (other than body image) of fat
people reflect the diversity that occur among the nonoverweight. Others contend there are substantial
differences between the personality characteristics of
fat, thin and normal people. Part of the problem here
is that until recently all overweight people were
grouped together as if they were all alike. More
recently, however, attempts have been made to see if
there are personality differences bewteen the clinically
obese (around 10% overweight), excessively obese (around
20% overweight), and the grossly obese (around double
the normal weight of a person of a given height and
stature). Recent attempts have also been made to determine personality differences among different types

of overeaters such as food addicts, compulsive overeaters, sporadic overeaters, phasic cyclical overeaters,
and the like. Such finer distinctions may be very important in treating obese people since overall the rate
of obese people returning to a normal weight and staying
there is quite low. Estimates of successful slimming,
defined as losing weight and staying at that weight,
usually range around five to ten percent. Many fat
people can lose some weight for a while, but often return to their original obesity.

For example, a formerly fat psychiatrist, Theodore
Rubin, contends there are three types of overeaters:
(1) those addicted to overeating; (2) those addicted
to fatness; and (3) those addicted to both overeating
and fatness. The first group is the easiest and most
successfully treated with decreasing success with the
next two groups. Those addicted to overeating are
characterized most by big appetites in all areas of
life that is expressed with exuberance, abandon, zest
and sensuality. They have strong feelings and emotions
and are sensitive people who enjoy showing their ex-
pressiveness in a variety of ways. Those addicted to
fatness have more emotional problems that they often
unconsciously mask by eating too much. They may eat
because of the anxiety they would suffer in their social
life if they became thin. They may be afraid of thinness because it represents a lack of substance and power
they equate with obesity. These food addicts often have
a repressed anger, difficulty in asserting themselves,
immature social reactions and poor self-esteem. But to
lose weight would produce anxieties of dealing with a
new image, new social relationships and not having a
rationalization of why they are not more successful.
The third group, those addicted to both overeating and
fatness, are the hardest to change because they not only
have bad and excessive eating habits but their obesity
satisfies a number of unresolved emotional conflicts.
All three groups are caught in what Rubin calls a
"double bind." They take on cultural attitudes of
hating fatness and therefore they hate themselves.
Hating themselves as "fatslobs" leads to even more
overeating, weight gain and more self-hate. Because so
much of their focus is on their body image, it is difficult to sustain a positive image of themselves while
thinning because they hate themselves. It is difficult
to escape from this destructive body image according to
Rubin.[17]

A number of studies have been done which relate the physiology of hunger signals to the psychology of eating. One significant difference stands out: normal weight people usually only eat when they experience intense hunger signals while overweight people have many fewer such signals and tend to respond to external cues for inducing them to eat. Obese people are more likely to eat when there are external cues such as the presence of food, TV commercials showing good food, when they are offered second or third helpings, when the food tastes or smells good, and when the amount of food available is very plentiful and would go to waste if not eaten. Obese people also get fewer internal satiety cues which signal them to stop eating when they are full. Erika Wick believes that there are five patterns of overeating with each underlain by a particular psychic dynamic: (1) sporadic overeaters only eat more occasionally as a coping mechanism to deal with transitory stressful situations; (2) impulsive binge-eaters use periodic engorgement as an escape mechanism from strong emotions and internal conflicts when they do erupt; (3) continuous overeaters tend to be reared in fat families where food is a sign of love and a culturally learned habit; (4) repetitive, compulsive overeaters have developed a personal food addiction syndrome that acts as a protective mechanism against emotional conflicts and feelings of depression, rejection, anger, despair and helplessness; and (5) the uncontrolled indulgent eater is a primal addict whose central pleasure is in eating the food he craves and who escapes from problems in his life by excessive indulgence. People can shift from one category to another. However, with the progression through these stages they show an increasing propensity to feeding disturbances that are deeply embedded in their personalities.[18]

Stereotypes About Obese People

Numerous stereotypes exist about fat people and most of them are bad. No attempt is made here to catalogue all of them. Rather the purpose is to illustrate that prejudices do exist which affect deeply the self-images of fat people in our society and the discriminatory behavior people exhibit toward them.

Several interesting studies have been done to show that the dislike of fatness begins early and that these attitudes are often learned from parents. In 1979,

Dr. Susan Wooley, a psychologist, told a convention of the National Association to Aid Fat Americans,

Children appear to develop attitudes about fat at a very early age, which probably persist through life. Some previous studies have shown that chubby children are regarded by their peers as ugly, stupid, mean, sloppy, lazy, dishonest, and frequently teased. Children indicate a desire to keep a greater personal distance from overweight than from average or thin children. Samples of adults including groups of health professionals, as well as children, rate obese children as less likeable than children with a variety of handicaps, disfigurements, and deformities.

We were interested in how early such attitudes develop and did a study in our lab... One of the measures was a preference test to see whether 2-to-5year olds preferred a thin or a fat rag doll; 53 out of 56 children as young as two years of age picked the thin doll...

We also studied ratings of fat and thin children and obtained similar results. We had wanted to use photographs, and the most interesting feature of this study is what became of that plan. In order to get the photographs, we went to shopping centers, amusement parks, places where there were many children. We had a brief consent form, saying that we needed photographs of children for a study and asked every parent who passed by to let us photograph their children. No parent of a thin child ever refused consent. No parent of a fat child ever gave consent. Sometimes parents permitted their thin child to be photographed, while hiding their fat child behind them. We ended up with hundreds and hundreds of photographs of children, and not one of them was fat.

Since many food junkies are addicted, but to a normally accepted household good, their addiction is not always seen as serious as the alcoholic's or drug addict's. But because they are addicted to daily routines of eating this makes treatment quite difficult.

211

They have lost control of a portion of their life in the minds of many. Self-control of one's feelings and expression and even more of one's behavior is viewed as important in a rational bureaucratic society. As one psychiatrist comments,

> The thin person, on a conscious level, and particularly on an unconscious one, is seen as possessing self-control and a predisposition to being responsible and reliable, while the fat person is seen as having no control in eating, and therefore as potentially chaotic and ir-responsible in all areas of life. When fat people turn out otherwise, they are regarded as exceptions and are sometimes viewed with surprise and even bewilderment. ("But he's so fat, how can he be so responsible?") If openness and a ready demonstration of feeling is coupled in a particular person with fatness— and that person then reveals obvious ability and evidence of responsibility, much confusion ensues in people who are predisposed to stereotyped thinking.[19]

Probably at no point in their lives are people more aware of the meaning of excess weight than when they are adolescents and teenagers. Many young people, especially women, feel that their identity as persons is tied to their bodies. If the young woman wants dates and wants to be attractive she needs to have a good figure. While curves are important they must not be excessive or she will be denied the good things in life like love and success. Most men and women treat over-weight women as asexual creatures. (Some fat women do use their obesity as an escape mechanism from husbands they want to avoid or to cover other feelings of in-feriority. And while a few thin or normal men are attracted to obese women, most see them as potential "friends" only.) They believe they don't care about sex or themselves or they "wouldn't let themselves go." Normal women often treat obese women as confidantes about their own romantic escapades because they won't offer them any competition.

While the severely obese may have a lower sex drive or interest in sex and greater difficulties in carrying out sexual intercourse, Marvin Grosswirth contends that most overweight people have the same interest in sex that people of normal weight do. Furthermore, he con-

212

tends that the two contradictory stereotypes of fat people—that they are good lovers and that they are poor lovers—do not stand up to the facts. For him as a fat person, the mechanics of sex are little different than for people of average weight.[20]

In the last half century we have come to idolize thinness, youth, agility and beauty. Thousands of advertisements advise us to slim down so we can enjoy life. Television commercials, movies, musical themes and weight watchers' clubs all equate the good life with youthfulness and thinness. The message is made clear to all: if you are fat, you are also ugly and old looking and too big to move with the speed of youth. You cannot "make out" in sports or in education or in work or in love if you are overweight. The result is often devastating on those who can't remain slim. One woman, whose weight has yo-yoed over the years, recalls how she felt in college when she was overweight:

> I was furious with myself then, and with anyone who came near me. I felt that fatness was ignoble, and that it made me unfit for love; that if I had no discipline for something as mechanical as a diet, I could never have it for any worthier enterprise of the will. As long as I was fat, I did not feel entitled to a "real" life.[21]

An interesting review of the literature on attitudes toward fatness was done by William DeJong. For example, he reports that when children were shown full-body silhouettes of thin ectomorphs, muscular mesomorphs and fat endomorphs, the fat endomorphs were least likely to be chosen as "best friend" or as having lots of friends. When asked to describe the endomorphs, the typical adjectives used were "lazy," "cheats," "forgets," "sloppy," "dirty," "ugly," "argues," and "stupid." DeJong then carried out several experiments to determine attitudes toward obesity and to see if these attitudes were linked to popular beliefs about obesity being caused by character defects like a lack of responsibility and a lack of will power rather than the complex etiology that is actually responsible for obesity. A sample of California children were shown four photographs: (1) an obese girl whose fatness was explained by a thyroid condition, (2) an obese girl with no thyroid problem, (3) a pale normal-weight girl whose paleness was attributed to a thyroid con-

dition, and (4) a pale normal weight girl whose paleness was attributed to a poor photograph. The obese
girl with no thyroid problem was most likely to be seen
as more self-indulgent and lazy on rating scales used
and was also the least liked. The normal-weight persons, in contrast, were seen to be both more attractive
and happier. As a result of his experiments, DeJong
concluded

> the perception of responsibility does play
> a large role in reactions to the physical
> stigma of obesity. It is not the mere fact
> that obese people are physically deviant
> which causes them to be derogated, but that
> they are assumed to be responsible for their
> deviant status. In this respect the obese
> have much more in common with those who pos-
> sess a characterlogical stigma than those who
> are physically handicapped or disfigured.[22]

Thus, while fat people are highly identifiable and
could be classified as a physical attribute minority,
they are best classified as a behavioral minority since
most people assume they have indulged in a voluntary behavior, overeating, which has caused their fatness.
Certainly their large size makes them a physical attribute minority; but the cause of this is attributed
to a character defect in most instances--being unable
to control the amount they eat.

Discrimination Against Fat People

Discrimination against fat people appears to be
both extensive and subtle. It occurs in noticeable ways
between fat and thin in everyday encounters as well as
in a variety of institutional encounters when fat people
are trying to gain entrance to a college, or get a job,
or rent an apartment, buy clothing or insurance, get
medical care, or go to a restaurant. At the same time
they provide a huge market for the thinning industry--
from health parlors to diet aids. This industry sells
the hope that thinning will transform "fatslobs" into
happy, sexy, successful people. But since so few permanently lose weight, they can count on the "repeat"
business of around seventy five million Americans. This
may be an undercount. Since so many Americans are fearful of becoming overweight, and few people think of
themselves as slim and trim, the market is very large.
Not many people are so thin they don't feel fat or think

214

they are fat.

In interpersonal encounters the obese are treated as many other minorities. Seen as inferior in will power, basically lethargic, sloppy and uncaring about themselves, they are talked about, joked about, shunned and dismissed as people who are not fully in control of their lives. Marvin Grosswirth believes that no other group is as extensively subjected to "good sportism" as are fat people. They are subjected to a variety of humiliations and then expected to go along with this in the name of being "a good sport." He says that good-sportism takes three forms: the nickname, the joke, and "the discussion." Overweight people are often given derogatory nicknames — fatso, buddha, beast, chubby, tiny, porky, skinny, jumbo, blimp — and expected to accept them in fun as if they did not hurt. In the same way they are expected to endure cruel jokes about "fatslobs" which impugn their willpower, their intelligence and their motives. Lastly they are expected to have their privacy invaded by those who want to "discuss" their "weight problem." They are quietly taken aside as if they were errant children who had done some naughty thing. People want to impugn the obese person's motives, eating patterns, family experiences, appearance, appetite, dieting attempts, and medications as if they have supervisory powers over their lives. Grosswirth's view is that, unfortunately, many fat people go along with these humiliations. They become a self-derogatory "fattie" who "makes fun of himself, he puts himself into situations which make him look ridiculous, he becomes the life of the party, the jolly fat boy, the guy who is always good for a laugh, as a prank, or a gag - that most miserable of self-hating people, the good sport."[23]

The differential treatment of the overweight occurs throughout the life cycle. It occurs on the playground where fat kids are frequently teased and occurs in the elementary and secondary classrooms where teachers often advise medical help for those with a weight problem. We might assume that entrance into a college would be determined by measures of scholastic aptitude and ability, not girth. But according to one study carried out by a noted nutritionist, there was marked discrimination by college interviewers against overweight adolescents, especially females. This differential discrimination against fat females trying to get into Ivy League schools was thought to rest on the general but often unconscious prejudice that exists against obese women.[24]

In 1975 Oral Roberts University developed a mandatory weight reduction program for its students as part of its program to develop the mind, body and spirit of its students. Each year the students undergo an annual body fat exam. A female having more than 35% body fat or a male with more than 25% is considered obese. If they are found obese, students must sign a contract pledging to lose a pound or two a week. If they fail to reach that goal they face probation and eventual suspension. In the first two years of the program, four students were suspended. One student with a high grade point average was suspended because she was too fat. She joined the Oklahoma's Coalition of Citizens with Disabilities to request HEW to review the school's policy to determine if it was discriminatory.[25]

The obese face employment handicaps too. Llewellyn Louderback in Fat Power surveys dozens of reports and case studies of employment discrimination against fat people in industry and the professions in the 1960's. A Maryland legislator, Raymond Dypski, who reduced his weight from 370 pounds to 260 on his five foot - eight inch frame in 1974, pushed a study of discrimination against fat people in his state to determine if other fat people had the same kind of problems he did. The director of the study, David Tucker, reported "Discrimination exists in terms of employment where the overweight are significantly less employed and less well paid." Tucker reported that the obese "also are put into public contact positions less frequently. In Maryland, we found that when we surveyed employment agencies, every one agreed that discrimination exists" against fat people. He cited one example of a female secretary, 50 pounds overweight, who was told she was qualified for the job she applied for over the telephone. However, when she went for a job interview, the excuse the personnel director gave her for not hiring her convinced her she was turned down because of her weight.[26]

Marvin Grosswirth reviews a number of cases of job discrimination agains the obese—a California physical education teacher who was dismissed because at 220 pounds she was considered too heavy to do her job, the dismissal of eight Long Island teachers, six of them fat, supposedly due to budgetary cuts, the inability of a young man in New York City to obtain a civil service post, despite his high score, because he was obese.[27]

Daphne Roe reported to the 77th annual meeting of the Society for the Study of Social Problems her findings on 469 upstate New York women who were on Aid to Families with Dependent Children. She found that unemployment was directly associated with obesity—and that it increased as women became more obese.

One overweight writer tells of being turned down for jobs by many companies. He explains his view after visiting many employment agencies and firms while doing research on job discrimination against the fat:

> When a fat person is denied employment, he is rarely told the true reason for that denial. If the prospective employer makes any reference to weight at all, it is always in conjunction with the requirements ostensibly laid down by the Insurance Company (the term always seems to have capital letters when used in this context) which covers the firm's employees.[28]

He visited a major insurance company and found that they had no such rule for their own employees nor, by implication, did they have it for other firms which insured with them. Grosswirth illustrates this with his own jobhunting endeavor as an overweight writer:

> The first employment agency interview I encountered told me that she represented only the largest publishing companies, all of which had major medical coverage for their employees. Inasmuch as the most cusory observation revealed my inability to pass the physical, there was no point in her trying to place me. When I informed her that I had worked for a publisher that offered similar coverage and that there had been no problem, she refused to believe me, although I offered to give her the firm's name so that she could check herself. When I suggested that I already had sufficient health and life insurance and was therefore willing to forego the company plan, she replied that this was "impractical." She was one of the most unpleasant but honest interviewers I have ever encountered.[29]

We might assume that physicians are mainly concerned with the medical aspects of obesity—the threats to health and longevity that it presents—rather than the aesthetic aspects of it. But Dr. Theodore Rubin

argues that doctors are just as prejudiced against fat
people as are other members of our society obsessed
with thinness. Even "doctors who are fat themselves
are full of self-hate and, without conscious awareness,
project much of their own feelings to their fat patients
whom they evaluate and treat with considerable prejudice—even outright dislike and contempt."[30] Rubin
goes on to point out that some doctors victimize patients by running "weight - reduction mills" and
inflicting on "innocent victims all kinds of extreme,
fad, and inappropriate diets" some of which are useless
and some hazardous. Most of the multi - million dollar
weight reduction business run by people inside or outside the medical establishment is economically motivated
and often lacks a concern for their clients' welfare.[31]
Rubin elaborates on the forms that physicians' prejudice
takes:

> My main concern in this connection is
> the legitimate, and even well-meaning quali-
> fied doctor. Many of them are prejudiced
> against fat people... It takes various forms;
> some, in the process of exaggerating the
> danger of fatness, become so obsessed with
> fat that they neglect and even overlook
> other important medical problems. Others,
> viewing a fat person, cannot see beyond
> the fatness... The fat patient is lumped
> together with a general population of other
> fat people in the doctor's mind and prac-
> tice and, in effect, loses his medical
> individuality and identity. Some doctors,
> even while viewing fat patients with dis-
> taste and loss of medical interest, simply
> become resigned to the condition and abandon
> any effort to encourage weight reduction.
> Others become overzealous, even sadistic
> and vindictive, producing weight-obsessed
> patients who become guilt-ridden, masochistic
> and obsessed with their condition. Depression
> and anxiety are not unusual in these victimized
> patients, and complications due to such de-
> pression and anxiety are often misinterpreted
> as being provoked by fatness. This produces
> more guilt and anxiety, completing a disastrous
> vicious cycle. In many cases doctors and their
> fat patients form sado-masochistic relationships
> that go on for years without conscious aware-
> ness on either side of the role each one is

218

playing in this destructive drama.[32]

While obesity is sometimes seen as a disease
(and diseases are usually assumed not to be motivated)
by physicians, very often it is looked upon as an addiction for which the patient is responsible. Like
alcoholics, the patient, the victim if you will, is
blamed for his condition even though his fatness may
be due to hereditary factors, endocrine disturbances,
brain lesions or childhood obesity which is quite difficult to reverse. Despite this, physicians and
dieticians "speak of their puffy patients in almost the
terms used by proponents of lily-white supremacy for
allegedly inferior ethnic minorities... It makes possible projection on the patient of full responsibility
for the failure of the weight reduction program being
advocated."[33]

The attitudes of health care workers toward fat
patients is revealing. In one survey it was found that
32% of the medical professionals working with fat people
believed they "do not have will power," while 74% believed obese patients had "family problems" and 87%
viewed them as "self indulgent." Eighty eight percent
of the medical professionals believed "eating as compensation" was typical of obese patients, while 70%
thought overweight persons had emotional problems.[34]
Thus, nonconformity in the form of excessive weight is
generally interpreted by health professionals as stemming from emotional disorders. Physical deviance is
medicalized by attributing it to personality flaws. As
a result, a behavioral minority is created by attributing their "weight problem" to character defects rather
than to the pejorative attitudes of normal weight
people.

While the weight reduction industry makes millions
of dollars off the obese, clothing manufacturers have
generally not responded well to the special needs of the
overweight. Large sizes in shoes, coats, pants,
dresses, suits and underwear are hard to find, often
unfashionable, available mainly in somber colors for
"mature" people, and located in the "back" sections of
department stores. In big people's stores and cata-
logues the mannequins remain slim. Salesclerks often
treat overweight people not as good customers but people who will tarnish the image of the store if they are
seen. Clerks frequently show a disinterest in them as
customers or take them to the "back room" to see if

219

they have "anything in their size" or show them old
models out of fashion. Grosswirth believes the origins
of these practices may be economic:

> Whatever its origins, there is no doubt
> that slimness was fashionable, perhaps only
> faddish, in the post World War I era. En-
> couraged by the merchants of America, the fad
> gained ground, and burst into full bloom with
> the advent of the boyish Flapper looks of the
> Roaring 20's. The economic rationale was
> obvious: it did not require a mathematical
> genius to discover that a bolt of fabric
> yields more dresses in size 12 than it does
> in size 18 or 20.[35]

The way that the medicalization of thinness can
end up in discrimination can be seen in the story of
Barbara and Gordon Ray who had been married for seven
years as of 1979. They wanted children. After medical
testing revealed Gordon had a low sperm count, they decided to adopt a child, even an older child if necessary.
However, when they went to their Wisconsin district
adoption agency, they were told they would be unable to
adopt children unless they lost weight. Both are big
boned. At 5'7" and 210 pounds Barbara was told she was
40 lbs. overweight; Ray was 25 lbs. overweight at 6'2"
and 220 lbs. They both were working, owned their own
home and had modest savings. They were hurt and
angered when the social worker at the adoption agency
said that they were too overweight for adoption and
that their overweight problem might present health problems in the course of rearing a child. Upon checking
with their State Senator, they found their district
adoption agency was the only one in the state to use
insurance guidelines on height and weight to determine
the future health of prospective parents. They went
public with their story through Wisconsin newspapers
that pointed out that nearly one-half of the parents in
this country were overweight and would be ineligible to
adopt children and would be seen as risky parents. The
state senate rescinded the rule on weight and said
weight guidelines were to be used in the future only if
an M.D. testified that prospective parents' fatness
would shorten their life as parents.[36]

Much of America's architecture, especially seats,
is made for the nonhandicapped, nonobese majority. Yet
the obese minority may be growing in numbers even as the

American population as a whole is getting bigger. In Boston in 1960, over 25% of the young men were over 6 feet tall compared to 4% in 1900. From 1940 to 1960 the average weight of adult American males went up ten pounds, in the next decade it went up six more pounds. Yet very big people have more trouble getting into and out of cars, through turnstiles, and through some bus doors. Desks with narrow leg entrances present problems as do regular sleeping bags, springy mattresses and seats everywhere: theaters, airplanes, classrooms, ballparks, buses, restaurant booths, bar stools. In airplanes the obese often have to get seat belt extenders to be able to buckle up.[37]

The thinning industry is estimated to be a 15 billion dollar a year enterprise that helps to create a national obsession over thinness. In The Overweight Society Peter Wyden gives detailed attention to the many commercial ventures in girth control. At the same time these profit-making ventures to help people lose weight are matched by other commercial enterprises who want to sell more food and capture a larger portion of the market. These two industries are working at cross purposes. Because many people do not know about the technicalities of vitamins, proteins, carbohydrates, fats, calories or the role of exercise and diet in weight control and health, they are prone to easy manipulation by the weight control industry. The American population has been subjected to diet plans that may be harmful, fraudulent weight control gimmicks and aids, and misinformation. Wyden argues that "The case for diet and exercise, however, remains riddled with charlatanism, commercialism, racketeering, professional jealousies and indifference."[38]

Recently the state of Maryland has taken steps to control the weight reducing aid industry. A state-sponsored investigation of this industry argued that it should be required to advertise its success rate, its failure rate, its attrition rate and its safety. Since the average American dieter goes on 2.3 diets a year, it is quite apparent the dieting plans have a low success rate. Raymond Dypski, the state Senator, who was sponsoring legislation to control the weight-control industry, said, "I want to try to get these diet companies and these expert people who tell you how to lose weight and don't have documented proof. They're like snake - oil salesmen in the old West."[39]

Lower Status

Overweight people as a rule exhibit a lower status, less income, more unemployment, fewer promotions and raises than other people. And as their degree of obesity increases so also does their stigmatized identity and lessened opportunities. Of course there are exceptions for those with unusual talent. Kate Smith, Winston Churchhill, Orson Wells became successful as have many others who were overweight. But like other minorities, the barriers to success which they face are often higher than for other groups. The lower economic position of people 10% or more overweight is revealed in one telling statistic: 40% of the men in the $10,000 to $20,000 annual income bracket are overweight compared to only 9% of the men in the $25,000 to $40,000 annual income range.[40]

Reactions to Stigmatized Identities

The reactions of the obese to their stigmatized identities fall into two major categories. Probably a majority of the obese accept the views of the dominant group that not only are overweight bodies ugly and less healthy but they have character flaws in being unable to control their love of food and wild eating binges. Even those who don't fully accept the stereotypes about them cannot but help know they exist and tend to have negative images of their body if not their character. While some of these people live in quiet desperation, many join a variety of weight control groups like TOPS (Take Off Pounds Sensibly) or Overeaters Anonymous or Weight Watchers. They want to lose weight, join the dominant group, be integrated into the weight-controlled stratum of society that is normatively approved as healthy, slim and beautiful.

A smaller group do not want to change their weight. To them fat is beautiful. They want to change society by ridding it of its deprecation of fat people and eliminating discrimination against them. They are more likely to join the National Association to Aid Fat Americans to protest the derogatory stereotypes to which they are subjected and to fight institutional policies which discriminate against them. This group undoubtedly contains some defectors from those who have repeatedly tried to lose weight but always unsuccessfully in the long run.

The self image of many if not most of the overweight comes from the larger society. Fat people often
look down on themselves because they lack the body
image of the "beautiful" people. The problem is more
acute for women because more women are overweight and
a double (sexist) standard is applied to women as sex
objects in our society. Women more than men seem to
be overweight because of differences in hormones and
body construction and chemistries and because of sex
differentials in cooking and food-shopping and simple
exposure to the presence of food. Many fat people
come to hate themselves because of their conspicuous
size, the limitations this imposes when severely obese,
and their seemingly uncontrollable eating binges. Like
many other addicts, they often end up lying to themselves and others about the fact or the motivations for
their midnight forays in the refrigerator. While often
internally miserable, fat people often try to compensate
for their obesity by developing above-average job
skills, by purchasing extensive wardrobes, by engaging
in elaborate grooming rituals to undercut the stereotype of being sloppy, or by cultivating a seemingly
happy forceful personality to mask their insecurities.
Others however withdraw into seclusion where they can
avoid stigmatizing looks and verbal barbs from others.
Fat people often become depressed but from two different
sources. They become depressed because they are seen
by society as ignorant, weak-willed, slobs. But when
they go on a diet they often become depressed because
one of their major sources of comfort and pleasure has
been taken away from them. In addition they feel that
the substantiality of their person is being reduced
away. And the very change in their pattern of living
and eating may be highly stressful if they are unable
to adjust to these central changes in their life style.[41]

William J. Fabrey knows well how people feel about
fatness. He comments, "Not only is a fat and beautiful
woman like my wife supposed to be embarrassed in public
places, especially when wearing a bathsuit; a slim man
like me is supposed to be mortified to be seen in public
places escorting a fat woman."[42] Grosswirth points out
that public attitudes help to create the vicious cycle
of self-hatred that many obese people experience:

"I'm fat and ugly. Everybody says so.
Why should I bother trying to be good looking,
when my fatness, by itself, is ugliness? The
hell with it. I'm just a fat slob. Why should

223

I be anything else? Why bother? I'll dress
in any old thing, stop fussing about personal
care. Fat is fat. Fat is sloppy. That's
me. A fat slob."[43]

In his hilarious account of his own battle with
dieting—of losing many pounds by a great mental concentration to be followed by gorging and weight gain,
Herbert Greene in the Diary of a Food Addict, deli-
neates the torture that many overweight people go
through. One anonymous fat man he talked to said, "I
call nighttime radio talk shows... The only time you
feel equal is when nobody can see you." Before this
the same fat person said,

"But it is the present, the todays,
the everydays, that are the torment of the
fat person. He thinks he's worse than other
people because his looks are distorted. A
person can hide almost anything he's deeply
ashamed of unless he's fat. There he is,
naked: convicted of greed, indulgence,
weakness, sloth. A self-made caricature.
He waddles when he might be walking. He
gasps when he could be breathing. He
cringes wondering what others think about
his sex life. He endures the humiliation
of euphemism such as 'portly' or 'ample' or
'outsize' when shopping for clothes and never
permits himself a whim for a style or a witty
design. He can't suddenly hop or skip or jump
for the sheer hell of it. And the ordinary
things such as a theater seat, an automobile
ride a place on a park bench, bending to
smell a rose, become extraordinary events
requiring lavish exhibitions of nonchalance.
The only peace he knows is loneliness. Yet
he needs someone, some human contact, He
finds it by dialing information and asking
for his own number again and again."[44]

Many fat people join dieting clubs, visit health
spas or secretly buy one of the hundreds of books available on dieting to try to pull themselves out of
overweight despair by their own efforts. Most are not
successful—at least permanently. Only about twenty to
thirty percent lose weight and less than half of these
can permanently stay thin. Most of the people who join
Overeaters Anonymous (OR), or Take Off Pounds Sensibly

(TOPS), or Weight Watchers (WW) or other similar groups
are women.

The dynamics of such groups operate much like that
of Alcoholics Anonymous. In fact, Esther Manx who
founded TOPS in 1945, got the idea for it by reading an
article on Alcoholics Anonymous while waiting to see
her doctor about the 210 pounds on her 5'2" frame in
1948. She recalled how effective the prenatal classes
had been in controlling her weight when she was pregnant a few years earlier with her third child. The
group sessions of these prenatal classes had provided
the competition and group support the women needed to
control their weight gain during pregnancy. For a
year Mrs. Manz met with these other women each
weighing over 200 pounds. They drank a lot of black
coffee and supported each other to reduce each week
before their weekly weigh-ins. Soon after the Milwaukee
Journal published a story that the four of them had lost
a total of 224 pounds in a year, 100 of it on one woman, the number of clubs grew rapidly. By 1963 there
were 2,481 chapters; by 1979 there were 12,399 chapters
in the U.S., Canada and other countries. This nonprofit
organization has five facets to its program. (1) It
requires that each member obtain diet regimens since no
one diet is applicable to all people. (2) Like
Alcoholics Anonymous its major emphasis is upon group
therapy, weekly programs with periodic weigh-ins dedicated to weight control, and mutual support among
members between meetings to aid in girth control. (3)
It emphasizes competition by giving periodic prizes and
recognition to women (and a few men organized into SIR
TOPS clubs) who have lost the most weight at chapter,
area, state and international levels. (4) It provides
reinforcing recognition of the biggest weight losers at
the various levels of organization. (5) It provides
funds for obesity research. Some of the groups have
weekly weigh-ins, paste cardboard piggies on those who
have gained weight and engage in a number of other similar group activities to maintain motivation to reduce
or control one's weight. For example, when a member
has reached her medically prescribed weight she is
graduated to TOPS "honor society" called KOPS (Keep Off
Pounds Sensibly) which emphasizes not backsliding into
TOPS. The organization's literature is adorned by
"Topsy," a thin, graciously curved nude who symbolizes
the transformation its members hope to achieve. In
1974 TOPS reported that its 347,584 members lost
2,238,341.47 pounds. This averages out to about 6.5

pounds per member. However, there appear to be a number of backsliders, some of whom drop out of the
organization. Yet, this method appears as effective as
many of the more costly commercial enterprises devoted
to helping people lose weight.[45]

While TOPS was the first self-help group oriented
to changing the minority to become like the majority,
others have followed. One that grew quickly and had
served two million people by 1970 was Weight Watchers.
Its founder was Jean Nidetch who in 1961 weighed 214
pounds but lost 72 pounds in a year following a diet
prescribed by the New York City Department of Health
Obesity Clinic. After going from a dress size over 20
to an "imperfect 12" she believed "talk" needed to be
added to the program so that people could gain en-
couragement for weight loss from honest people who had
lost weight themselves. Her Weight Watchers movement
grew from a basement self-help group into a major
commercial venture that has transformed the lives of
thousands of people following significant weight loss.
In its first eight years it came close to serving two
million members. It publishes diet books, magazines,
runs a summer camp for overweight girls and sells
scales for weighing food. It provides diet plans to
members who are advised to have them adjusted by their
individual physician. It emphasizes not skipping meals
but eating balanced meals with no exceptions made to the
prescribed dieting plan. It forbids the use of alcohol
or appetite suppressants. It encourages attendance at
its weekly meetings to hear the success stories of those
who have had their lives dramatically improved by substantial weight loss.[46]

Overeaters Anonymous is explicitly modeled on
Alcoholics Anonymous with no records kept and only the
first names of participants used. In Such a Pretty
Face: Being Fat in America, Marcia Millman looks at
this group's promise to transform obese females (largely
working class women) into svelte women if they abstain
from certain foods and come to believe that fatness and
compulsive overeating are personal failings that can be
altered. She also looks at a summer camp run for overweight teenagers which promises to turn chubby ducklings
into lissome swans. But by segregating these people
from mainstream temptations, she believes the camp may
do more harm than good. Their exclusion from normal
social life further reinforces their deviance. Because they are sent there by parents, dieting is often

interpreted as punishment. But eating to oversize can be a form of rebellion by any age group. It sometimes is the way that youngsters can show their independence from their parents.[47]

Sometimes the very obese resort to more drastic medical procedures in order to lose weight. One of these involves wiring the jaws shut and living on an all-liquid, low-calorie diet for an extended period of time. Another technique is extended fasting. An even more drastic procedure is used by over 20,000 people annually. It involves intestinal bypass surgery where all but 30 inches of twenty-some feet of intestine is removed so that fewer calories are absorbed into the bloodstream. It is often reserved for those who weigh twice as much as they should. But about 5 out of 150 die from the operation and many others are bothered by complications from the surgery which appears to reduce the body's immunity system from attack from rashes and rheumatoid arthritis.[48] Such extreme measures are more often as detrimental to health as is fatness.

Not all groups of fat people agree with the stereotypes about either their unsightliness or their character defects. One of these groups is the National Association to Aid Fat People (NAAFA), organized in 1969 to combat derogatory stereotypes and discrimination against them. By 1980 its membership had grown slowly to 1500 people from 48 states. While it does try to help people lose weight if they want to, they argue that for a majority of people weight loss is nearly impossible and not a satisfactory solution to their problems. NAAFA's stated purposes are: (1) "To assist the large number of people regarded by the medical profession as 'persistently or incurably overweight' to adapt to themselves and increase their self-confidence;" (2) to promote tolerance toward fat people and fight discrimination; (3) to serve as a forum where problems of fat people can be openly discussed; (4) to disseminate knowledge about the many aspects of being fat; and (5) to sponsor research about the sociological, psychological and medical aspects of obesity.[49]

In addition to providing its membership with periodic newsletters, meetings, a dating service, book discount services, NAAFA uses civil rights tactics to promote equal opportunity for overweight people. It testified at the Maryland hearings to pass state legislation to investigate discrimination against fat people.

It testified before two state human relations commission meetings reviewing complaints of job discrimination. In the Pennsylvania case a 300 pound woman was not hired because she was overweight while in Rhode Island a 210 pound woman was fired because of obesity. NAAFA was not entirely happy that in both cases the basis for finding an employer at fault was discrimination against a person with a handicap--in this case obesity. But they did testify that this disability does not automatically mean a person cannot perform a job. In both cases job performance per se was not at the root of the problem but rather the assumption that overweight people are handicapped. NAAFA Executive Secretary Lisbeth Fisher testified at the Florissant, Missouri, city council meeting hearing in 1979 about that city's policy of firing and harassing city employees who were overweight according to standard height and weight charts. Because of the bad publicity this policy brought, it was rescinded by the Mayor who started it.

The basic philosophy of NAAFA is found in the lapel pins some of its members wear: "Fat Pride", "Fat can be Beautiful," "Fat People Unite--You Have Nothing to Lose!" "How DARE You Presume I'd Rather Be Thin," and "Fat Power." But its rather small membership suggests that most fat people are either assimilationist or isolationist in their self identities rather than taking pride in their size and being willing to fight what they see as uncalled-for pressures to be like others. NAAFA has no weight limits in any direction. Its president has noted that this sometimes results in reverse prejudice within the organization— that some people are not considered "fat enough" to experience the problems of very heavy people and therefore questions arise as to whether they should be members.

Obesity: A Medical Problem or Social Problem?

Obesity remains an enigma. While some of its causes are known in general, they are not always identifiable in a given person. This makes appropriate treatment primarily a guessing game. Some people appear to inherit either a tendency to fatness or genes which had survival power in man's evolution. A few people have endocrine disorders which lead to perpetual obesity. Metabolic differences vary considerably so that some people burn up calories at a higher rate than others. If people periodically diet, some evidence indicates that when they go off that diet that more of the weight that is gained is fat. Once people have more fat cells they appear to be there for life. Dr. Orland Wooley, a clinical psychologist at the Clinic for Eating Disorders at the University of Cincinnati College of Medicine, summarizes the findings which indict dieting for some types of people:

> 1. Non-dieters whose overeating is not preceded by a period of caloric restriction gain very little weight.
>
> 2. People re-feeding after weight loss gain weight very easily, and the regained weight is mostly fat.
>
> 3. Obese people gain weight much more easily than non-obese people.
>
> 4. Obese people almost always have a long history of dieting.[50]

Thus it appears that once people have engaged in periodic dieting they have a proneness to obesity because their bodies have developed adaptive mechanisms to conserve calories in the face of shortages. While some people are able to become thin by dieting and remain thin through caloric restriction and exercise, others are not. This suggests to Wooley that there are two solutions to obesity: medical and political. The <u>medical solution</u>, weight loss, works for some—but apparently only for a minority of obese people as the low success rates for dieting suggest. The <u>political solution</u> is for society to come to the recognition that not all people can be forced into a weight/height mold of conformity. The political solution requires greater tolerance for and a recognition of a wider range of weights as normal. Rather, fat people must take the initiative in altering the intolerable stereotypes held about them and discrimination denying them equal opportunity. Certainly a medical solution is often preferable for the individual, if it works, because it will extend life on the average. On the other hand, if it does not work permanently, it often produces high stress among periodic dieters who may find such stress more damaging than the prospect of a shorter life. Futhermore, dieting sometimes leads to anorexia nervosa (self-starvation), especially among teenagers, or binge vomiting which can be even more damaging to health than

than being overweight. Without a political solution
to the problem of obesity, the majority of the overweight who cannot lose weight for medical or psychological reasons will still be exposed to a second-class
citizenship. Most overweight people diet primarily for
the purpose of appearance than for medical reasons.
Perhaps the exception to this general rule is the very
obese—those double the normal weight who are the ones
most likely to suffer from diabetes, hypertension,
renal diseases, strokes and heart attack.

But how sound are the height and build desirable
body weights established by the Metropolitan Life
Insurance Company in its 1950s survey of 5 million insured Americans? They found that for people over age
forty that death rates increased proportionately with
obesity. Those 10% overweight had a 10% higher mortality rate, those 20% overweight had a 20% higher
mortality rate and so on. However, Dr. Reubin Andres
of the National Institute on Aging found in a review
of 17 studies done since that time that there is no
relationship between obesity and shortened life ex-
pectancy. He speculated that the obese are less prone
to suicide and schizophrenia and that the obese are
better prepared for the extreme weight loss that accompanies the treatment of some types of cancer. Other
doctors agree that "mild" obesity may not be harmful
if it is not accompanied by other disorders such as
diabetes, hypertension and high cholesteral levels.
Two recent surveys show that the lowest death rates
were among those 25 to 35 percent overweight and 15 to
20% overweight respectively. Very thin people have
somewhat shorter lives. The Society of Actuaries is
now revising the ideal weight charts that are now
nearly three decades old. They may be increased by as
much as 10 to 20% for each height and weight category.[51]
The standards and practices of medical science are
often made relative by new findings.

If the medical evidence on the standards for
obesity and its causes and effects appear enigmatic and
relative, the appearance factor may be even more relative. In societies where there was always a danger of
starvation, overweight persons, up to a point, were
seen as prosperous, of having "king" or "queen"
dimensions. The magnificently obese, like Daniel
Lambert of Leicester, England, in the nineteenth century,
are usually considered "freaks." Lambert weighed 739
pounds, his "waist" measured 112 inches, each thigh 37

inches and it took ten strong men to carry his coffin which measured four feet across. The Guiness Book of World Records lists ten men who surpassed 800 pounds. That fat was both beautiful and erotic in some European societies is seen in Venus, the fattening of women for marriage, and Federico Fellini's movies 8½ and Satyriion.[52] Fatness in our society is relative also. Men forty pounds overweight are considered "heavy" while women fifteen pounds overweight are often considered "fat." With a growing national obsession with thinness, the relativity of beauty has been pushed to a thin extreme. In the process a minority has been created whose status primarily has more to do with appearance than either health or performance in a variety of human activities. Who sets our aesthetic standards of beauty by weight? Are those standards relevant to human happiness and productivity?

One of our nation's leading nutritionists, Jean Mayer, makes an observation about our national obsession with obesity that is a fitting conclusion to this chapter. He writes,

> The old view of medicine, that patients
> are sick because of their sins, including
> their lack of self restraint—a view which
> has been generally abandoned in the Western
> world even in the matter of alcoholism—still
> dominates as far as obesity is concerned.
> Obesity, almost alone among all the pathologic
> conditions, remains a moral issue. Therapists
> and propagandists, conscious of their own
> lower weights and presumably purer natures,
> adopt either a sternly censorious or a
> pityingly superior attitude toward their chubby
> charges. Not infrequently, usually dispas-
> sionate physicians and dieticians speak of
> their puffy patients in almost the terms used
> by proponents of lily-white supremacy for
> allegedly inferior ethnic minorities.[53]

Appendix I Footnotes

Chapter 1 Sociological Perspectives on Deviant and Minority
Statuses: A Comparison

1. Reece McGee. Sociology: An Introduction, (2nd Ed.), New
York: Holt, Rhinehart and Winston, 1980, p. 459.

2. Arnold M. Rose and Caroline B. Rose (eds.). Minority Problems, (2nd Ed.), New York: Harper and Row, 1965.

3. Edward Sagarin, "From the Ethnic Minorities to the Other
Minorities," in Edward Sagarin (ed.). The Other Minorities,
Waltham: Ginn and Co., 1971, pp. 1-19.

4. Louis Wirth, "The Problem of Minority Groups," in Ralph
Linton (ed.). The Science of Man in the World Crisis. New
York: Columbia University Press, 1945, p. 347.

5. Charles Wagley and Marvin Harris. Minorities in the New
World: Six Case Studies. New York: Columbia University
Press, 1958, p. 10.

6. Anthony Gary Dworkin and Rosalind J. Dworkin. The Minority
Report. New York: Praeger Publishers, 1976, p. 23.

7. Simon Dinitz, Russel R. Dynes and Alfred C. Clark. Deviance:
Studies in Definition, Management and Treatment, (2nd Ed.),
New York: Oxford University Press, 1975.

8. Edward Sagarin and Fred Montanino (eds.). Deviants: Voluntary Actors in a Hostile World. New York: General Learning
Press, 1977.

9. Sagarin and Montanino, op. cit.

10. Sagarin and Montanino, op. cit.

11. Graham C. Kinloch. The Dynamics of Race Relations: A Sociological Analysis. New York: McGraw-Hill Book Co., 1974,
p. 50.

12. Ibid.

13. James Vander Zanden. American Minority Relations: The
Sociology of Racial and Ethnic Groups, (3rd Ed.). New York:
Ronald Press, 1972.

14. Gwynn Nettler. Explanations. New York: McGraw-Hill Book
Co., 1970.

15. Marshall B. Clinard and Robert F. Meier. Sociology of
Deviant Behavior, (5th Ed.), New York: Holt, Rinehart
and Winston, 1979.

233

16. Clinard and Meier, op. cit.; Norman Denzin. The Research Act. Chicago: Aldine, 1970.

17. Sigmund Freud. A General Introduction to Psychoanalysis. Garden City: Garden City Books, 1952; Clinard and Meier, op. cit.; Donald Webster Cory, "Homosexuality," in Albert Ellis and Albert Abarbanel (eds.). The Encyclopedia of Sexual Behavior. New York: Hawthorn Books, Inc., 1967, pp. 485-97.

18. Carol Tavris and Carole Offir. The Longest War: Sex Differences in Perspective. New York: Harcourt Brace Jovanvich, Inc., 1977.

19. Clinard and Meier, op. cit.

20. Peter Conrad and Joseph Schneider. Deviance and Medicalization: From Badness to Sickness. St. Louis: C. V. Mosby Co., 1980; Charles S. Suchar. Social Deviance: Perspectives and Prospects. New York: Rinehart and Winston, 1978.

21. Robert K. Merton. Social Theory and Social Structure. New York: Free Press, 1967; Charles H. McCaghy. Deviant Behavior: Crime, Conflict and Interest Groups. New York: Macmillan, 1976.

22. Richard A. Cloward, "Illegitimate Means, Anomie and Deviant Behavior," American Sociological Review, 24 (1959), 164-76; Richard A. Cloward and Lloyd E. Ohlin. Delinquency and Opportunity: A Theory of Delinquent Gangs. New York: Free Press, 1960.

23. Charles McCaghy, op. cit.; Clinard and Meier, op. cit.; Ronald L. Akers. Deviant Behavior: A Social Learning Approach, (2nd Ed.). Belmont: Wadsworth Publishing Co., 1977.

24. Akers, op. cit.; Suchar, op. cit.

25. Clinard and Meier, op. cit., p. 83.

26. Stuart L. Hills. Demystifying Social Deviance. New York: McGraw-Hill, 1980; Akers, op. cit.

27. Akers, op. cit.; Clinard and Meier, op. cit.

28. Akers, op. cit.; Clinard and Meier, op. cit.

29. Edwin M. Lemert. Human Deviance, Social Problems and Social Control, (2nd Ed.). Englewood Cliffs: Prentice-Hall, 1972; McCaghy, op. cit.

30. Howard S. Becker. Outsiders: Studies in the Sociology of Deviance. New York: Free Press, 1963.

31. Becker, op. cit., p. 14.

32. Akers, op. cit.; Lemert, op. cit.; Sagarin and Montanino, op. cit.

33. Edwin M. Lemert. Social Pathology: A Systematic Approach to the Theory of Sociolpathic Behavior. New York: McGraw-Hill, 1951, pp. 75-76.

34. Becker, op. cit.

35. Akers, op. cit.; McGaghy, op. cit.; Clinard and Meier, op. cit.

36. Akers, op. cit.

37. Travis Hirschi. Causes of Delinquency. Berkeley: University of California Press, 1969.

38. Akers, op. cit.; Clinard and Meier, op. cit.

39. Edwin H. Sutherland and Donald R. Cressey. Criminology, (10th Ed.). Philadelphia: Lippincott, 1978, pp. 80-82.

40. Akers, op. cit.

41. See, for example Edward Sagarin (ed.), op. cit.

Chapter 2   The Handicapped Minority: The Physically Impaired

1. John Gliedman and William Roth. The Unexpected Minority. New York: Harcourt Brace Jovanovich, 1980.

2. Robert L. Burgdorf, Jr. "Who Are 'Handicapped' Persons?" in Robert L. Burgdorf, Jr. (ed.). The Legal Rights of Handicapped Persons. Baltimore: Paul H. Brooks Publishers, 1980, pp. 2-3.

3. M. E. Worthington, "Personal Space as a Function of the Stigma Effect," Environment and Behavior, 6 (1974, 289-94.

4. Robert Kleck, "Emotional Arousal in Interaction with Stigmatized Persons," Psychological Reports, 19 (1966), 12-26.

5. Robert Kleck, "Reactions to the Handicapped--Sweaty Palms and Saccharine Words," Psychology Today, 9 (Nov., 1975), 122.

6. Robert Kleck, et al, "Effect of Stigmatizing Conditions on the Use of Personal Space," Psychological Reports, 23 (1968), 111-18; Robert Kleck, et al, "Physical Appearance Cues and Interpersonal Attraction in Children," Child Development, 45 (1974), 305-10; A. G. Miller, "Role of Physical Attractiveness in Impression Formation," Psychonomic Science, 19 (1970), 241-43; D. W. Novak and M. J. Lerner,

"Rejection as a Consequence of Perceived Dissimilarity,"
<u>Journal of Personality and Social Psychology</u>, 9 (1968),
147-52.

7. Gliedman and Roth, <u>op</u>. <u>cit</u>., p. 28.

8. Gliedman and Roth, <u>op</u>. cit., p. 29.

9. Jerome R. Dunham and Charles S. Dunham, "Psychosocial
    Aspects of Disability," in Robert M. Goldenson (ed.),
    <u>Disability and Rehabilitation Handbook</u>. New York: McGraw-
    Hill, 1978, p. 14.

10. Sonny Kleinfield. <u>The Hidden Minority</u>: America's Handi-
    <u>capped</u>. Boston: Little Brown, 1979.

11. Gliedman and Roth, <u>op</u>. cit., pp. 41-2.

12. Gliedman and Roth, <u>op</u>. cit.

13. Gliedman and Roth, <u>op</u>. cit., pp. 3-4.

14. Leo Buscaglia, <u>The Disabled and Their Parents</u>: A Counseling
    <u>Challenge</u>. Thorofare, N. J.: Charles B. Slack, Inc., 1975,
    p. 107.

15. Buscaglia, <u>op</u>. <u>cit</u>., p. 187.

16. Quoted in Kleinfield, <u>op</u>. <u>cit</u>., 15-16.

17. Marcianne Miller, "The Real Barriers for the Handicapped,"
    <u>Boston Globe</u>, March 3, 1980, p. 6.

18. Barbara Burtoff, "A Hidden Bias in Children's Books,"
    <u>Boston Globe</u>, January 19, 1980, p. 6.

19. Buscaglia, <u>op</u>. <u>cit</u>., p. 107.

20. Buscaglia, <u>op</u>. cit.

21. James Haskins. <u>The Quiet Revolution</u>: The Struggle for the
    <u>Rights of Disabled Americans</u>. New York: Thomas Y. Crowell,
    1979.

22. <u>Ibid</u>.; also see Frank Bowe, <u>Rehabilitating America</u>. New
    York: Harper and Row, 1980.

23. Haskins, <u>op</u>. cit.

24. Department of Health, Education and Welfare. <u>The White
    House Conference on Handicapped Individuals</u>: <u>Summary</u>.
    Washington: U. S. Government Printing Office, 1978; Bowe,
    <u>op</u>. <u>cit</u>.

25. Gliedman and Roth, <u>op</u>. <u>cit</u>.

26. Gliedman and Roth, <u>op</u>. <u>cit</u>.; Haskins, <u>op</u>. <u>cit</u>.

27. Gliedman and Roth, <u>op</u>. <u>cit</u>.; Haskins, <u>op</u>. <u>cit</u>.

28. Gliedman and Roth, op. cit., p. 207.

29. Gliedman and Roth, op. cit.

30. Nicholas Hobbs, The Futures of Children. San Francisco: Jossey-Bass, 1978, p. 3.

31. Hobbs, op. cit., p. 4.

32. Kleinfield, op. cit.

33. Sar A Levitan and Robert Taggart. Jobs for the Disabled. Baltimore: Johns Hopkins University Press, 1977.

34. Monroe Berkowitz, William C. Johnson and Edward Murphy, Public Policy Toward Disability. New York: Praeger Publishers, 1976.

35. Bowe, op. cit.

36. Gopal C. Pati and John I. Adkins, Jr., "Hire the Handicapped --Compliance is Good Business," Harvard Business Review, 58 (Jan-Feb, 1980), p. 15.

37. Haskins, op. cit.; Gliedman and Roth, op. cit.; Kleinfield, op. cit.

38. Kleinfield, op. cit.

39. T. R. Wilson and J. A. Richards. Jobs for Veterans with Disabilities. Alexandria, Va.: HUMPRO Manpower R and D Monograph 41, 1975; Max Cleland quote found in Kleinfield, op. cit., p. 150.

40. Levitan, op. cit.; Haskins, op. cit.

41. "What's Being Done for 35 Million Handicapped?" U. S. News and World Report, 83 (Aug. 29, 1977), p. 58; "Rights for the Handicapped--New Rules Stir Turmoil," U. S. News and World Report, 82 (May 9, 1977), p. 84.

42. Gliedman and Roth, op. cit., pp. 302-03.

43. André Lussier, "Psychological Aspects of Handicap," Appendix I in Gliedman and Roth, op. cit., p. 316.

44. Charles S. Dunham, "Social-Sexual Relationships," in Goldenson, op. cit., pp. 28-29.

45. Haskins, op. cit., p. 3.

46. Quotes, without further reference, are found in Kleinfield, op. cit., pp. 26-27.

47. Jerry Flint, "Handicapped No Longer Act Like It." New York Times, (October 2, 1977), p. 8.

Chapter 3   The Unseeing Minority: The Blind

1. Robert Scott. The Making of Blind Men. New York: Russell
    Sage Foundation, 1969.

2. Blindness and Services to the Blind in the United States.
    Cambridge, Ma.: Organization for Social and Technical Inno-
    vation, Inc., 1971.

3. Ibid.

4. Ibid.

5. Scott, op. cit.

6. Scott, op. cit.; Jerome Dunham, "Blindness and Visual Impair-
    ment," in Robert M. Goldenson (ed.). Disability and Rehabil-
    itation Handbook. New York: McGraw-Hill, 1978, pp. 249-65;
    Gabriel Farrell, The Story of Blindness. Cambridge:
    Harvard University Press, 1956.

7. Kenneth Jernigan, "To Everything There is a Season: Discrim-
    ination Against the Blind," Vital Speeches, 43 (Aug. 15,
    1977), 667.

8. Michael E. Monbeck. The Meanings of Blindness: Attitudes
    Toward Blindness and Blind People. Bloomington: Indiana
    University Press, 1975.

9. Jernigan, op. cit., p. 669.

10. Alexander Alexanian, "An Investigation Into Public and
    Private Attitudes Held Toward Various Handicapped Groups:
    Stutterers, Cerebral Palsied, and the Blind," unpublished
    Ph.D. dissertation. Boston University, 1967.

11. Scott, op. cit.

12. Scott, op. cit., p. 14.

13. Scott, op. cit., and Monbeck, op. cit.

14. Deborah Zook. Debby. Scottdale, Pa.: Herald Press, 1974,
    pp. 91-92.

15. Zook, op. cit., p. 98.

16. Scott, op. cit.; Blindness and Services to the Blind in the
    United States. Cambridge: Organization of Social and
    Technical Innovation, Inc., 1971. Also see Sar A. Levitan
    and Robert Taggart. Jobs for the Disabled. Baltimore:
    Johns Hopkins University Press, 1977.

17. Scott, op. cit.

18. Scott, op. cit., p. 77.

19. Scott, op. cit.

20. Scott, op. cit., p. 116.

21. Kenneth Jernigan, "Blindness: of Visions and Vultures," Vital Speeches, 43 (October 15, 1976), p. 20

22. L. D. Baker, "Authoritarianism, Attitudes toward Blindness and Managers: Implications for the Employment of Blind Persons," The New Outlook for the Blind, 68 (1974), pp. 308-14.

23. W. H. Nichols, "Blind Persons in Data Processing: The Attitude of Industry," The New Outlook for the Blind, 64 (1970), pp. 293-96.

24. Quoted in Kenneth Jernigan, "Blindness: Of Visions and Vultures," op. cit., p. 21.

25. James Haskins. The Quiet Revolution. New York: Thomas Y. Crowell, 1979.

26. Kenneth Jernigan, "To Everything There Is a Season: Discrimination Against the Blind." op. cit.

27. Charles E. Buell, Physical Education and Recreation for the Visually Handicapped. Washington: American Alliance for Health, Physical Education and Recreation, 1973, p. 4.

28. Kenneth Jernigan, "Blindness: Of Visions and Vultures," op. cit., pp. 20-21.

29. H. Robert Blank, "Psychosocial Problems of the Blind and the Rehabilitation System," in Blindness and Services to the Blind in the United States, op. cit., p. 182.

30. Farrell, op. cit.

31. Florence Weiner, Help for the Handicapped Child. New York: McGraw-Hill Book Co., 1973; Farrell, op. cit.

32. Farrell, op. cit.,; Haskins, op. cit.

33. Kenneth Jernigan, "To Everything There is a Season: Discrimination Against the Blind," op. cit., p. 666.

Chapter 4 The Invisible Minority: The Hearing Impaired

1. My discussion of the "nature of deafness" draws on the following sources: Richard Carmen, Our Endangered Hearing. Boston: G. K. Hall and Co., 1978; K. P. Murphy, "Hearing, Deafness, and Recent Research," an appendix in David Wright, Deafness. New York: Stein and Day, 1969, pp. 203-13; Helmer R. Myklebust, The Psychology of Deafness. New York: Grune and Stratton, 1960; John Ballantyne, Deafness, (3rd Ed.). Edinburgh: Churchill Livingstone, 1977.

2. Robert M. Goldenson (ed.). Disability and Rehabilitation Handbook. New York: McGraw-Hill, 1978, pp. 765-66.

239

3. "Hearing Problems in the U. S.," _Intellect_, 104 (Jan 1976), pp. 285-6.

4. Richard Carmen, _op. cit._

5. James A. Pahz and Cheryl S. Pahz, _Total Communication_. Springfield, Illinois: Charles C. Thomas Publisher, 1978.

6. _Ibid._

7. _Ibid._; Terrence J. O'Rourke. _A Basic Course in Manual Communcation_ (2nd Ed.). Silver Springs, Md.: National Association of the Deaf, 1973.

8. Pahz and Pahz, _op. cit._

9. Phyllis P. Phillips. _Speech and Hearing Problems in the Classroom_. Lincoln, Nebraska: Cliff Notes, Inc., 1975; Helmer R. Myklebust, _Your Deaf Child_. Springfield: Charles C. Thomas, 1950.

10. Boris V. Markovin. _Through the Barriers of Deafness and Isolation_. New York: Macmillan Co., 1960; Philip H. Van Itallie, _How To Live with a Hearing Handicap_. New York: Paul S. Eriksson, Inc., 1963.

11. David Wright. _Deafness_. New York: Stein and Day, 1969, pp. 134-35.

12. Wright, _op. cit._

13. _Ibid._

14. _Ibid._

15. Wright, _op. cit._, pp. 156-57.

16. Wright, _op. cit._; Ballantyne, _op. cit._

17. Pahz and Pahz, _op. cit._; Wright, _op. cit._

18. Hans G. Furth. _Thinking Without Language._ New York: The Free Press, 1966, p. 7.

19. Story Moorefield, "Opening a New Door for the Deaf." _American Education_, 10 (April, 19740, 30-32.

20. Myklebust, _The Psychology of Deafness_.

21. Pahz and Pahz, _op. cit._

22. G. B. Phillips, "An Exploration of Employee Attitudes Concerning Employment Opportunities for Deaf People," _Journal of Rehabilitation of the Deaf_, 9 (1975) 1-9; Wright, _op. cit._

23. "I Chose the Hearing World," an interview with James C. Marsters in Boris V. Markovin. _Through the Barriers of Deafness and Isolation_. New York: Macmillan Co., 1960.

24. "Subtitles for TV and Films," _American Education_, 13 (March, 1977), pp. 18-22.

25. _Ibid._

26. William C. Norris, "Technology and the Handicapped," Control Data Corporation Pamphlet, August, 1979.

27. James Haskins, _The Quiet Revolution_. New York: Thomas Y. Crowell, 1979; "Newsletter" of the National Center for the Law and Deaf, September, 1980.

28. Carmen, _op. cit._

29. Carmen, _op. cit._, pp. 109-10.

30. Pahz and Pahz, _op. cit._

31. Quoted in Frank Bowe, _Handicapping America: Barriers to Disabled People_. New York: Harper and Row, 1978, p. 146.

32. Bowe, _op. cit._

33. Ballantyne, _op. cit._

34. Mary Sarah King, "When You Can't Hear What's Going On," _Boston Globe_, May 26, 1977, p. 41; Hans G. Furth. _Deafness and Learning_: A Psychosocial Approach. Belmont, California: Wadsworth, 1973.

35. Wright, _op. cit._, pp. 6, 8, 81, 116, 202.

36. Trenton W. Batson and Eugene Bergman, _The Deaf Experience_, (2nd Ed.). South Waterford, Maine: The Merriam-Eddy Co., 1973.

37. Kathryn Meadow, "Sociolinguistics, Sign Language, and the Deaf Sub-Culture," in Terrence O'Rourke (ed.). _Psycho-linguistics and Total Communication: The State of the Art_. Washington: The American Annals of the Deaf, 1972, pp. 19-33; James C. Woodward, Jr., "Some Observations on Sociolinguistic Variation and American Sign Language," _Kansas Journal of Sociology_, 9 (Fall, 1973), 191-200.

38. Edward M. Gobble, "Breaking the Silence," _The Progressive_, 41, (Feb., 1977), p. 35.

39. Margaret Fisk (ed.). _Encyclopedia of Associations_. Vol. 1, (10th Ed.). Detroit: Gale Research Co., 1976.

Chapter 5 The Littlest Minority: Dwarfs and Midgets

1. Hy Roth and Robert Cromie. _The Little People_. New York: Everest House, 1980.

2. Joseph A. Bailey, II. _Disproportionate Short Stature_: Diagnosis and Management. Philadelphia: W. B. Saunders, 1973.

3. Sonny Kleinfield, "Dwarfs," Atlantic Monthly, 236 (Sep, 1975), 62-66; Marcello Truzzi, "Lilliputians in Gulliver's Land: The Social Role of the Dwarf," in Edward Sagarin (ed.). The Other Minorities. Waltham: Ginn and Co., 1971, pp. 183-204.

4. Bailey, op. cit.; Robert J. Goldenson, "Dwarfism," in Robert M. Goldenson (ed.). Disability and Rehabilitation Handbook. New York: McGraw-Hill, 1978, pp. 596-601.

5. Truzzi, op. cit.

6. Arthur J. Snider, "Giants and Midgets," Science Digest, 69 (Jan 1971), pp. 62-66.

7. Leslie Fiedler. Freaks. New York: Simon and Schuster, 1978, p. 39.

8. Roth and Cromie, op. cit.; Fiedler, op. cit.

9. Roth and Cromie, op, cit.

10. Roth and Cromie, op. cit.

11. Fiedler, op. cit.; Roth and Cromie, op. cit.; Victor A. McKusick and David L. Remain, "General Tom Thumb and Other Midgets," Scientific American, 217 (July 1967), 102-10.

12. Edward Sagarin. Odd Man In: Societies of Deviants in America. Chicago: Quadrangle Books, 1969, p. 197.

13. "A Short Police Story," Newsweek, 94 (Sep 17, 1979), p. 73.

14. Viola Osgood, "A Small Man Has Big Ideas," Boston Globe, May 16, 1980, p. 19.

15. Kleinfield, op. cit., p. 62.

16. Kleinfield, op. cit.

17. Quoted in Roth and Cromie, op. cit., p. 155.

18. Kleinfield, op. cit.; Alvin Adams, "The Little People--A Tiny Minority with Big Problems," Ebony, 20 (Oct 1965), pp. 104-13.

19. Quoted in Roth and Cromie, op. cit., p. 169.

20. Walter Bodin and Burnet Hershey. It's a Small World. New York: Coward-McCann, 1934.

21. Snider, op. cit.; McKusick and Remain, op. cit.

22. Joseph Rogers and M. D. Buffalo, "Fighting Back: Nine Modes of Adaptation to a Deviant Label," Social Problems, 22 (Oct 1974), 101-18.

23. Truzzi, op. cit., pp. 191-92.

24. Truzzi, op. cit., p. 192.

25. Ibid.

26. Margaret Fish (ed.). *Encyclopedia of Associations*, (10th Ed.). Vol. 1 Detroit: Gale Research Co., 1976; Roth and Cromie, op. cit.; Kleinfield, op. cit.; Goldenson, op. cit.

27. Sagarin, op. cit.; Truzzi, op. cit.

28. Adams, op. cit.

29. Martin S. Weinberg, "The Problems of Midgets and Dwarfs and Organizational Remedies: A Study of the Little People of America," *Journal of Health and Social Behavior*, 9 (March 1968), pp. 65-71; Adams, op. cit.

30. Sagarin, op. cit., pp. 202-03.

31. Sagarin, op. cit., p. 204.

32. Sagarin, op. cit.

33. Fiedler, op. cit., p. 88.

34. Fiedler, op. cit., p. 90.

Chapter 6   The Ugly Minority: The Facially Disfigured

1. Paul Ekman and Wallace V. Friesen. *Unmasking the Face*. Englewood Cliffs: Prentice-Hall. 1975.

2. Frances Cook Macgregor, Theodora M. Abel, Albert Bryt, Edith Lauer and Serena Weissmann. *Facial Deformities and Plastic Surgery--A Psychosocial Study*. Springfield: Charles C. Thomas Publishers, 1953.

3. Macgregor, et al, op. cit.

4. Frances Cook Macgregor, "Facial Disgurgement," in Robert M. Goldenson (ed.). *Disability and Rehabilitation Handbook*. New York: McGraw-Hill, 1978, pp. 389-95.

5. Macgregor, et al, *Facial Deformities and Plastic Surgery*.

6. S. A. Richardson, A. H. Hastorf, N. Goodman, S. M. Dornbach, "Cultural Uniformity in Reaction to Physical Disability," *American Sociological Review*. 26 (1961), pp. 241-47.

7. Macgregor, "Facial Disfigurement," in Goldenson (ed.), op. cit.

8. Macgregor, et al. *Facial Deformities and Plastic Surgery*, op. cit., p. 67.

9. Edith Lauer, "The Family," in Macgregor, et al, op. cit., p. 116.

10. Macgregor, et al, op. cit.

11. Macgregor, et al, op. cit.

12. Macgregor, _et_ _al_, _op_. _cit_, p. 72.

13. Macgregor, _et_ _al_, _op_. _cit_., pp. 76-77.

14. Macgregor, _et_ _al_, _op_. _cit_., pp. 77-78.

15. Frances Cook Macgregor. _Transformation and Identity: The Face and Plastic Surgery_. New York: The New York Times Book Co., 1974.

16. Macgregor, _et_ _al_, _op_. _cit_., pp. 70-71.

17. Macgregor, _Transformation and Identity: The Face and Plastic Surgery_, _op_. _cit_.

18. Macgregor, _Transformation and Identity_, _op_. _cit_., pp. 49-53.

19. Macgregor, _Transformation and Identity_, _op_. _cit_., p. 53.

20. Macgregor, _et_ _al_, _op_. _cit_., pp. 84-85.

21. Macgregor, _et_ _al_, _op_. _cit_.

22. Macgregor. _Transformation and Identity_, _op_. _cit_.; Also see Frances Cook Macgregor. _After Plastic Surgery: Adaptation and Adjustment_. New York: Praeger Publishers, 1979.

23. Herbert Greene and Carolyn Jones. _Diary of a Food Addict_. New York: Grosset and Dunlop, 1974, pp. 19-20.

24. Macgregor. _Transformation and Identity_, _op_. _cit_.

25. Duane F. Stroman. _The Quick Knife: Unnecessary Surgery U. S. A_. Port Washington: Kennikat Press, 1979.

26. _Ibid_.: Kurt Wagner and Helen Gould. _A Plastic Surgeon Answers your Questions_. Englewood Cliffs: Prentice-Hall, Inc., 1972.

27. Stroman, _op_. _cit_.; Wagner and Gould, _op_. _cit_.; Sylvia Rosenthal. _Cosmetic Surgery: A Consumer's Guide_. Philadelphia: J. B. Lippincott Co., 1977; Sheldon Rothfleisch. _The No-Nonsense Guide to Cosmetic Surgery_. New York: Grosset and Dunlop, 1979.

28. James O. Stallings with Terry Morris. _A New You: How Plastic Surgery Can Change Your Life_. New York: Van Nostrand Reinhold Co., 1977; Kurt J. Wagner and Gerald Imber. _Beauty by Design_. New York: McGraw-Hill, 1979.

29. Colette Dowling. _The Skin Game_. Philadelphia: J. B. Lippincott Co., 1971; Kendall H. Moore and Sally Thompson. _The Surgical Beauty Racket_. Port Washington: Ashley Books, Inc., 1978.

30. Robert L. Burgdorf, Jr., "Who Are 'Handicapped' Persons?" in Robert L. Burgdorf, Jr. (ed.). _The Legal Rights of Handicapped Persons: Cases, Materials and Text_. Baltimore: Paul H. Brookes Publishers, 1980, pp. 1-52.

Chapter 7 The Growing Minority: Fat People

1. Gina Bari Kolata, "Obesity--A Growing Problem," _Science_,
    198 (Dec 2, 1977), 905-06; Milton V. Kline, Lester Coleman
    and Erika Wicks (eds.). _Obesity: Etiology, Treatment and
    Management_. Springfield: Charles C. Thomas Publisher,
    1976.

2. Jean Mayer. _A Diet for Living_. New York: David McKay Co.,
    Inc., 1975.

3. Marvin Grosswirth. _Fat Pride: A Survival Handbook_. New
    York: Jarrow Press, Inc., 1971; Mayer, _op. cit._

4. Mayer, _op. cit._; George A. Bray, "Obesity," _Disease of the
    Month_, Vol XXVI (Oct 1979), pp. 14-23.

5. Edward B. Johns, Wilfred C. Sutton and Lloyd E. Webster.
    Health for Effective Living, (3rd Ed.). New York: McGraw-
    Hill, 1962, p. 226.

6. Martha Demmick, "Obesity," in Robert M. Goldenson (ed.).
    Disability and Rehabilitation Handbook. New York: McGraw-
    Hill, 1978, pp. 496-502.

7. Mayer, _op. cit._

8. Mayer, _op. cit._

9. Kolata, _op. cit._; Theodore Issac Rubin. _Alive and Fat and
    Thinning in America_. New York: Coward, McCann and
    Geoghegan, Inc., 1978.

10. Evan Charney, Helen Goodman, Margaret McBride, Barbra
     Lyon and Rosalie Pratt, "Childhood Antecedents of Adult
     Obesity: Do Chubby Infants Become Obese Adults?" _New
     England Journal of Medicine_, 295 (Jul 1, 1976), pp. 6-9;
     Grosswirth, _op. cit._

11. William Stockton, "Conspiracy Against Fatness," _Psychology
     Today_, 12 (Oct 1978), pp. 82-88.

12. Grosswirth, _op. cit._; Patricia A. Sullivan, "Review of the
     Literature," in Kline, Coleman and Wick (eds.), _op. cit._,
     pp. 5-17.

13. J. Trevor Silverstone, Robert P. Gordon and Albert Stunkard,
     "Social Factors in Obesity in London," in Kline, Coleman
     and Wick (eds,), _op. cit._, pp. 318-25.

14. Kolata, _op. cit._

15. Kolata, _op. cit._

16. Ann Scott Beller. _Fat and Thin: A Natural History of
     Obesity_. New York: McGraw-Hill, 1977.

17. Rubin, op. cit.

18. Erika Wick, "Overeating Patterns Found in Overweight and Obese Patients," in Kline, Coleman and Wick (eds.), op. cit., pp. 18-33; Stanley Schacter. Emotion, Obesity and Crime. New York: Academic Press, 1971; Judith Rodin, "Social and Immediate Environmental Influences on Food Selection, International Journal of Obesity. 4 (1980), pp. 364-70.

19. Rubin, op. cit., p. 39.

20. Grosswirth, op. cit.; Also see, "For the Very Fat, Sexual Problems Are Largely Logistic," Psychology Today, 11 (Sep 1977), p. 33.

21. Judith Thurman, "Never Too Thin to Feel Fat," MS, 6 (Sep 1977), p. 48.

22. William DeJong, "The Stigma of Obesity: The Consequences of Naive Assumptions Concerning the Causes of Physical Deviance," Journal of Health and Social Behavior, 21 (March 1980), p. 85.

23. Grosswirth, op. cit., p. 22.

24. Grosswirth, op. cit.

25. "College Criticized for Get Thin Policy," New York Times, December 4, 1977, p. 31.

26. "Maryland Legislator Attempting to End Prejudice Against the Fat," New York Times, March 31, 1980, p. 12.

27. Grosswirth, op. cit.

28. Grosswirth, op. cit., pp. 137-38.

29. Grosswirth, op. cit., p. 137.

30. Rubin, op. cit., p. 26.

31. Rubin, op. cit., pp. 27-28.

32. Rubin, op. cit., pp. 28-29.

33. Grosswirth, op. cit., p. 30.

34. Lois A. Maiman, "Attitudes Toward Obesity and Obese Among Professionals," Journal of American Dietetic Association, 74 (March 1979), 331-334.

35. Grosswirth, op. cit., p. 26.

36. Elaine Markoutsas, "They Said We Were Too Fat to Adopt a Baby," Good Housekeeping, 189 (Sep 1979), pp. 96-99.

37. Mayer, op. cit.

38. Peter Wyden. The Overweight Society. New York: William Morrow and Co., 1965, p. 310.

246

39. "Maryland Legislator Attempting to End Prejudice Against the Fat." _New York Times_, March 31, 1980, p. 12.

40. Jean Mayer, _A Diet for Living_. New York: David McKay Co., Inc., 1975.

41. Rubin, _op. cit._; Madeline Lee, "Fat Is Still A Feminist Issue," _MS_, 8 (Feb 1980), pp. 50-51.

42. In the Foreword to Grosswirth, _op. cit._, p. 13.

43. Grosswirth, _op. cit._, p. 56.

44. Quoted in Herbert Greene and Carolyn Jones. _Diary of a Food Addict_. New York: Grosset and Dunlop, 1974.

45. Wyden, _op. cit._; and literature from TOPS, P. O. Box 07489, Milwaukee, Wisconsin, 53207.

46. Jean Nidetch. _The Story of Weight Watchers_. New York: W/W Twenty First Corp., 1970.

47. Marcia Millman. _Such a Pretty Face: Being Fat in America_. New York: W. W. Norton, 1980. Also see Karen R. _That First Bite: Journal of a Compulsive Overeater_. New York: Thomas Nelson, Inc., 1978.

48. Loretta McLaughlin, "Surgery to Control Obesity Dangerous, Scientist Warns," _Boston Globe_, May 29, 1980, p. 8.

49. William J. Fabrey. _What is NAAFA?_ (A Leaflet from NAAFA, P. O. Box 43, Bellerose, N. Y. 11426).

50. Wayne Wooley, "An Indictment of Dieting,"--address to NAAFA Convention September 2, 1979, mimeo, p. 3.

51. Stuart Wilk, "Leading Doctors Say . . . Your 'Extra' Pounds are Good For You," _National Enquirer_, August 7, 1979; "Fat May Keep You Fit, Study Finds," _Chicago Sun Times_, July 4, 1979.

52. Leslie Fiedler. _Freaks: Myths and Images of the Secret Self_. New York: Simon and Schuster, 1978.

53. Jean Mayer. _Obesity: Causes, Cost, and Control_. Englewood Cliffs: PrenticeHall, 1968, p. 1.